IN THE
DEVIL'S
TOOLBOX

THE HIDDEN TOOLS USED BY THE
DEVIL TO GAIN "LEGAL ACCESS" TO YOUR LIFE

Part One: Emotions—A Hiding Place for Demons

RICHARD E. OSWALT, J.D.

ELECTRIC
MOON
PUBLISHING

Copyright 2020 by Richard E. Oswalt, J.D.

Published by Electric Moon Publishing, LLC

©2020 *In the Devil's Toolbox: The Hidden Tools Used by the Devil to Gain "Legal Access" to Your Life, Part One: Emotions—A Hiding Place for Demons* / Richard E. Oswalt, J.D.

Paperback ISBN: 978-1-943027-45-3
E-book ISBN: 978-1-943027-46-0

Electric Moon Publishing, LLC
P.O. Box 466
Stromsburg, NE 68666
info@emoonpublishing.com

All Scripture is taken from *The Holy Bible, English Standard Version*, unless otherwise noted. Copyright © 2000; 2001 by Crossway Bibles, a division of Good News Publishers. Used by permission. All rights reserved.

Scripture quotations marked (NASB) are taken from the *New American Standard Bible*. Copyright © 1960, 1962, 1963, 1968, 1971, 1972, 1973, 1975, 1977, 1995 by The Lockman Foundation. Used by permission. All rights reserved.

Scripture quotations marked (NIV) are taken from the Holy Bible, New International Version®, NIV®. Copyright © 1973, 1978, 1984, 2011 by Biblica, Inc.™ Used by permission of Zondervan. All rights reserved worldwide. www.zondervan.com The "NIV" and "New International Version" are trademarks registered in the United States Patent and Trademark Office by Biblica, Inc.™

Scripture quotations marked (NKJV) are taken from the *New King James Version*®. Copyright © 1982 by Thomas Nelson. Used by permission. All rights reserved.

Scripture quotations marked (KJV) are taken from the *Authorized (King James) Version*. Rights in the Authorized Version in the United Kingdom are vested in the Crown. Reproduced by permission of the Crown's patentee, Cambridge University Press.

Scripture quotations marked (BSB) are taken from *The Holy Bible, Berean Study Bible, BSB*. Copyright © 2016, 2018 by Bible Hub. Used by permission. All rights reserved worldwide.

Scripture quotations marked (NLT) are taken from the Holy Bible, New Living Translation, copyright ©1996, 2004, 2015 by Tyndale House Foundation. Used by permission of Tyndale House Publishers, a Division of Tyndale House Ministries, Carol Stream, Illinois 60188. All rights reserved.

Scripture quotations marked (BLB) are taken from The Holy Bible, Berean Literal Bible, BLB Copyright ©2016 by Bible Hub. Used by Permission. All Rights Reserved Worldwide. http://literalbible.com/.

Quotes from the book of Enoch are taken from *The Book of Enoch, Translated from Ethiopian*, (Saltheart Pub. by R.H. Charles, 1906/2013).

Cover and Interior Design by Lyn Rayn / Electric Moon Publishing Creative Services

Printed in the United States of America

ELECTRIC MOON PUBLISHING

www.emoonpublishing.com

Dedicated to Reverend Royce Pope.

. . . lest Satan should take advantage of us;
for we are not ignorant of his devices.

2 Corinthians 2:11 (NKJV)

CONTENTS

Introduction

The road to hell is not labeled "Road to Hell." It is labeled "Road to Heaven." The devil is called the Great Deceiver, the Father of Lies—and he imitates everything our good God has created to deceive and destroy us.

Many people call these deeds of the devil *spiritual warfare*. And while some are aware of its presence, most are completely unaware of the unmanageable damage it may have caused in their lives.

For some, spiritual warfare may be that thing you can't quite put your finger on that keeps sabotaging your life. For others, it may be that unexplained grieving in your spirit or internal pain that won't go away. And still for others, it may manifest as an unnatural or uncontrollable urge or desire that is taking your life in a direction you don't want.

Billy Graham offered these words about this spiritual battle in his book *Angels*:

> "We live in a perpetual battlefield . . . The wars among the nations on earth are mere popgun affairs compared to the fierceness of battle in the unseen spiritual world. This invisible spiritual conflict is waged around us incessantly and unremittingly. Where the Lord works, Satan's forces hinder; where angel beings carry out divine directives,

the devils rage. All this comes about because the powers of darkness press their counterattack to recapture the ground held for the glory of God."

The devil hates God's creation and wants to destroy mankind to establish his own kingdom on this earth, which he intends to rule. Spiritual warfare is his plan to do just that.

He started this warfare against humanity several millennia ago and continues these assaults on us to this day through his army of fallen angels, demons, and earthly agents.

Many people, including myself, believe we are in a time when Satan is preparing his final assaults against mankind. His deception and assaults are growing in intensity and scope. And his final attack will leave all but those who are firmly grounded in truth totally unprepared.

What do you know about this spiritual battle that surrounds you daily? A battle which—

- cares not if you are aware of its presence
- doesn't play by man's rules but rages within its own set of spiritual guidelines
- if ignored, still pursues
- intensifies every passing day
- can destroy our lives if we are unprepared.

I have divided my book into four sections. Each section is designed to give you a look behind the curtain at how this spiritual system operates, and to give you a *general understanding* of how this warfare is used against us.

Section One

The first section is designed to educate you on the invisible spiritual battle we are all engaged in. For those who are unfamiliar with this spiritual battle, I will lay out its scriptural foundation. I will discuss the "three heavens" outlined in Scripture, which contain the areas where this spiritual warfare takes place, and will provide evidence from the scientific community proving the existence of these three physical realities. I will define the three separate spiritual entities we battle in this warfare—Satan, fallen angels, and demons—and I will discuss some characteristics of each. (Please note that I use the term *Satan, the devil, the Enemy,* and *the Evil One* interchangeably. I also use the terms *demon, evil spirit, foul spirit, unclean spirit,* and *lying spirit* interchangeably).

While all spiritual warfare is global in nature, I will discuss the methods of attack used by the Enemy to deliver his spiritual warfare against us personally. I will discuss the "Laws of the Spiritual Realm" and explain what conduct (all of which can be categorized as sin) gives the devil and his host of demons the "legal right" or a legal inroad to attack us. The mere fact that our conduct may give the Enemy "legal right" to our lives might be a new revelation for you, but it is something the Enemy preys upon, and something he would prefer you not know.

In keeping with the admonition from Proverbs 25:2 that says, *It is the glory of God to conceal things, but the glory of kings is to search things out,* I will discuss schemes of the Enemy that you may be familiar with, and will outline schemes of the Enemy that you may know nothing about. These schemes will be revealed in this book, Part One of *In the Devil's Toolbox: Emotions—A Hiding Place for Demons,* as well as in the second book, Part Two of *In the Devil's Toolbox: The Coming Deception—When the Second Heaven Invades Earth.*

Section Two

In the second section of this book, I will highlight one of the devil's most effective tools used in this spiritual battle to implement his schemes: our "emotions." I will disclose the various ways the devil uses our emotions against us and why our emotions are such an effective tool. I will discuss how emotions can enable the devil to gain a "legal right" or "legal access" to our lives and our family's lives through our thoughts and actions. Also, I will discuss three different levels of spiritual deception that we may succumb to and the symptoms associated with each of these three levels. If you are dealing with spiritual deception and have succumbed to spiritual strongholds or spiritual bondages, hopefully after reading Section Two, you will recognize what conduct opened the door to this attack, and then learn how to set yourself free from it grips in the next section.

Section Three

The third, and I believe most important section of this book, outlines God's defenses to protect us from all the wiles, schemes, and devices of the Enemy. I discuss God's instructions on how to recognize spiritual deception and the bondage it creates, and I discuss how to set yourself free from this bondage. I also address the power and authority we have as Christians over the Enemy. God is quite aware of this spiritual battle zone we live in. He has not left us defenseless or abandoned us in this battle but has given us as true Christian believers the power and authority of the Holy Spirit,[1] promises in His Holy Word,[2] and the privilege of prayer to triumph over the forces of evil.[3]

Section Four

The fourth section of this book is titled In The Devil's Toolbox. Here I will outline fifteen common emotions used by the devil and his host to gain "legal access" to our lives. I will outline how these emotions differ from our God-given emotions, how to tell if we have succumbed to these counterfeit emotions, and how—if left unchecked—these emotions can actually become entry points for the devil and his host of demons.

One final note: If the information disclosed in this book were widely known and commonly taught through the mainstream churches, there would be no need for this publication. The world in which we live is, in reality, a spiritual battlefield. A basic understanding of this genuinely real battle, the participants, and the rules of engagement are central to the outcome of our lives and our eternity.

So as you read this book, if you find this information completely new and are challenged in some way by the positions offered, you are right where I was and possibly right where the Enemy wants you to be—unaware and unprepared for his schemes and devices. Ask yourself, "Who would benefit most from my ignorance of the schemes outlined in this book?"

Accordingly, I would suggest that you simply take your time as you read, taking nothing by suggestion; do your own homework, and come to your own biblically-based conclusions on the topics discussed. And, of course, take everything contained in this book to the Lord in prayer. This book represents the conclusions that I have arrived at and what I believe to be true.

With all of this in mind, I hope this book will make you look at the world a little differently and, if you're bound in any way by the Enemy, help set you free.

The Invisible Battle

What Devil?

Every night, we lock our doors and bolt our windows to prevent a thief from entering our homes, but we do little, if anything, to protect ourselves from the master thief—the one who robs our unsuspecting soul daily of God's greatest gifts to us, including our happiness, our peace of mind, our love, and, if we allow it, even our life.

Why do we make such a mistake? Because we won't protect ourselves from an Enemy we don't know about or believe exists. Therein lies the devil's first line of defense: disbelief. It's his ultimate cover. By allowing his influences to go unnoticed, people are left blaming each other for their messed-up lives and for every hardship they encounter. We see this played out every day in the nightly news. Man against man, authority against authority, and nation against nation.

I'm not implying that we don't have a choice regarding how much influence the devil has on us—I believe we do. But we won't screen him out of our lives if we don't believe he exists, we don't believe he has access to us, or we don't know how to detect his influence in our lives. We're dealing with a tasteless, odorless, non-physical spirit that inhabits the earth similar to you and me. It's time we learned a little bit about our adversarial neighbor.

2

Isn't the Devil Confined to Hell?

I f you're like me, you may be completely surprised to find out that the devil has access to us in this life. You may also be surprised to find out that nowhere in Scripture does it tell us that the devil, the fallen angels, or his cast of demons (spiritual entities different from fallen angels) currently reside in hell. In fact, this misconception is exactly what the devil wants you to believe. At some future time, all these evil entities will be confined to hell, but that is not the world we live in today.[4]

A closer look at Scripture actually reveals Satan is not only alive, but an inhabitant of our world. In fact, Job 1:6-7 tells us that one day, when the sons of God (angels) came and presented themselves before the Lord, Satan also came among them. The Lord said to Satan, *"From where have you come?" Satan answered the* Lord *and said,* **"From going to and fro on the earth, and from walking up and down on it"** (emphasis added). God didn't question the devil's response. The devil, a spiritual being, is actually inhabiting the same place we call our physical heavens—the earth, the sky, or the air—only in spiritual form.

That's what the apostle Paul is talking about when he says, *And you were dead in the trespasses and sins in which you once walked, following the course of this world, following the* **prince of the power of the air**, *the spirit that is* *now at work in the sons of disobedience—*[5] (emphasis added). The "prince of the power of the air" is, of course, our Enemy the devil.

The devil's presence is again evidenced by the apostle Peter's instruction in 1 Peter 5:8 to be self-controlled and alert because our Enemy the devil *prowls around like a roaring lion, seeking someone to devour*[6] (emphasis added). If this invisible enemy wasn't present in this world, why would Peter give us such a warning?

In Ezekiel 28:12–19, we are told of the devil's original rebellion against God. Later, in the book of Revelation 12:3–4, we are told (according to the understanding of most biblical scholars) that one-third of the angels in heaven sided with the devil in his rebellion and were thrown to the earth. This Scripture says, *And another sign appeared in heaven: behold, a great red dragon, with seven heads and ten horns, and on his heads seven diadems.* **His tail swept down a third of the stars of heaven and cast them to the earth** . . .[7] (emphasis added).

As stated above, many biblical scholars believe that the stars referred to in this Scripture were the angels (now known as fallen angels) that defected with Satan. These entities are very powerful in nature, often having power over certain geographical areas, and causing great havoc upon earth. Thus, both the devil and his legion of fallen angels have an active presence with us here on earth.[8]

In addition, as we will discuss later in this section, there is another entity of evil that we deal with in this world known as evil (unclean) spirits or demons. These evil spirits or demons, are a completely different entity than fallen angels. They are limited to earthly activities, and have apparently been around since the days of Noah.

We see evidence of the demons' involvement with mankind (and Christ's showing His authority over these evil entities) throughout the New Testament.[9] Jesus spoke directly to these evil spirits, commanding them to depart from people during His ministry here on earth.[10] Likewise, Christ gave His disciples authority over demons, and commissioned them to cast demons out of people—a commission that would have been unnecessary if demons didn't inhabit this world.[11]

So, our physical world coexists with the spiritual world, and this spiritual world includes not only God and His holy angels, but also the devil, his fallen angels, and demons. This may be old news to some of you, but to others, it may be your first understanding that we share our world with a host of spiritual entities. If so, buckle up because there's more.

The Three Heavens

Okay, are you ready for this? The Scriptures refer to three heavens. If you are like me, you missed that the first time through—and although some scholars disagree over the labeling of these three separate areas, few scholars deny their existence. This is why I have chosen to use the term "heavens," which I believe is biblically-based. We needn't go any further than the very first verse in the Bible for evidence of multiple heavens. Genesis 1:1 tells us, *In the beginning, God created the heavens and the earth.* Notice that the verse says "heavens" (plural tense) not "heaven," certainly indicating more than one heaven.[12]

However, when most of us hear the word "heaven," we think of our future dwelling place with the Lord. The Bible actually calls this the "third heaven." This third heaven is paradise; God's heaven. In 2 Corinthians 12:2–4, Paul is talking about his own revelation when he says, *I know a man in Christ who fourteen years ago was caught up to the **third heaven**—whether in the body or out of the body I do not know, God knows. And I know that this man was caught up into paradise—whether in the body or out of the body I do not know, God knows—and he heard things that cannot be told, which man may not utter* (emphasis added). So paradise is the third heaven.

But this leaves a first and second heaven. And make no mistake, both heaven number one and heaven number two are battlegrounds where God's angels clash with Satan's demonic angels and demons in a war for your salvation and well-being. How you interact with these heavens is the difference between life and death, happiness and despair.

So let's briefly discuss these three heavens, and examine both their location and the composition of each. I will begin this discussion with heaven number three because it is the easiest for most people to understand.

The Third Heaven (God's Dwelling Place)

The third heaven is where God the Father and His Son, Jesus Christ—and all who have been redeemed of their sins reside. That perfect place in which we all strive to dwell forever. There is no power struggle there. Satan and his host of fallen angels have been cast out of this heaven. As a result, unlike the other two heavens, no evil exists in the third heaven. It's a perfect place, with perfect love, joy, and peace. The Lord has all power and authority forever and ever in the third heaven. And as believers, we have spiritual access to this heaven when praying in the Spirit, but we have no spiritual authority in this heaven.[13]

The Second Heaven (The Spiritual Realm)

Now let's jump to heaven number two: the spiritual world. This is the spiritual realm that co-exists with our physical world and spans from right here on earth all the way to the gates of heaven, but no farther. Most people are aware of this realm but don't really understand it, and oftentimes are frightened by it. This domain contains Satan and his host of evil entities, both fallen angels and demons. But it also contains God's holy angels. Scripture tells us that **we battle not with flesh and blood, but with principalities, powers, and evil forces in heavenly places.** Many of these battles take place in the second heaven, or what the Bible refers to as "heavenly places."[14]

Isn't it interesting that the devil's spiritual domain has been established right between God's heaven (heaven number three) and our own physical world (heaven number one)? What better place could there be to run interference between God and His people? In the second heaven, the devil and his legion use every tool at their disposal against mankind.

Let's look at two verses that demonstrate the spiritual battle that rages in this unseen realm referred to as the second heaven, and that shows us that God provides angelic protection over us in this spiritual realm.

The first example comes from Daniel 10:1–21 in Daniel's vision by the Tigris River. While he was standing at the Tigris River, Daniel was visited by a mighty angel who told Daniel he had been held up from delivering God's message for twenty-one days by the prince of the kingdom of Persia. Daniel 10:12–13 states it this way:

> *Then he said to me, 'Fear not, Daniel, for from the first day that you set your heart to understand and humbled yourself before your God, your words have been heard, and I have come because of your words. **The prince of the kingdom of Persia withstood me twenty-one days,** but Michael, one of the chief princes, came to help me, for I was left there with the kings of Persia . . .* (emphasis added)

In Daniel 10:20–21, after delivering his message to Daniel, the angel said he would return to continue his battle against this demonic prince.

> *Then he said, "Do you know why I have come to you? **But now I will return to fight against the prince of Persia;** and when I go out, behold, the prince of Greece will come. But I will tell you what is inscribed in the book of truth: there is none who contends by my side against these except Michael, your prince.* (emphasis added)

Clearly, no human prince can do battle with a mighty angel of the Lord—especially for twenty-one days. Scripture refers to one instance when the angel of the Lord, in one night, struck down 185,000 men in the camp of the Assyrians.[15] So battling just one *human* prince would be child's play. In summary, this means that Satan's demonic angel, known as a prince, fought with God's messenger for twenty-one days to prevent the Lord's message from being delivered to Daniel.

Our second example in the Bible also demonstrates how God provides angelic protection over us in this spiritual realm (second heaven), and is ready to come to our rescue in the physical world (or as we will discuss, the first heaven) when necessary. For this example, let's look to Elisha, a prophet of God and a man of great faith who lived in the eighth century before Christ and was the successor to the great prophet Elijah.

Although most men in their normal state cannot see into the spiritual realm or other dimensions, the Bible tells us that this was not the case with Elisha. Apparently, Elisha was fully aware of this other "spiritual" dimension and the angelic protection that God provided for him through it. Elisha's servant that had accompanied him, however, was not keenly aware of this spiritual dimension.[16]

The king of Aram, who was at war with Israel at the time, was in pursuit of Elisha for revealing his military plans to Israel. Although the king would discuss his plans in secret, Elisha, a prophet of God, would know these plans and disclose them to Israel, enraging the king. Being informed that Elisha and his servant were staying in the city of Dothan, the king dispatched a large army with many chariots and horses to surround the city and seize Elisha.

When Elisha's young servant got up early the next morning and went outside, he saw King Aram's troops, horses, and chariots everywhere. The young man in distress cried out to Elisha.[17] Elisha, knowing of God's angelic protection over him and his companion, calmly spoke to his servant:

'Do not be afraid, for those who are with us are more than those who are with them.' Then Elisha prayed and said, 'O LORD, please open his

eyes that he may see.' So the LORD *opened the eyes of the young man, and he saw, and behold, the mountain was full of horses and chariots of fire all around Elisha.*

Although not visible in the physical realm, Elisha knew the Lord had His angels (in the second heaven) present and ready to jump into action on his behalf and that of his companion at a moment's notice. As the Aramean army advanced toward him, Elisha prayed to the Lord, and the Lord struck the Aramean army with blindness.[18]

So, both the story of Daniel and Elisha make clear that angelic forces battle on our behalf in heaven number two. And, although it is debated what authority man has in battling evil spiritual entities in the second heaven, I believe Scripture makes the argument that this battle is primarily the Lord's, not man's—let me explain.

Man's Apparent Lack of Authority in the Second Heaven

I believe man's lack of authority in this realm is clearly evidenced in the books of Daniel and Jude. Take for instance the above story of Daniel at the Tigris River. Gabriel, God's messenger, never requested Daniel's help or prayers in resisting this demonic prince. In fact, Gabriel tells Daniel that no one supports him against this evil entity except the archangel Michael (Daniel 10:21 NIV says, *No one supports me against them except Michael, your prince*). I believe this gives us some very clear understating that this battle in the second heaven is not our battle and is way out of our spiritual league to fight.

Secondly, in the book of Jude, we are told that when the archangel Michael was arguing with Satan over Moses' body, Michael did not dare bring a slanderous statement against Satan but said, *"The Lord rebuke you!"* (Jude 1:9). If the archangel doesn't dare rebuke Satan—the evil leader of this spiritual realm—then we clearly shouldn't either.

The book of Jude goes even further to warn us of the dangers of slandering and abusing these spiritual entities in the second heaven when it says: Yet these people slander whatever they do not understand, **and the very things they do understand by instinct**—as irrational animals do—**will destroy them** (Jude 1:10 NIV, emphasis added). A very stern warning indeed.

So, we can fast, pray, and ask God to deal with these entities, but attempting to do spiritual warfare battle ourselves by cursing against and/or praying against these principalities, powers and evil forces that are located in the second heaven, appears to be stepping outside our realm of authority and can be extremely dangerous. That is, unless called upon by God specifically for this purpose. An excellent resource on this topic can be found in the late John Paul Jackson's book *Needless Casualties of War.* [19]

The First Heaven (the Physical World)

Let's now focus on heaven number one: the physical world in which we live. This heaven includes everything we can see and even the physical things we can't. It's the heavens we gaze at when we look up at the stars. Psalm 19:1 says, *The heavens declare the glory of God, and the sky above proclaims his handiwork.* This world and everything in it is God's handiwork and comprises the first heaven. It stretches, as the psalmist suggests, from our earth to the farthest point in the universe.

Earlier, I referenced the apostle Peter's warning for us to be self-controlled and alert, because our Enemy the devil *prowls around like a roaring lion, seeking someone to devour.* [20] Even though Satan and his demonic army roam around [21] in the second heaven, they look for opportunities, or "legal rights," to *jump from heaven number two into heaven number one,* our physical world, to kill, steal, and destroy us and to inflict harm on our lives. [22]

The book of Revelation makes the point that Satan has a presence in this world. The apostle John is instructed to write to the angel of the church in Pergamum. He says, *I know where you dwell, where Satan's throne is.* [23] Pergamum was an Ancient Greek kingdom on the coast of Asia Minor. It was a very influential Roman city at the time of John's writings, and its ruins can be found today in modern-day Turkey. Although known in the first century for its culture and external beauty, this city was one of the darkest and most evil cities in the Roman Empire.

Apparently at that time, Satan actually located his earthly base in Pergamum, where he had great access to the world and its people. Even though the devil and his host of fallen angels and demons are spiritual in nature, as we will see, they clearly have access to this physical world. And they never stop prowling around and looking for any "legal rights" we might give them to infiltrate our lives in this physical realm, resulting in demonic strongholds, bondages, and torment. For those who are uneducated about this spiritual reality, Satan thrives undetected and uninhibited.

So for all practical purposes, heaven number one is where the rubber meets the road—where Satan's agents jump into our reality (through surrendered legal rights) and engage in physical and mental combat with mankind, where the outcomes of these battles are manifested in godly triumphs and demonic tragedies. Often, we see these victories and defeats played out before us daily.

Fortunately, as believers in Christ, the Lord has not left us defenseless in this battle.

Man's Authority in the First Heaven

In this world (heaven number one), we have been given authority by the Lord to fight and prevail over all the forces of the Evil One. Our authority over evil in this world is a reality that all Christians possess, and one that we should fully understand. I will discuss more on this important topic in Section Three.

At this point, you might be wondering if there is any actual scientific evidence to support the claim that these "three heavens" or three separate realities actually exist. The answer is yes, there is. Let's take a look.

4

Scientific Evidence of the Three Heavens

The string theory was first studied in the 1960s, eventually becoming known as the "Superstring Theory," or—as some in the scientific community call it—"The Theory of Everything." With this theory, the scientific community unwittingly reinforced the sovereignty of God as Creator, and simultaneously provided evidence supporting the existence of the three heavens. I am obviously not a physicist, or have a scientific background. However, I will highlight below a brief history of this theory's development.

This theory, which is still evolving, is the scientific community's great attempt to merge the three forces of nature found in quantum mechanics (*electromagnetism*, the *strong force*, the *weak force*) with the fourth force of nature (*gravity*), into one universal formula. Put another way, prior to the discovery of the string theory, Einstein's theory of relativity, which was his mathematical formula for the big stuff (gravity and space time) could never explain how the small stuff worked (quantum mechanics). Likewise, the math for the small stuff (quantum mechanics) could not explain how the big stuff worked. In other words, these formulas did not mathematically mesh.

The beginning of the solution to this problem came about in 1968, when Gabriele Veneziano, an Italian theoretical physicist, made a breakthrough. Veneziano discovered a centuries-old scientific formula that explained some of the data he had been collecting in his study of the quantum *strong force.*[24] A few years later, in 1974, three physicists using Veneziano's discovered formula, found what appeared to be vibrational motions of energy that resembled strings, hence the string theory name. [25]

Interestingly, the formula suggested the existence of massless particles that no one had ever discovered. These massless particles,[26] that appeared to be from another dimension, were precisely the massless particles predicted by the string theory.

This discovery, that perfectly merged the mathematical formula for the big stuff (gravity and space time) with the mathematical formula for the small stuff (quantum mechanics), indicated the startling fact that our universe is comprised of ten dimensions—four of these spatial dimensions (height, width, depth, and time) that form the world in which we live, and six other spatial dimensions previously unknown to man.

Interestingly, this equates to three separate realities (heaven number one, heaven number two, and heaven number three) each containing height, width, and depth, which result in nine dimensions, and the tenth dimension being time, which runs through each dimension. And if two of these realities—heaven number one (our physical world) and heaven number two (the spiritual world)—are next to one another, as the string theory suggests is possible, this could explain how angels, both good and evil, seem to appear and disappear instantly in our physical reality.[27]

It's interesting to note that a Hebrew sage by the name of Nachmonides, writing in the thirteenth century, through simply studying the book of Genesis also predicted our universe was made up of ten dimensions—*four knowable by man, and six that were unknown to us.*[28]

And even though more recent evidence has hypothesized there may be well in excess of ten dimensions,[29] we must remember that God can do as He wishes for His own glory. We cannot put Him in a box. He could have created 10,000 dimensions. And, as we discussed before, no matter whether ten or 10,000 dimensions exist, He is the Lord of them all.

And although man, with few exceptions, is limited to existing within his own worldly dimensions, angels, on the other hand, are not, and appear to be able to jump between these dimensions at will. We know that three angels appeared in human form and ate dinner with Abraham and Sarah to inform them about their coming son,[30] and we know two angels came as men to warn and remove Lot and his family from the coming destruction at Sodom and Gomorrah.[31]

This ability to jump between dimensions apparently applies not only to God's holy angels but to Satan's fallen angels as well. As we will discuss in the second book in this series, *In The Devil's Toolbox: The Coming Deception— When the Second Heaven Invades Earth*, the ability to jump between realities will be explored more, and will explain the many stories we hear about fallen angels appearing out of nowhere, physically encountering mankind, and then disappearing into thin air.

Further Scientific Evidence of Additional Dimensions

The European Organization for Nuclear Research (CERN) is one of the world's largest and most respected centers for scientific research.[32] Even if you haven't heard of it, you've probably heard of its Large Hadron Collider or their discovery of the Higgs Boson Particle (a.k.a., "The God Particle") in 2012.[33] But it has also made other interesting discoveries, such as weak neutral currents, light neutrinos, and antimatter.

But what some find even more interesting than these discoveries are the comments made by Sergio Bertolucci, director of research and scientific computing, regarding the potential existence of other dimensions, and their expectation to possibly bridge these interdimensional boundaries. Mr. Bertolucci told reporters in September 2009, while discussing this topic of interdimensional boundaries, "Out of this door might come something, or we might send something through it."[34]

So interestingly, one of the overall expectations of the largest scientific project ever undertaken by man, involving over 12,500 scientists and more than 110 nationalities,[35] is to potentially bridge our dimensional boundary, and make contact with another dimension—another dimension that the string theory has proven to exist. One must ask, "Why would such an institution search for another dimensional reality, if this other worldly dimension did not exist?" The answer is, they wouldn't.

If you were unaware of these other dimensions, the reality of these three heavens, and how they can interact with your life, you may be exactly where I was many years ago—unaware, bewildered, and somewhat alarmed, to put it mildly. When I first learned of these spiritual dimensions and the spiritual warfare that was raging within them, I was flat out spooked. But as I studied and learned more about this reality and how it works, I became much more at ease. I realized I had no reason to be alarmed by this new revelation, and I actually became comfortable with this understanding, knowing that God is the Creator of all of these dimensions—both visible and invisible—and He knows their purpose and has them all under His authority and control. We only need to look at the Bible to see these truths.[36] And God, as He demonstrated with Elisha and Elisha's servant in protecting them from King Aram,[37] provides His angels to protect all who walk closely with Him, and who call upon His name.[38]

I came to understand that as children of Christ and inheritors of His spirit, we not only have God's angelic protection promised by His Scriptures but also assurance of victory over the demonic players in this spiritual realm. Scripture tells us, *For he who is in you is greater than he who is in the world.*[39] In other words, the Holy Spirit, who lives inside each believer, is greater than the devil and his spiritual hosts that inhabit our world. But we must submit to Christ to assert this power.

If you're not a Christian, however, you don't have this protection or the power and authority over these evil entities. That's a scary thought. For some, simply understanding that this warfare is raging in heaven number one and heaven number two is a real eye opener. But this new understanding also causes us to ask the following question: Why was the devil allowed by God to gain access to our world in the first place?

We will address this question in the next chapter.

How Did Satan Obtain His Authority in This World Anyway?

Many people wonder why God even allows Satan the authority to exist in this world. This is an important question—one that needs to be answered. To do so, we will look first at Satan's claim that he has been given authority to operate within this world, and then look at how Satan supports his claim that he has obtained legal authority within this world.

Let's look first at Satan's declaration to Jesus that he had obtained authority in this world. Three of the four Gospels—Matthew, Mark, and Luke—discuss Jesus' temptation by the devil after His baptism and forty-day fast in the wilderness. In one of these temptations, Satan boasted about the authority he had over this world while tempting Christ in the wilderness. Look again at what Satan said as he brought Jesus to a high place to tempt Him showing Him all of the kingdoms of the world. Satan stated, *I will give you all their authority and splendor; it has been given to me, and I can give it to anyone I want to. If you worship me, it will all be yours.*[40]

Interestingly, Jesus didn't take issue with the devil's claim to exert authority over the kingdoms of the world. Since God never delegated this authority to Satan, how in the world did the devil gain this authority he claims to possess? Some Bible commentators point out that Satan is the father of lies and never possessed the authority that he boasted about to Christ. But I would disagree. I believe the Bible text supports the position that Satan did obtain authority in this world.

In the Garden of Eden, God gave man authority over this world and all that was in it.[41] In fact, Psalm 115:16 says, *The heavens are the* L*ord*'s *heavens, but the earth he has given to the children of man.* But God also gave man the free will to reject Him. When Adam and Eve chose to reject God's spoken Word as truth and believe Satan's lie, their choice caused them to "sin" against God, and in doing so, they surrendered (at least in part) their authority over this world to the Great Deceiver, Satan. At that moment, Satan obtained through this sin the "legal right" or authority he needed to enter this world—an authority Satan has enjoyed for several thousand years.

How do we know that man, through this sin, surrendered (at least in part) his authority over this world to Satan and that Satan entered our world at this point? Because when sin entered the world, man became separated from God, and man himself became cursed. Man's physical make-up changed. Man, which had been designed and coded only for life, was now coded for death.

In addition, the earth changed. Once a perfect dwelling where God Himself dwelt with man, it likewise became cursed.

Romans 8:19–23 also tells us:

*For the creation waits with eager longing for the revealing of the sons of God. For the creation was subjected to futility, not willingly, but because of him who subjected it, in hope that the creation itself will be set free from its bondage to corruption and obtain the freedom of the glory of the children of God. For we know **that the whole creation has been groaning together in the pains of childbirth until now**. And not only the creation, but we ourselves, who have the firstfruits of the Spirit, groan inwardly as we wait eagerly for adoption as sons, the redemption of our bodies.* (emphasis added)

Man's sin in the garden granted Satan the "legal right" and thereby the legal authority he needed to corrupt not only the world, but to enter into the very life of every man, as demonstrated by Satan's presence in this world.

But Christ, through His death on the cross and resurrection from the grave, stripped and disarmed Satan of much of his inherited worldly authority, and reclaimed this authority for His church. The Bible says that Jesus, *having disarmed the powers and authorities, he made a public spectacle of them, triumphing over them by the cross.*[42] Jesus also confirmed this when He told His disciples after His resurrection, *All authority in heaven and on earth has been given to me.*[43]

By the cross, Satan's rule on earth ended. Man would no longer be captive to Satan's authority. Said another way, by the cross, Jesus set us free from sin, the fear of death, man's subjugation to the Law, and the power of the Evil One.[44] Those who were previously held captive by the power of the Evil One, and fear of death, now had the ability to break free from this bondage.

But make no mistake, Satan still maintains his presence and a level of power in this world. As we have stated, the apostle Peter tells us in 1 Peter 5:8, *Be sober-minded; be watchful. Your adversary the devil prowls around like a roaring lion, seeking someone to devour*, a warning given to us after Jesus had risen from the cross and had made a public spectacle of Satan, and a warning that would have been unnecessary if Satan did not still have some level of access to mankind.

And man's continued disobedience has managed to further Satan's power and control in this world. We know this because we are told in Ephesians 2:1–3 (NIV), *As for you, you were dead in your transgressions and sins, in which you used to live when you followed the ways of this world and of the* **ruler of the kingdom of the air**, *the spirit who is now at work in those who are disobedient. All of us also lived among them at one time, gratifying the cravings of our flesh and following its desires and thoughts. Like the rest, we were by nature deserving of wrath* (emphasis added).

In the next several chapters, we will discuss how Satan uses his remaining worldly power and authority to further influence our way of thinking, and to sneak into our lives under the radar, so to speak, so we won't notice him and assert Christ's protection against him. So be alert, and on guard for this deception.[45]

To help understand what authority Satan possesses in this world, I have generated a seven thousand year timeline. This timeline will indicate the approximate level of Satan's worldly authority and access to mankind, along with the events that changed his access to our lives, and can be found in the Appendix at the back of this book.

So, if you are like me, you may be wondering, "If all of this spiritual warfare is really going on all around me, then why in the world wasn't I told about it?"

Why Didn't Someone Tell Me about Spiritual Warfare?

Twenty-five years ago, I didn't know anything about spiritual warfare. Maybe that's where you are right now, so let's get specific about what it means. Spiritual warfare may be defined as follows: the warfare going on between Jesus Christ and His army of elect spiritual beings (angels), and the devil and his army of evil spiritual beings (fallen angels and demons).

As spiritual beings, we are involved in this warfare to the fullest extent. In fact, we are the object of this warfare. But for many of us, this is taking place without our knowledge, and it is tough to win a war you don't know you're involved in. I have come to understand two basic reasons Christians neglect this important topic.

First, I learned that even though spiritual warfare has been a church doctrine from the days of the first-century church, it appears it has not often been taught in many seminaries. Knowing that the early church's converts almost always came from cities and towns with severe demonic strongholds like Ephesus (the book of Ephesians), and that a basic practice of the church was personal deliverance from these demonic strongholds, it was hard for me to understand how American churches had lost this critically important teaching.

Second, because the topic of spiritual warfare is so sensitive, I believe the church doesn't discuss this topic during worship for fear of scaring people off. To me, that's the same as purposely neglecting to inform your army of soldiers that the enemy may have chemical weapons, and that you had better prepare accordingly. It might unsettle them a bit, but at least they are aware of the situation and can adequately prepare themselves for battle. Without this information, these soldiers are completely and unknowingly exposed, just like we are if we are unaware of the devil's schemes. A spiritual position that Paul warns against when he advises us in 2 Corinthians 2:11 (NKJV) *lest Satan should take advantage of us; for we are not ignorant of his devices.*

If you are wondering if this spiritual warfare described above could really exist, take another look at the Scriptures. Spiritual warfare is discussed throughout the Bible, from Eve's deception in the Garden of Eden to the end times' battle of Armageddon. Jesus acknowledged our battle with the devil and these demonic spirits and repeatedly showed His dominance and authority over them.[46]

In almost every circumstance in which Christ told His disciples to preach the good news of the gospel, He accompanied His command with the charge that they also cast out demons[47]—a charge that confirms our earthly battle with spiritual beings and Christ's authority over these demonic adversaries.

If you're like me and were blind to all this, you have also succumbed to the devil's number one trick: to stay so well-hidden and below the radar that most people either don't believe he exists, or they think he isn't active in our everyday lives. The devil is equally pleased with both positions.

With this in mind, let's pull back the curtain, and examine the three sources of attack the devil uses against us in this world.

Our Three Sources of Attack: The Devil, the World, and the Flesh

The Great Deceiver cleverly delivers his attacks against us today using the same methods he used 2,000 years ago. While these three methods are very predictable, they're also very effective.

- **The Devil (and the demons who serve him)**
- **The World (which the devil has been given access to)**
- **The Flesh (our sin nature): Lust of the Flesh, Lust of the Eyes, and the Pride of Life**

Sower of the Seed and our Three Sources of Attack

Christ revealed these three methods of attack in the Parable of the Sower.

And when a great crowd was gathering and people from town after town came to him [Jesus], he said in a parable, 'A sower went out to sow his seed. And as he sowed, some **fell along the path** *and was trampled underfoot, and the birds of the air devoured it. And some* **fell on the rock,** *and as it grew up, it withered away, because it had no moisture. And some* **fell among thorns,** *and the thorns grew up* *with it and choked it. And some fell into good soil and grew and yielded a hundredfold.' As he said these things, he called out, 'He who has ears to hear, let him hear.'*[48] (brackets added, emphasis added)

The Devil

In Matthew 13:19, Christ explained to His disciples that the seed **sown on the path** is like *anyone who hears the word of the kingdom and does not understand it, the **evil one** comes and snatches away what has been sown in his heart. This is what was sown along the path.* (emphasis added) The Evil One is, of course, the devil.

The World

Jesus continued in Matthew 13:20–21 to explain that the seed which **fell on rocky ground** is like *the one who hears the word and receives it at once with joy, yet he has no root in himself, but endures for a while, and **when tribulation or persecution arises** on account of the word, immediately he falls away.* (emphasis added) This persecution and tribulation comes from the **world**. Scripture tells us that the world is under the influence of Satan.[49] And we know the world will reject and persecute the believer, just as it did Jesus. That is why Jesus tells us in John 15:20 . . . *if they persecute me, they will persecute you. . .*

The Flesh

Christ further explained in Matthew 13:22 that the seed **sown among the thorns** is like the one who hears and accepts the Word of God, *but the cares of the world and the deceitfulness of riches choke the word, and it proves unfruitful.* (emphasis added) It's our **fleshly desires** (lust of the flesh, lust of the eyes, pride of life) that chase after worldly riches, that arouses in us anxiety about such things, and that separates us from God's will for our lives.

So, it is important that we are aware of and understand these three means of attack the Enemy uses against us, including the resources he uses to draw us away from the saving grace of Jesus Christ and the fulfilling life that God has provided for us through His Spirit.

Let's get started and examine these three sources of attack starting with our first source: the **devil**.

Our First Source of Attack
The Devil (and the Demons Who Serve Him)

Our Thought Life

As Christians, we possess Christ's power to overcome the devil, *because greater is He who is in you than he who is in the world* (1 John 4:4, NASB). But we can still be influenced by his deception if we aren't aware of his schemes against us.[50] Many people believe that when they become a Christian, they are protected in all ways from demonic influence. This is true to an extent. When we become Christians, we are given power over the Enemy and do inherit God-given protection. But, once you become a Christian, this also puts you directly in the line of fire of the devil's attacks because now you are in opposition to his kingdom. The apostle Paul expresses his concern for us in this area when he says, *But I am afraid that as the serpent deceived Eve by his cunning, your thoughts will be led astray from a sincere and pure devotion to Christ.*[51]

Satan can attack us in a number of ways, even if we are a Christian. One of these ways is through our thoughts. Paul was aware that the devil could influence our thoughts as well as place thoughts into our mind (a tactic we're all subject to). He knew we had to **protect our minds** from these fiery darts of Satan by staying focused on God's Word or we would become open game for the devil's mental assaults.[52] Let me give you a few biblical examples as to the reason for Paul's concern. The first example comes from the apostle Peter.

Satan "Sifting" Peter to deny Christ

Peter was a Christian, yet the devil placed thoughts into his mind that provoked Peter to tell Christ "not to be crucified." Christ's response was, *get behind me, Satan!*[53] Those are strong words for someone who Christ just minutes before had given the keys to His church.[54] This tells us two things:

1. Your status as a Christian gives you no defense from the devil placing thoughts into your mind.
2. Peter didn't even realize that it was the devil who placed this thought in his mind, but Christ knew.

Later, Christ told Peter that the devil had demanded to **sift you like wheat,**[55] but Christ told Peter He had prayed for him that he might be saved. Peter had no idea what this "sifting" might look like. Even with Christ's forewarning, the devil "sifted" Peter's mind and emotions, and Peter denied Christ three times, as Christ said he would. His mind was sifted by the devil, but Christ's prayers sustained him.

Satan "Incited" David to Number Israel

Next, consider King David—the same David who as a boy slew Goliath, and who God proclaimed as *a man after my heart.*[56] The devil's attack on the mind of King David is found in 1 Chronicles 21:1 (emphasis added), *Then Satan stood against Israel and **incited David to number Israel.***[57] Going against the advice of Joab, his military commander, David submitted to this mental and emotional prompting from the devil, and ordered Joab to count Israel—a sign of David's reliance on human power and authority, not God's. This act was displeasing to God. Seventy thousand men of Israel died as a result of a census conceived by the devil.

The deceptions you and I have encountered probably do not come with such dire consequences as this, but if the devil can do this to King David, do you think he will have any problem with us?

Satan "Filled the Heart" of Ananias and Sapphira to Lie to the Holy Spirit

Third, remember that the devil attacked the mind of Ananias, a property owner in the early Christian church. Within the early Christian community, believers willingly sold all their possessions and brought the proceeds before the apostles, and the proceeds were distributed to each according to need.

As described in Acts 5:3, Ananias apparently sold a piece of his property. He retained, with his wife's knowledge, some of the purchase price and took the remainder to the apostles as full payment for the property. Peter said to him, *Ananias, why has Satan **filled your heart** to lie to the Holy Spirit and to keep back for yourself part of the proceeds of the land?* (emphasis added). When Peter confronted Ananias about this deceit, Ananias fell dead at his feet. Likewise, when his wife, Sapphira, was brought to the apostles, she also tested the Spirit of the Lord and lied to them about the proceeds of the land, instantly falling dead. Again, our surrender to the devil's deceptions doesn't usually have such immediate consequences, but as you can see, the devil planted this seed of deception in the heart's and mind's of Ananias and Sapphira, and it cost them their lives.

Satan "Placed into the Heart" of Judas to Betray Christ

And last, let's look at one more story I'm sure you will recognize. Before Christ was handed over to the Pharisees and put to death in the city of Jerusalem, He was betrayed by one of His disciples, Judas. Why did Judas commit such an act? John 13:2 tells us that *During supper, **when the devil had already put it into the heart** of Judas Iscariot, Simon's son, to betray him* ... (emphasis added). Once again, Scripture tells us that it was the devil who planted this seed into the heart of Judas to betray Christ. A deception that led him to take his own life.

So Satan Can Plant Thoughts into Our Minds

In these four examples, the devil deceptively *sifted, incited, filled,* and *placed* into the unsuspecting hearts, minds, and emotions of men his own agenda. If the devil can deceive these men and women, he can certainly deceive you and me. We all have areas of emotional vulnerability and spiritual weakness in our character. The devil knows about these areas and preys on them. The devil also knows that if we become aware of his ability to place thoughts into our mind, stirring our emotions, it will become more difficult for him to slip his life-destroying deception into our minds.

By learning the devil's schemes, we block the devil's most effective method of attack—obscurity. By learning that all our thoughts are not our own, and by quickly dismissing those which are not in line with Scripture, we establish a strong first line of defense against the deception of the Great Deceiver.

If you're like me, it's a total shock to learn that your mind is not your own. The mind has been characterized by some as a playground in which three people play: yourself, God, and the devil. Your mind is as accessible to God and the devil as the breeze is coming in through a window.[58] If you don't know or believe this, you are being misled. That's what the devil wants.

Please allow me to clarify one point. Although I don't believe we are responsible for every evil thought that comes into our minds, I do believe we are responsible for what we do with these thoughts. It is ultimately your decision which thoughts you choose to follow or dismiss. Even though your thoughts may not be one hundred percent your own, your decision or will to follow them is. If you dwell on, nurture, or act on sinful or evil thoughts—that is your fault, and you are responsible for this conduct no matter where the thought arose from. But again, if you are blaming yourself for every evil or sinful thought that pops into your mind, then you are probably being much too hard on yourself.

Our Second Source of Attack
The World (Which the Devil Has Been Given Access To)

I don't know about you, but I always believed the world was under God's control. In the big scheme of things, it is. But as we covered earlier, God has allowed the devil direct access to the world, which means he can have a direct influence in our lives. Scripture reveals this in multiple places.

As we have previously discussed in Chapter Five, the devil took Jesus to a high place and showed Him all the kingdoms of the world in all their glory, and offered these kingdoms to Jesus if He would worship him.[59] When I first read this, I wondered how the devil could give away the kingdoms of the world. What right does he have? He can't give something away that he doesn't own. But take notice, as we stated before: Christ didn't argue with the devil about ownership rights.[60] Adam and Eve, through their choice of disobedience to the Word of God in the Garden of Eden, allowed the devil to obtain a "legal right" to this world.

God, in His ultimate wisdom, has allowed the devil to co-exist with us in this world to achieve His ultimate plan for mankind, so, the devil shares this world with us, at least for a time. A good way to think of this is that God is the rightful owner and landlord of our world and the devil is the permitted tenant. The tenant has full rights (within God's set limits) to use this property, this world, as he chooses during the term of his lease. But the moment the lease ends, the landlord, Jesus Christ, will return and expel the tenant and resume full control of His property. But during his residency, the devil uses this world to lure us away from God and His truth.

The devil deceives us by leading us to believe that our joy, peace, happiness, and love can be achieved through the accumulation of material goods. But material goods lead to a false sense of security. You might become comfortable by accumulating many things, but joy, peace, and happiness are not by-products of wealth.

We are all spiritual beings, designed by God with a spiritual gap. This gap is designed to be filled by the Holy Spirit, and that comes from our accepting Christ as our Lord and Savior. Physical things can never fill a spiritual gap.

Scripture makes it clear that only our relationship with Christ can produce what we truly desire, and were created for—the Spirit of love, joy, peace, patience, kindness, goodness, faithfulness, gentleness, and self-control.[61] This is why we are told that we are complete in Christ.[62]

This world also leads us to believe that acquiring a position of power or authority or earthly wealth will bring us joy, peace, and happiness. Again, it cannot. Jesus turned down the world and all its riches as a poor imitation of the glory to be given Him by God. Interestingly, many of us spend the majority of our time and talents devising ways to accumulate the very same earthly treasures Jesus rejected as a fraudulent substitute for the true joy and peace He offers us on the cross—an exchange Jesus refused to make and we should as well. Now let's look at the devil's third source of attack.

Our Third Source of Attack
The Flesh (Our Sin Nature):
Lust of the Flesh, Lust of the Eyes, and the Pride of Life

When Adam fell from God's grace in the Garden of Eden, mankind fell from grace. This means every human born after the fall of man was born with a sin nature. This doesn't mean we sin the minute we are born, it means we're born with a sin nature or the propensity to sin.

Everyone would agree it can be easier to be bad than good. We don't have to learn how to be bad. But we do have to learn how to be good. Why? Because of our sin nature—that internal tendency or predisposition to act out of selfishness (the flesh), rather than love.

And although we break the power hold that sin has over us at our conversion,[63] we still feel the gravitational pull that our old sin nature exerts over us. The closer to Christ we become, the less power this pull has. Paul described his battle with his own sin nature when he said, *For I do not do the good I want, but the evil I do not want is what I keep on doing.*[64]

Unless we are keenly aware that we can be easily deceived through our own fallen nature, we can be easily led into temptation through our former wants and desires.[65] Scripture tells us that we *once lived in the passions of our flesh, carrying out the desires of the body and the mind, and were by nature children of wrath, like the rest of mankind.*[66] Scripture goes on to list certain characteristics of the flesh: *sexual immorality, impurity, sensuality, idolatry, sorcery, enmity, strife, jealousy, fits of anger, rivalries, dissensions, divisions, envy, drunkenness, and orgies,* just to name a few.[67] But Scripture gives us the remedy for this problem. It tells us that if we walk in the Spirit, we will not fulfill the lusts of the flesh.[68] In other words, if we submit our thoughts to Christ, think about and act upon His precepts, surrendering our heart and will to the Lord, we will walk through life in line with the Spirit.[69] Characteristics of a Spirit-filled life include love, joy, peace, patience, kindness, goodness, faithfulness, gentleness, and self-control.[70]

However, left unchecked, our sin nature will automatically open us up to the devil's influences, suggestions, and nudges. He cleverly blurs the lines between our actual needs and desires with his excessive and addictive needs and desires. These excessive needs and desires are then sold to us by the devil as legitimate. God calls these excessive desires *lust.* We can lust for a person, drug, alcohol, money, food, praise, possession, sex, or any number of things.

Scripture tells us, *Love not the **world**, neither the things that are in the **world**. If any man love the **world**, the love of the Father is not in him. For all that is in the **world**, the lust of the flesh, and the lust of the eyes, and the pride of life, is not of the Father, but is of the **world***[71] (emphasis added).

Merriam-Webster defines lust as a usually intense or unbridled sexual desire. The Greek word for lust is *epithumos*. The prefix *epi* means to "add to," telling us that something has been added to our normal desire. Adding to our normal desire is one of the devil's specialties—just ask anyone hooked on pornography, illicit sex, drugs, alcohol, gambling, and the list goes on.

The devil knows that our physical bodies become addicted to these stimulants, so he lures us into these excesses until our physical bodies demand that we continue the process. His objective is to elevate these desires above all else, including God. When our God-given natural desires get distorted into unnatural and unhealthy desires, the devil has his hooks in us.

We are warned repeatedly in Scripture about succumbing to such things. That's what the apostle Paul was referring to when he said, *For whatever overcomes a person, to that he is enslaved*[72]—an enslavement that usually has its roots in a spiritual stronghold mindset. But this mindset oftentimes has a physical component as well. Let's look at some science that supports this position.

The Science behind God's Word

I always find it tremendously satisfying when someone presents scientific facts and explanations that confirm God's great Words. Such are the below facts on why the pursuit of *lust of the flesh* produces an entirely different outcome in people's lives than those who live their lives pursuing the *works of the Spirit* as defined in God's Word.

Such was the wonderful explanation of the difference between two of mans' most sought after emotions—the emotion of *pleasure* and *happiness* as described by Dr. Robert Lustig, a professor in the Department of Pediatrics in the Division of Endocrinology at the University of California, San Francisco.[73]

Dr. Lustig explains that the stimulus that creates the emotion of *pleasure* (produced the chemical dopamine) is quite different than the stimulus that creates the emotion of *happiness* (produced by the chemical serotonin). Dr. Lustig also explains that these two stimuli and the body's reaction to each couldn't be more opposite. Dr. Lustig discusses his findings in an interview, as well as in his book *The Hacking of the American Mind, The Science behind the Corporate Takeover of Our Bodies and Brains*.[74]

Although Dr. Lustig's interview, discussion, and writings on these two emotions do not reference Scripture, nor does he discuss them in this context, his findings are quite consistent with what we find in the Word of God.

Dopamine and the Feeling of Pleasure

Dr. Lustig reports that substances such as alcohol, drugs, pornography, and other such material things we crave, all promote a neurochemical reaction that increases levels of dopamine in our brain.[75] This produces the feeling of *pleasure* that according to Dr. Lustig, tells us *"this feels good, I want more."* This feeling can be the driving force behind lust. Dr. Lustig goes on to explain the chemical dopamine excites the next neuron—and neurons, when they're excited too much, too frequently—tend to die. So the neuron has a defense mechanism. It's a process that Dr. Lustig notes as *down regulation*. What the body does is reduce the number of receptors that are available to be stimulated in an attempt to try and mitigate the damage.

So the next time, a bigger and bigger amount of the same stimuli is required to get the same erotic feeling, because there are less receptors available to be stimulated. This then becomes a vicious cycle which results in becoming more and more dependent on whatever substance is used to get the high, erotic feeling until huge doses of stimulus produce no high at all. Dr. Lustig says that when people find themselves not being able to concentrate on their job or on their family because their craving calls to them, and it interferes with their daily life in some fashion or in their work—that's usually a sign of addiction. This is a condition the devil would love for us all to be trapped in: chasing after the *lust of the flesh* and *lust of the eyes*. Promises that never satisfy.

Serotonin and the Feeling of Happiness

According to Dr. Lustig, the feeling of *happiness*, is produced by the release of the chemical serotonin in the brain. Interestingly, according to Dr. Lustig, serotonin works on a completely different basis than dopamine. Serotonin stimulates the nerves with a sensation that produces the feeling of contentment or satisfaction and this chemical does not overload or damage the receptors. Interestingly, Dr. Lustig notes, this chemical produces *"no craving for more"* of this stimuli—only contentment.

Interestingly, acts that are consistent with what the Bible indicates as the *fruit of the Spirit*, such as doing things for others, unselfish love, and acts of kindness—all appear to induce this chemical (serotonin) that produces the feeling of happiness and contentment in one's life known as serotonin.

There is No Cost to a Spirit-Filled Life

Jesus tells us, *whoever drinks the water I give them will never thirst.*[76] There is no cost for a Spirit-filled life. We know that God works in mysterious ways, and sometimes it's just fun to get a look inside and see how His Word actually manifests in even these tiny biochemical systems of our body.

So, if you absolutely have to have something—and you have to have it now—you're probably being duped. The devil's solution to this craving will never lead you toward peace or happiness. Instead, it will always lead you toward satisfying your desires with a replacement god—the addiction.

So why do some people struggle with bigger issues than others? And why are some attacks of the Enemy so effective against us and others are not? It has a lot to do with how much "legal access" we have given to the Enemy to influence us.

Let's examine how we give "legal access" to the Enemy. I'll start with a brief examination of the laws of the spiritual realm, and how violating these laws can create a "legal right" for the Enemy to invade our lives.

8

Laws of the Spiritual Realm

Most of us are aware that God is a God of love, but also a God of law and order. Jesus gave us the new commandment that we love one another, but He also came to fulfill that Law and the precepts that God has given us, and that we are to strive to follow. Even though as believers in Christ we have been freed from the Law,[77] (i.e., we are saved by faith and not by adhering to the Law)[78] we are still subject to the *spirit* of the Law,[79] for Christ came to fulfill the Law, not destroy it.[80]

Let me explain. When Christ freed us from the Law, He freed us to live by a more excellent standard, the *spirit* of the Law.[81] The *spirit* of the Law is based on our love for God,[82] and Jesus' new commandment that we love one another.[83] This new standard is revealed in Jesus' comment to us when He stated *everyone who hates his brother is a murderer . . .*[84] and that *everyone who looks at a woman with lustful intent has already committed adultery with her in his heart.*[85]

This more excellent standard, the *spirit* of the Law, goes much deeper than the Law, it goes to the **heart** of man. So even, though we are freed from the Law, if we violate the *spirit* of the Law, we still sin. But we know that Jesus died for our sins. So the question arises: If we are forgiven for our sins, what, if any, is the consequence of our sin, and does our sinning really matter?

1st Law—*Sin Can Always Provide a "Legal Right"*

So, if we are saved by grace—through our faith in Jesus Christ, and not by following the Law or the *spirit* of the Law—does our sinning matter? Or put another way, does grace give us a license to sin? The answer is, of course not. Grace provides no place for intentional sinning. The apostle Paul explained this exact point to the disciples in the book of Romans when addressing this question: *What then? Are we to sin because we are not under law but under grace? By no means!*[86]

Sin is defined as "actions by which humans rebel against God, miss His purpose for their life, and surrender to the power of the evil rather than God."[87] Yet we all sin every day. And if sin in our lives provides a "legal right" to the Evil One, how then do we protect ourselves?

God Protects the Believer

One of the greatest truths in the Bible is that Jesus died to take away all of our sins—our past sins, our present sins, and our future sins.[88] And by accepting Jesus' sacrifice, our sins are forgiven, and have been nailed to the cross. Through our confession of faith in the risen Lord, not only is our salvation secured[89]—an incredible privilege, but our relationship with the Lord also greatly protects us from the Enemy. First John 5:18 tells us, *we know that everyone who has been born of God does not keep on sinning, but he who was born of **God protects him, and the evil one does not touch him*** (emphasis added).

So why is this protection important? Because we all continue to sin daily. Even if our actions are noble and pure, who among us can claim that our *thoughts* are always pure? No one can. And sin breaks our fellowship with God. And anytime we have a break in our fellowship with God, we provide the possibility of a foothold for the devil to come into our lives.[90] The more we sin, the more opportunity we give the adversary to access our life.

So the question that arises is this: If we are a believer and under the grace of the Lord Jesus, our sins are forgiven, and we are told the Enemy cannot touch us, **then how does our sinning provide an opportunity, or a "legal right" to the Enemy?**

But We Can Still Provide a "Legal Right"

Put another way, is there a point in one's sinning in which a Christian opens the door to the Enemy, providing "legal access" to the devil and his host of demons? And if so, at what point in our sinning is this place of "legal access" reached? Do we cross this point based on the type of sin we commit, or is it based on our intent in the sin? Or is it based on our indifference to the sin (hardened heart), or the length of time we remain in the sinful state?

All great questions, and the honest answer is "I simply don't know," and I'm not sure anyone else does either. But we do know, as believers there is a limit to our sinning that once reached, puts us smack in the arms of the Enemy. Guessing at what point this is reached is almost like trying to guess "How much pressure does it take to pop a balloon?" You simply aren't sure, but you do know that it will eventually happen, if you keep applying pressure.

In fact, the apostle Paul, in a similar fashion on two separate occasions, "turned over" a member of the Christian church, who continually insisted on sinning, and hardened their heart against the Lord, to Satan for reprove. Paul stated, . . . *you are to deliver this man to Satan for the destruction of the flesh, so that his spirit may be saved in the day of the Lord* (1 Corinthians 5:5, emphasis added). And again in 1 Timothy 1:20, the apostle Paul stated, regarding two other church members, . . . *among whom are Hymenaeus and Alexander, whom I have* **handed over to Satan** *that they may learn not to blaspheme* (emphasis added).

I would certainly argue that what Paul is talking about here when he states: "hand this person over to the devil," *is not* handing this person over to what I have labeled in Chapter Fourteen as level one spiritual warfare—meaning subjection to spiritual mental strongholds, because we are all potentially subjected to this. I would suggest that Paul is talking about handing this church member over to what I have labeled in Chapter Fourteen as level two spiritual warfare—or a level of spiritual warfare that subjects the individual to inhabitation by a demonic spirit, with all of the torment, compulsions, and bondage that it represents.

But notice, Paul is doing this so that the brother's **spirit** may be saved. It appears this verse means one of two things: Either this brother has lost (or is in danger of losing) his salvation, and Paul is hoping that by handing him over to Satan he will suffer greatly in the flesh and will repent and return to his prior salvific state. Or, that the Church is turning over this man to Satan for destruction of his body, for preservation of his spirit, which is to remain safe in God's hands for the day of redemption. If it is the latter, then it reveals for us the distinction between Satan having access to one's body and mind, yet at the same time being prevented from accessing the man's spirit—where some believe the Holy Spirit resides—which remains for the redeemed believer in the Lord's sole possession. (emphasis added)

The above two Scripture verses are excellent examples of what can happen in the spiritual realm to Christians who persist with their sinning. As you read through the remaining laws of the spiritual realm, remember this first spiritual principle: Sinning can always provide a "legal right" to the Enemy.

I have listed below our standing as believers (and non-believers) before Christ, and how this standing can greatly protect us from the Enemy.

BELIEVERS	NON-BELIEVERS
• Continue to sin[91]	• Continue to sin
• Sins are forgiven[92]	• Sins are unforgiven
• Have been removed from the curse[93]	• Are under a curse
• Not judged under the Law, but are under grace[94]	• Judged under the Law
• Required to uphold the *spirit* of the Law[95]	• Required to uphold the Law
• Access to the Enemy is greatly restricted[96]	• Access to the Enemy is much greater

2nd Law—*God's Laws and Precepts Transcend into the Spiritual Realm*

So how does sin provide a "legal right" to the Enemy? We all know that violating man's laws sometimes has an immediate or direct consequence in this world. We see and hear about this daily with those committing sins or crimes against another and being led off to jail. However, our sins appear to go unnoticed.

What most of us are unaware of and don't understand, is that God's Laws and commandments transcend into the spiritual realm. And unlike in the world, where our violation of man's laws often times go unnoticed, our violation of God's Laws and precepts **never goes unnoticed in the spiritual realm**, and *always* has the potential to cause a spiritual consequence. Let me explain.

In the Lord's Prayer, we ask for forgiveness for our trespasses. What is a trespass? *Merriam Webster's Dictionary* offers the definition as "a violation of moral or social ethics... TRANGRESSION; especially: SIN.[97]

Transgressing against the *spirit* of the Law of the Lord makes us a spiritual trespasser. As such, we lose certain rights and protections that we enjoy when we remain within the Lord's spiritual domain. Venturing into these unauthorized areas can make us subject to the devil and his hosts while we remain in that trespass. And anytime we trespass into the devil's domain, we potentially lose certain protections the Lord provides for us against the Enemy.

Further evidence that God's Laws and precepts transcend into the spiritual realm, is made apparent for us as we examine the next spiritual law—"Thoughts Matter."

3rd Law—*Thoughts Matter; We Can Sin Mentally*

When most people think of sin, they think of some wrongful action or conduct, and this would be correct. But did you know we can also sin mentally?

We know through Scripture that the Lord not only knows our thoughts,[98] but He examines our thoughts.[99] Thoughts that are contrary to the Spirit such as lust, covetousness, hatred, prolonged anger, unforgiveness, intentional desire to pursue evil, or holding onto any emotion that is contrary to the Spirit of God, can open one up to the harassment, oppression, or possibly even some level of control by the Enemy.

I'm a lawyer by trade. In criminal law, intent to commit a crime is one of the many elements that is required for the accused to be found guilty. The legal term for this is called *mens rea* or "guilty mind." However, it is only when this intent is coupled with an illegal act of some type that the accused can be found guilty of a crime. One's mental intent alone (or guilty mind) is not enough for a finding of guilt.

In the spiritual realm, however this rule doesn't apply. In the spiritual realm, *mens rea*—a guilty mind—is not *one* of the many elements required to be guilty of sin—it can be the **only** element required to be found guilty of sin.

As pointed out earlier in this chapter, the Lord made this clear to us when He said *I say to you that everyone who looks at a woman with lustful intent has already committed adultery with her in his heart.*[100] Looking by itself is not a sin, but the one who does so lustfully—with a heart that desires to commit adultery—sins. No physical act is required.

Another example is stated in 1 John 3:15 (NIV): *Anyone who hates a brother or sister is a murderer, and you know that no murderer has eternal life residing in him.* Obviously, this is quite a serious statement—especially for someone who hasn't performed a physical act.

A third example of how our mental state alone can create an opening to the Enemy can be found in Ephesians 4:26–27: *Be angry and do not sin; do not let the sun go down on your anger, and give no opportunity to the devil.* Anger is an emotional state that may or may not be followed by action. But as we can see, this emotional or mental state itself can create a "legal right" to the Enemy.

A fourth example can be found in the Ten Commandments. We are told not to covet our neighbor's wife.[101] Nobody in the physical world really knows if we are committing this act of coveting, but the Lord knows. And this sin, even though it is invisible in the physical realm, can provide the devil with a "legal right" and "legal access" to us in this world.

Please understand your mental state *can* provide an open door to the Enemy, even if it is not coupled with action. Many are completely unaware of this spiritual law, which is exactly what makes it such a successful and useful weapon of the Enemy in the spiritual warfare game, and one of the primary reasons why our emotions are such an effective tool in the hand of the Enemy.

4th Law—*Ignorance is Not an Excuse*

Sin, whether committed through ignorance or intent, can provide a "legal right" for the devil and his host to attack us. As children of God, we have been given the Word of God (the Scriptures) and the Spirit of God to live by. Whether we violate God's precepts intentionally or violate these precepts *out of ignorance* makes little difference to the devil. A violation of God's precepts is still a sin, and can provide an open door to the Enemy. Our failure to follow Jesus' command to love God with all of our heart, soul, and mind, and love our neighbor as ourselves (in which all of the laws and the precepts are based)[102] can provide just such an open door.

In the Old Testament book of Leviticus chapter four verse two, God specifically outlined purification procedures to atone for those who had sinned out of ignorance. In addition, Leviticus 5:17 says, *If anyone sins, doing any of the things that by the Lord's commandments ought not to be done, though **he did not know it**, then realizes his guilt, he shall bear his iniquity* (emphasis added). Knowledge of God's Word gives us hope for stopping the Enemy's influence in our lives. The prophet Hosea recognized the danger of these unintentional sins when he said, *My people are destroyed for lack of knowledge.*[103]

I do believe that God looks at our heart, and takes into consideration if we sin unknowingly. But to the devil, our ignorance of our transgression makes little difference. He views every sin as a "legal right" to assault and deceive us. This may not seem right, or even fair, but believe me it's true, I learned this one the hard way.

What Conduct Opens Us up to the Enemy?

Exactly what sinful thoughts and actions can provide such a "legal right" into our lives? The next chapter contains an incomplete, but general list of examples as to how the Enemy can gain "legal access" to us and our families. This list, will be broken down into the following six basic areas: *unscriptural thoughts, sinful actions, occult/witchcraft, drug use, sexual abuse, and at God's own discretion or permission.* Although, as stated above, this list is not intended to be comprehensive of all the possible entry points the Enemy may access, it will hopefully provide a general understanding that such entry points exist, and can be used against us.

I believe it is important to point out that far worse than providing "legal access" to the Enemy in this life, is being turned over to the Enemy for all of eternity in the next life. One who rejects Jesus Christ and the forgiveness He offers, and one who chooses to live a life of continual sin without repentance will not only suffer Satan's harassment in their everyday life, but will be given over to him permanently for all eternity by the Lord—a very, very sobering thought, and one that all should weigh very carefully when choosing whom they will serve each day.

9

Identifying the Devil's "Legal Access" Points (*Thoughts, Actions, Occult/Witchcraft, Drug Use, Sexual Abuse, and At God's Discretion*)

The fact that the devil uses access points to gain ground into the hearts and minds of mankind is not new. As we discussed in Chapter Seven, even though the sources of the devil's attacks on us hasn't changed—the world, the flesh, and the devil—his techniques for delivering this deception have. In this chapter, I will outline a list of areas in which we may surrender ground to the Enemy. While this is not a complete list, it is a generally agreed upon list of areas in which we may give "legal access" to the Enemy. I will expand on this topic further in Chapter Thirteen when we explore our "Three Emotional Vulnerabilities" where the devil seems to focus his assaults against us. However, for the purposes of this chapter we will focus on the specific **areas of conduct** that can give the Enemy "legal access" to our life.

As we previously discussed, all sin may provide a "legal right" to the Enemy, even if you're a Christian. So knowing, understanding, and following God's Word is important if you desire to remain free of the devil gaining access to your life. Remaining within the will of the Lord and placing His armor over our lives on a daily basis, as we will discuss in Chapter Nineteen, is the best way to remain free from Satan's grasp.

Over the next several pages, I will break down into six basic areas actions that give the devil and his demons the "legal access" they need to gain a foothold in our lives. These six areas include:

1. Unscriptural Thoughts,
2. Sinful Actions,
3. Occult/Witchcraft,
4. Drug Use,
5. Sexual Abuse, and
6. At God's Own Discretion or Permission.

Engaging in these activities does not guarantee that Satan or his evil host of demons will assault you, but it certainly may give them the "legal right" they need to do just that.

Unscriptural Thoughts

As we will discuss here, and again in Section Two, "Our Emotions," the spiritual battlefield takes place in our heart and mind. Our thoughts matter, and thoughts have a by-product—emotions. So if our thoughts are the seeds, our emotions are the fruit. And just like an apple seed will only produce an apple tree, a positive thought can only produce a positive emotion. Likewise, a negative thought can only produce a negative emotion. Unscriptural thoughts and emotions can and often do create entry points for the devil to enter our lives.

Unscriptural thoughts over time can create what is known as a mental stronghold. Mental strongholds by definition are beliefs that are based not on the truths of Scripture but on the lies of Satan. A stronghold usually originates at some point in our lives (typically during our youth) when we have been exposed to or told some untruth (such as a negative comment, insult, or lie) that we assume to be true. Depending on the length of time someone has held onto this false mind-set, ridding oneself from such a stronghold may be as simple as changing one's thinking, or as hard as changing one's basic beliefs.

Our emotions seem to play a big part both with mental strongholds, as well as spiritual bondages, a topic that we will also discuss later in Section Two of this book. Emotions tend to originate from the dominant thoughts we hold and focus upon. And whether positive or negative, these thoughts tend to feed our emotions, which can and often do propel us into action. These actions, if sinful in nature, may themselves also create entry points for the Enemy.

If you are interested in knowing how much ground, if any, you may have surrendered to the Enemy, here's a quick and easy way to *self-test*, and see where your mind is taking you on a daily basis. Take a pen and paper and set the timer on your phone to alert you every fifteen minutes for one full day—preferably on a weekend when you don't have work-related tasks that will dominate your mind. Every time your phone alerts you, write down what you're thinking about—your dominant thought. What you are recording is what you think about when your mind is in an idle state, or what your mind defaults to. This will give you a good indication of what your mind is pre-occupied with, which is a good indication of how much ground (if any) you may have surrendered to the Enemy. Proverbs 23:7 (NASB) tells us: *For as he* [a man] *thinks within himself, so he is* (brackets added). We become what we continually think about or focus on, whether positive or negative. If you are continually thinking negative thoughts or having negative emotions about others or your current life situation, you have probably surrendered ground to the Enemy, and your life is probably headed in the exact direction your thinking and focus is taking you. Depending upon the length of time you have remained in this state of mind, you may have given the Enemy "legal access" to your life in this area of focus.

Sinful Actions

As we just discussed, actions are normally a direct result of our thoughts and emotional mindset. Most of us are fully aware that actions *can* have consequences in this physical realm in which we live. If we break a law, we may be punished for this trespass. As previously discussed, many are unaware that sinful actions *always* have consequences in the spiritual realm. If we purposefully and intentionally take action we know is against the Word and will of God, we run the risk of taking ourselves out from under the protection of the Lord and give the devil "legal access" to our life—a dangerous place to be for sure.

To outline a list of actions that would give the devil access to our lives is unnecessary. We only need to say that if a certain conduct is prohibited by the Word of God, then engaging in that conduct (or mentally pursuing such conduct as explained in Chapter Eight, Laws of the Spiritual Realm), can provide access to the devil. Again, our ignorance that such conduct is a sin in God's eyes and contrary to His Word may matter to God, but it certainly doesn't matter to our adversary, the devil, who accuses us before God day and night[104] and looks for every "legal right" to gain access to our mind, body, and soul.[105]

Occult/Witchcraft

The occult can be defined as "involving or related to the supernatural, mystical or magical powers or phenomenon, [or a person who is] a follower of occult practices similar to voodoo," according to the *Oxford Dictionary of English*.

Occult bondage can occur when you voluntarily submit yourself to the influences of Satan in one or more of the following areas: witchcraft, Satanism, New Age, shamanism, taking mind-altering drugs, Spiritism, voodoo, Eastern religions, having contact with demonic entities (discussed further in the second book in this series Part Two *In the Devil's Toolbox*), or belonging to any organization that derives their power and authority from the devil and his legion. Many, I assume, dabble in these types of activities just for fun or in disbelief, not knowing the true essence behind this veil.

If you're doing this, the clearest way that I can put it is this: you are inviting the forces of hell to come into your life. This can be as simple as visiting a medium (We are specifically told in Isaiah 8:19 not to consult the dead for the living.) or as involved and intentional as taking an oath to the devil. It should not be a surprise to anyone that people who participate in the occult and the above-referenced practices can open themselves completely and totally to the Enemy. They are, by their actions, asking or petitioning for the direct indwelling of the devil and his host of deceivers.

Please understand me, I'm not saying that everyone that goes to a psychic, takes a mind-altering drug, or plays on a Ouija board will incur a demonic presence in their lives. I don't believe this to necessarily be true. What I am saying is that it can happen. Sin, especially when intentional and habitual, allows the Enemy to gain strongholds into our lives. These strongholds can turn into spiritual bondage, or what I refer to as "level two" spiritual warfare, which can be a very problematic state that we will describe more in Chapter Fourteen.

Anyone who practices or is engaged in this type of conduct might as well be flashing a "vacancy" light over their head for the Enemy to see. Dabbling in these things does not guarantee you will be harassed by demons, but you are certainly mentally and spiritually exposing yourself. Satan's forces will usually respond to such an invitation, and in some cases, leave the individual in bondage to the deceiving spirits.

Anyone who has studied or understands anything about the occult will admit that supernatural knowledge can be imparted by the devil and his host of fallen angels and demons, but this supernatural knowledge is used only to further the kingdom of darkness, ruled by the devil. It is totally and completely in direct opposition to God's kingdom. That's why Scripture, as we referenced above, instructs us, *Do not turn to mediums or seek out spiritualists, for you will be defiled by them. I am the* LORD *your God.* (Leviticus 19:31 NIV)

If you are dealing with the occult/witchcraft, you have chosen sides and are warring against the Lord. If you find yourself in this state or have participated in such conduct through intent or ignorance, you should fully repent, renounce all your occult associations, actions, and words, and submit yourself fully and completely to the Lord.

There may be no protection from the devil's wrath for those who voluntarily submit themselves to the occult. In my opinion, God will not intervene to rescue someone who willfully and intentionally chooses to embrace the occult lifestyle, unless that person renounces (an outwardly verbal declaration) all association with the occult and wholeheartedly asks for His forgiveness, indwelling, and protection.[106]

God will never override our free will, so deliverance without a heart-filled desire for repentance and change, will have no effect in your life. Satan will maintain his "legal right" to you, and God will not act to remove him.

Additional Consequences of Involvement in the Occult/ Witchcraft

There is an additional consequence that few consider when dealing with the occult. Those involved in the occult not only give the devil full and complete access to their lives, but they may also give the devil "legal access" to their children, grandchildren, and great grandchildren. Deuteronomy 5:9 says the Lord visits *the iniquity of the fathers on the children to the **third and fourth generation** of those who hate me* (emphasis added). Exodus 20:5 gives us the same warning: *I the* LORD *your God am a jealous God, visiting the iniquity of the fathers on the children to the **third and the fourth generation** of those who hate me* (emphasis added). We will see this warning manifesting over and over in the second book of this series, Part Two of *In the Devil's Toolbox*, where it appears evident that there is a direct link between children suffering the same demonic involvement and harassment experiences in their lives as did their parents.

This "legal access" or "legal right" to children and children's children need not remain an open door. Children can completely and forever extinguish this "legal right" created by their parents, grandparents, great-grandparents, or great-great-grandparents. Accordingly, we are told, *But if they confess their iniquity and the iniquity of their fathers . . . if then their uncircumcised heart is humbled and they make amends for their iniquity, then I will remember my covenant with Jacob . . .*[107] Likewise, we are also told, *Fathers shall not be put to death because of their children, nor shall children be put to death because of their fathers.*[108] And *The son shall not suffer for the iniquity of the father, nor the father suffer for the iniquity of the son.*[109]

So this "legal right" of the Enemy may be terminated by the children, grandchildren, or anyone in the family line who renounces any and all associations or generational ties of any type with Satan and his host of demons, and submits themselves fully and completely to God, confessing their faith in the risen Jesus Christ as their personal Lord and Savior. In fact, we are told that God will extend blessings, not a curse, to the children and grandchildren of the righteous.[110]

For those who believe they may be suffering from a curse of witchcraft or the occult, an interesting and informative source on the topic may be found in Mary L. Lake's *What Witches Don't Want Christians to Know (Expanded Edition).*[111]

Cleansing Your Home

A much less talked about, but important topic in the area of giving "legal rights" to the Enemy, is on clearing our home of spiritual darkness. If we close off all of the spiritual doors in our lives to the Enemy, yet maintain items or symbols in our homes that invite in the forces of evil, we may find ourselves in a position where no matter what we do, we can't seem to rid ourselves of spiritual heaviness, or persistent issues which keep resurfacing in our home. What may be occurring is we may have unknowingly collected, or are hoarding something of spiritual significance, that is providing a legal entry point for evil entities to inhabit our home.

Although this may sound a bit far-fetched for some, as we go through the Bible, we are repeatedly warned about possessing idols, due to the entities they represent. Deuteronomy 7:26 (KJV) states: *Neither shalt thou bring an abomination into thine house, lest thou be a cursed thing like it: but thou shalt utterly detest it, and thou shalt utterly abhor it; for it is a cursed thing.* Without going into great detail on this issue, ask yourself, "Do I have any items in my home that represent some religion other than my Christian faith? Do I possess any symbol that has been prayed over by someone of another faith? Do I possess any item that has demonstrated any unnatural qualities?" If you answer "yes" to any of these questions, I would suggest cleansing your home of such things. Two good sources of information on the dangers of idols, and how to rid your home of the spiritual darkness are the books *Ridding your Home of Spiritual Darkness* and *Protecting You Home from Spiritual Darkness* by Chuck D. Pierce and Rebecca Wagner Sytsema.

Drug Use

There is little question that drugs open a door to the Enemy. Throughout history, the many cultures that have existed before us—from shaman, to witch doctors, and those involved with the forces of evil—fully understand that drugs can open one up to the spiritual world. If you are taking drugs, your natural body's defenses have been altered, and your spiritual defenses greatly compromised. Making you a great target for the Enemy. This is not a good position to be in.

Let me relate a short story. Many years ago, I had the opportunity to speak with a group of adults in an alcohol and drug rehab program. The topic was on how drugs open a spiritual door for the Enemy to come into our lives. After my discussion, one of the attendees came up to me and told me he wanted to share an experience he had while taking cocaine.

He related to me that one evening, after snorting cocaine, he was driving his vehicle on the highway. He stated that he began to hear some voices in the back seat. Alarmed, because he was alone, he glanced in the review mirror, only to see his back seat full of demons. He was so startled, he opened his driver's door and immediately jumped from the vehicle while it was moving at full speed down the road.

A gentleman in a vehicle behind his, saw the entire event. He slammed on his breaks and ran to see if this man was alright. After checking his condition, and attending to his needs, the gentleman asked about the other people in his car. The gentleman said he had seen several people in the backseat of the car, and wondered if they were alright. Alarmed to say the least, the attendee told me after he finished his story, "You don't have to convince me that drugs open a door to demons; I *know* they do."

Additional Considerations

I should note at this point that any mode of manipulation that influences our thoughts and our mind has the potential to affect our emotions, and therefore our behavior. This also includes the controversial topic of transhumanism, which is the altering of our minds and bodies with genetics, robotics, artificial intelligence, nanotechnology, synthetic biology, neuropharmacology, or other similar means, all with the described goal of producing a "more improved" humanity.[112]

However, all such methods of genetic manipulation, especially that which encourages the connecting of one's body and mind to The World Wide Web of intelligence through some type of brain-computer interface technology (BCI), offers a potential two-way gateway, or doorway to the human mind that may not be reversible, and may provide unlimited "legal access" to our mind by spiritual sources (the Enemy).[113]

In addition, such technologies may also have the potential to change our DNA, moving us away from the "Image of God" in which we were created.[114] Both potential consequences of genetic manipulation that one should be warned about, and will be discussed in more detail in Part Two of this series.

Sexual Abuse

Another area that, according to those who have much experience in deliverance ministries, seems to provide an access point into one's life is sexual abuse, especially if this occurs as a child.[115] Somehow, this abuse not only fractures one's psyche, but it can apparently open the door (give a "legal right") for demons to come into the life of and torment the victim.[116] The duration, severity, and age at which this sexual abuse occurred may have an effect on how much access the Enemy has been granted. This abuse may be accompanied by physical abuse and psychological abuse (more discussion on psychological abuse can be found in the last section of this book under the Rejection tool).[117] This is certainly not the fault of the victim, but it can, nonetheless, be a source of mental torment. If a demon has entered one's life through such abuse, this torment can persist in one's life until this "legal right" is severed. Severing this "legal right" (commonly known as deliverance) is one of the many reasons our Lord and Savior came on this earth—to set the captives free.[118]

Deliverance from such demonic torment is available for all who have accepted Jesus Christ as their personal Lord and Savior, surrendered their life to Him, and earnestly call upon His name. The devil does not like giving up his ground (hold over the person's life). Accordingly, this area of deliverance (sexual abuse) may well require the assistance of one who is trained in the area of Christian deliverance ministry. Psychological counseling will only deal with the mental issues of such abuse, and will have no effect on severing the "legal right" of these demons if a "legal right" has been given, and demons are present in the person's life. These spiritual entities will only respond to an authority greater than their own—that of Jesus Christ. Those who are freed from this torment (and from any demonic torment) fully understand the saving grace of the Lord Jesus Christ and understand what it means to be "set free."

This type of spiritual torment certainly is not fair to the victim, nor is it the victim's fault, but then again, Satan never cares about fairness, only about what "legal rights" he has to kill, steal, and destroy humanity.[119]

Just because someone has suffered sexual or physical abuse this does not mean this person is dealing with a demonic presence in their life. One would need to examine their life to determine what they may be dealing with if any ongoing trauma exists.

It's interesting to note that Mary Magdalene, a faithful follower of the Lord Jesus Christ—and the one that Jesus appeared to first after He rose from the dead—was herself delivered from seven demons by Jesus.[120] So if you find yourself in need of deliverance from a demonic condition, it is not shameful. And as stated, it may not even be your own fault. But living your life in this condition is unnecessary—and is a surrender to the Enemy—when Christ has already paid the price to set you free.

At God's Own Discretion or Permission

The last area that we will discuss is a list of four examples in Scripture where it appears God allowed man to be turned over to the Enemy at His own discretion or permission. I will list four examples in Scripture where it appears God allowed man to be turned over to the Enemy.

For Testing

The first example is in the Old Testament book of Job. Job 1:1 tells us, because Job was a blameless and upright man, who feared God and shunned evil, God blessed him greatly. Satan challenged God that if He removed His favor from His servant Job, Job would curse God. God disagreed, and allowed Satan access to all Job possessed to test him.[121] After Job successfully endured the test, in Job 42:10, God restored Job's health and blessings, making him twice as prosperous as before.

For Chastisement or Disobedience

The second example can be found in the Old Testament book of 1 Samuel, where we are told that God directed an evil spirit into the life of King Saul to torment him.[122] But why would God do this to King Saul—a king that was appointed by God himself? It was due to Saul's repeated disobedience.

Saul's first act of disobedience occurred when he was instructed by the prophet Samuel to go to Gilgal and prepare to fight the Philistines. Saul was instructed to wait for seven days for Samuel's return before entering the battle. After waiting seven days for Samuel to return, Saul's men had seen the size and scope of the Philistine army, and became fearful and began to scatter. Saul, seeing Samuel had not yet arrived, hastily presented a burnt offering himself to the Lord, instead of waiting for God's chosen prophet Samuel to do so.[123] Upon his return a short time later, Samuel saw what Saul had done, and angrily announced to Saul that because of his disobedience, God would now strip Saul's kingdom away from him.[124]

Next, the prophet Samuel is instructed by God to have Saul attack and totally destroy the Amalekites.[125] But Saul disobeyed, and brought back King Agag, the best of the sheep, cattle, and lambs—everything that was good.[126] At this, Samuel announced to King Saul that God has rejected him as king of Israel[127] because of his disobedience. And not only did God withdraw His Spirit from Saul, the once anointed king of Israel, but the LORD sent a harmful spirit to torment him.[128]

For Humility and Dependence upon the Lord

In our third example we also know the Lord allowed the apostle Paul to have a "thorn in his flesh" (a demonic messenger of Satan) to torment him throughout his ministry. We also know that the apostle Paul asked the Lord on three separate occasions to remove this "thorn" from him, but the Lord responded, *"My grace is sufficient for you, for my power is made perfect in weakness"* (2 Corinthians 12:7-10). So at least in Paul's case, the Lord allowed him to be tormented by what appears to be a demon, to accomplish His purpose of keeping Paul humble, and dependent upon the Lord.

All three of the above examples are instances of God allowing either Satan or what appears to be a demon's access to His anointed servants for testing, chastisement, and humility. While we can't (nor will we attempt to) fully comprehend God's reasoning and purpose behind these allowances, such instances appear to be quite rare, but nonetheless demonstrate God's discretion and use of Satan and his host of demons for God's purpose within His chosen people.

To Follow Their Debased Mind

The fourth example, and one that should wake us all from our slumber, is found in the New Testament book of Romans. Here, we are given two separate circumstances in which God apparently may allow man to be **"given over"** to the Enemy. A scary thought indeed. Let's look at the verses that tell us of the circumstances in which God would take such a drastic step with man. Roman 1:24–28 tells us:

> *Therefore **God gave them up** in the lusts of their hearts to impurity, to the dishonoring of their bodies among themselves, because they exchanged the truth about God for a lie and worshiped and served the creature rather than the Creator, who is blessed forever! Amen.*
>
> *For this reason **God gave them up** to dishonorable passions. For their women exchanged natural relations for those that are contrary to nature; and the men likewise gave up natural relations with women and were consumed with passion for one another, men committing shameless acts with men and receiving in themselves the due penalty for their error.*
>
> *And since they did not see fit to acknowledge God, **God gave them up** to a debased mind to do what ought not to be done.* (emphasis added)

Those who refuse God's truth, who harden their hearts and set their minds on foolish and sinful things, run the terrible risk that God may "give them over" to their debased minds. Should you find yourself in such a precarious position, renounce your sinful thoughts and actions, repent, and submit yourself fully to the Lord for forgiveness and restoration.

For Judgment

So, as we have discussed in Chapter Eight, being a Christian gives us great immunity from Satan and his host of demons,[129] but it does not give us absolute immunity from the Enemy gaining "legal access" to our lives. The Lord may show us incredible grace and mercy in our ignorance and unbelief; however, as we have mentioned in Chapter Eight, those who believe they can habitually and intentionally sin, and remain under the full protection of the Lord, are sorely mistaken.

If one continues to sin, and harden his/her heart against the Lord, as stated above, God may "give them over" to their sinful ways. But, as stated above, there is a greater danger than being "given over" to one's sinful ways, or even being "turned over" to the Enemy in this life—that is to be turned over to the Enemy for all eternity.

The Bible makes it abundantly clear that the Enemy can never take us (a believer) out of God's hands, *I give them eternal life, and they will never perish, and no one will snatch them out of my hand* (John 10:28). But can we, through our own deliberate, persistent, and habitual sinning remove our self from God's hand? I'll let you decide your own position on this controversial issue. But I believe the following Bible verses indicate that such a "falling away" from the Lord's grace is possible when one whom was once saved by faith, yet whole-heartily and deliberately, with no desire for repentance, later chooses to live a life of continual sin.

Such a verse can be found in Hebrews 6:4-6:

For it is impossible, in the case of those who have once been enlightened, who have tasted the heavenly gift, and have shared in the Holy Spirit, and have tasted the goodness of the word of God and the powers of the age to come, and then have fallen away, to restore them again to repentance, since they are crucifying once again the Son of God to their own harm and holding him up to contempt.

Hebrews 10:26-27 also gives us a similar warning:

For if we go on sinning deliberately after receiving the knowledge of the truth, there no longer remains a sacrifice for sins, but a fearful expectation of judgment, and a fury of fire that will consume the adversaries. Anyone who has set aside the law of Moses dies without mercy on the evidence of two or three witnesses. How much worse punishment, do you think, will be deserved by the one who has trampled underfoot the Son of God, and has profaned the blood of the covenant by which he was sanctified, and has outraged the Spirit of grace? For we know him who said, "Vengeance is mine; I will repay." And again, "The Lord will judge his people." It is a fearful thing to fall into the hands of the living God.

Although many Christians disagree with this position, holding fast to the "once saved always saved" doctrine, I believe the two Scripture verses below, given to us by the apostle Paul, are a strong warning that one cannot willfully remain in sin, after receiving salvation from the Lord, without the expectation of dire consequences.

*Or do you not know that **the wrongdoers will not inherit the kingdom of God**? Do not be deceived: Neither the sexually immoral nor idolaters nor adulterers nor men who have sex with men nor thieves nor the greedy nor drunkards nor slanderers nor swindlers will inherit the kingdom of God* (1 Corinthians 6:9–10, NIV, emphasis added).

*The acts of the sinful nature are obvious: sexual immorality, impurity and debauchery; idolatry and witchcraft; hatred, discord, jealousy, fits of rage, selfish ambition, dissensions, factions and envy; drunkenness, orgies, and the like. I warn you, as I did before, that those who live like this **will not inherit the kingdom of God*** (Gal. 5:19–21, NIV, emphasis added).

These two verses reflect the condition that many of us were in before we were washed, sanctified (set apart), and justified (acquitted of our sins) in the name of the Lord Jesus Christ, and by the Spirit of God (see 1 Corinthians 6:11).

But now, having been saved by the Lord from this prior condition, can we willingly return to such conduct, and still claim to remain in a salvific state of grace? Can we yet expect to live under the privilege, provision, and protection of the Lord, while at the same time disregarding His Holy Word, truth, and Spirit?

Some make the argument that those who persist in such sin have never had the spiritual conversion that salvation brings, and therefore have never been saved in the first place. An argument to which only the Lord knows the answer.

What we do know is, for those whom transgress into the areas listed above, or into **any conduct that is in opposition to the word of the Lord,** and repents—there **is forgiveness.** Yet, those whom harden their hearts toward the Lord, abandon God's truths, and choose to perpetually live in such sins, are not only in danger of being turned over to the Enemy in this life, but for all of eternity. A condition from which there is no deliverance.

A Final Point to Remember

And last, it is important to note that **I did not say** being a Christian and having protection from the Enemy **prevents you from being harassed by Satan** and his host of demons. As we have discussed earlier in Chapters Five and Seven, Satan still maintains a certain level of authority in this world, and has the ability to both harass us and plant thoughts into our mind. So, we all live under the Enemy's harassment, or what I label as "level one" spiritual warfare.

With this in mind, and with a new understanding of the realities of this invisible battle, let's now examine the main focus of this book, and one of the devil's most deceptive and incredibly effective tools against us in the spiritual warfare battle: *our emotions.* As we will uncover, not only does the devil use our emotions against us for self-destructive purposes, but he also tries to use our emotions to gain permanent "legal access" into our lives.

Our Emotions

10

Our Emotions Can Be Used Against Us

God made us emotional beings for a reason. Our emotions can empower us, enable us, bring us great pleasure, and bring us closer to God. In fact, they are one of our God-given gifts that assist us to live the way God intended, experiencing the fullness of the fruit of the Spirit.[130] Some of the great men of the Bible were quite emotional: David, Elisha, Moses, and the apostle Paul. Even Jesus demonstrated righteous anger when He knocked over the tables of the money changers in the temple.[131] Jesus also displayed great sorrow when He *wept* over the death of Lazarus.[132] But, as emotional beings, we must be the master over our emotions, and not let our emotions be the master over us.

Emotions are defined in Webster's New World Dictionary as: any specific feeling; any of various complex reactions with both physical and mental manifestations of love, hate, fear, anger, etc.[133]

Our outward expression or manifestation of emotions is extremely healthy, if shared in a constructive manner. In fact, failing to express our emotions can have a negative effect on our lives.[134] The act of stuffing our emotions can lead to mental instability with the result of unhappiness, dissatisfaction with life, feeling weighed down, overwhelmed, cheated, abused, taken advantage of, and defeated. That's not how God intended for us to live. Scripture tells us to cast all our anxieties on Him, because He cares for us.[135]

So be honest with your emotions. To deny our real feelings is just plain being deceitful with ourselves. The Bible tells us to know the truth and the truth will set us free.[136] I personally believe, if we are not even being truthful and honest with ourselves about our own feelings, it will make it harder to be truthful and honest with the liberating Word of God. So be honest about the way you feel, either good or bad, but monitor your expression and how you act out on these emotions.

With that being said, let's get to the heart of this book and discuss how the devil can, and does, use our emotions against us. I divided this chapter down into three sections.

- Scripture Verses that Prove Satan Can Use Our Emotions Against Us
- Opening Spiritual Doors by "Harboring" Destructive Emotions
- Emotions: A Hiding Place for Demons

Scripture Verses that Prove Satan Can Use Our Emotions Against Us

I would suggest that emotions may be one of the most *effective* and *overlooked* tools of the Enemy to impact our lives. I say "overlooked" because our emotions are so intertwined with our personalities that many refuse to examine them, and sometimes we even defend them, saying, "That's just the way I am." Effective, because when this occurs, we can provide persistent "legal access" to the Enemy without our knowledge. The Bible gives us several examples of how our emotions can be door-opening avenues for the Enemy. Let's look at three of them.

Anger

Our first clue to this emotional deception is found in Ephesians 4:26–27, where the apostle Paul tells us, *Be angry and do not sin; do not let the sun go down on your anger,* **and give no opportunity to the devil** (emphasis added). This may be just one Bible verse, but it reveals great insight into the workings of the devil that many people fail to realize.

First, it tells us that the devil has access to us in this life. Second, it tells us that the devil uses our emotions to gain access into our lives—more specifically into our minds. Third, it makes it clear that if we don't follow God's guidelines for our anger, then we leave room for the devil to fill our minds with his substitute emotion of resentment, hatred, and rage. All insights that the devil would rather you not know, which would give him unfettered access to your life.

Unforgiveness

Our second clue to this emotional sabotage is found in 2 Corinthians 2:10–11. Here, the apostle Paul tells us, *Anyone whom you forgive, I also forgive. Indeed, what I have forgiven, if I have forgiven anything, has been for your sake in the presence of Christ,* **so that we would not be outwitted by Satan;** *for we are not ignorant of his designs* (emphasis added).

Here again, we are given a similar warning. When we fail to forgive someone and remain bitter toward that person, we open the door for the devil to gain access to our hearts and our minds through this unscriptural mindset of unforgiveness. Unforgiveness has a unique way of turning into bitterness, resentment, and even hatred if cultivated for too long.

Worse yet, most of us are totally unaware that by doing so we have allowed the devil "legal access" to our minds. He subtly substitutes one of our God-given emotions of forgiveness for his counterfeit emotion of unforgiveness.

Jealousy

Our third insight comes in the form of a warning on jealousy and selfish ambition. The apostle James tells us, *But if you have bitter jealousy and selfish ambition in your hearts, do not boast and be false to the truth.* **This is not the wisdom that comes down from above, but is earthly, unspiritual, demonic.** *For where jealousy and selfish ambition exist, there will be disorder and every vile practice* (emphasis added).[137]

Clearly, jealousy is a very powerful emotion. One that I believe we can fairly say has ruined countless lives. It's fleshly by nature—an emotion that screams in our minds, "Me first" and "Why not me?" Only bad things can come from a mindset that is constantly focused on jealousy and selfish ambition. The apostle James is telling us that we should be aware of the source of our emotional influences because some of these influences are the work of the devil.

Opening Spiritual Doors by "Harboring" Destructive Emotions

As we have stated, although God gives us emotions for our good, the devil can use our emotions against us. One way the Enemy does this is by getting us to hold onto, or harbor destructive emotions.

We all experience fear, anger, regret, guilt, or unforgiveness for short periods of time, all of which are normal in the ordinary sense. These emotions usually display themselves outwardly, and then subside over a few hours or days. Problems arise, however, when we remain in these emotional states much longer than God intended. I refer to this as "harboring" destructive emotions because of the length of time some people remain harbored in them. Let me give you a brief example. Fear can be a good thing. It can protect us from trying activities that might be dangerous to our well-being, or it can awaken the warrior inside of us to respond in a time of great need. However, fear can be a tremendously destructive emotion as well, paralyzing us and robbing us of our love, joy, and peace if we remain in its constant grasp.[138] The devil knows this and uses all sorts of fears and phobias to repress and oppress people and to keep them from enjoying life and full-filling their God-given purpose.

The other example we discussed is the emotion of anger. As we also know, the emotion of anger can transform into bitterness, unforgiveness, or even hatred simply by remaining in this state for an extended period of time. This is why the apostle Paul in Ephesians 4:26–27 warned us about remaining in a state of anger because it gives the devil a foothold or "legal right" to enter our minds. This is a very clear warning on how remaining in this emotional state can open the door to the Enemy.

Interestingly, Paul's warning on anger, and Jesus' advice for us to forgive one another not only keeps us from providing a "legal right" to the Enemy, but as we will read below, it also benefits our physical make-up. This is but one more affirmation that the God who created us always knows what is best for us.

More Science behind God's Word

Another very interesting fact about harboring negative emotions has been studied by Dr. Jerry Tennant, M.D. founder of the Tennant Institute. Dr. Tennant has discovered that negative emotions persisting in one's life normally result in illness. How does he come to this conclusion? Dr. Tennant explains that the body has a constant and normal electrical voltage, and maintaining that voltage is one major key to optimum health. According to his research, the body's normal electrical voltage is approximately -25 mV (millivolts). According to Dr. Tennant, when the body is damaged in any way or suffers an illness, it requires twice that voltage or approximately -50 mV, to repair itself.[139]

Interestingly, according to Dr. Tennant, negative emotions are one of the primary culprits of bad health and one of the primary inhibitors in this healing process. Dr. Tennant explains that these negative emotions create an electromagnetic field that actually blocks the flow of electricity into certain cells of the body, resulting in a severe drop in cellular voltage. This low voltage then greatly reduces the cells' ability to both repair and properly reproduce themselves, resulting in chronic illness. A process that, Dr. Tennant explains, can be both reversed and treated.

This may explain why unforgiveness is actually classified in medical books as a disease.[140] Dr. Tenant's conclusions that negative emotions are a precursor to compromised health are supported in the research by Dr. Michael Barry, a pastor and the author of the book *The Forgiveness Project: The Startling Discovery of How to Overcome Cancer, Find Health, and Achieve Peace.*[141] Dr. Barry states that of all cancer patients he researched, 61 percent had forgiveness issues. And out of that 61 percent, more than half struggled with *severe unforgiveness.* According to Dr. Barry, who arrived at the same conclusion as Dr. Tennant about the effect of negative emotions (but through a different medical diagnosis), harboring these negative emotions, this anger and hatred, creates a state of chronic anxiety. Chronic anxiety, according to Dr. Barry, then produces excess adrenaline and cortisol, which deplete the production of our natural killer cells, which are our body's foot soldiers in the fight against cancer.[142]

Regardless of which of the above medical diagnosis we use, these doctors mutually conclude that negative emotions are a precursor to compromised health. This is yet another example of how God's Word, which instructs us to forgive and to set our minds to think on things that are lovely and pure, perfectly aligns with what the medical community understands to be true.[143]

Emotions: A Hiding Place for Demons

There is another even more sinister (and for the most part overlooked) way our Enemy can use our emotions against us. As unusual as this may seem, our emotions can provide a hiding place for demonic spirits. If you're scratching your head on this one, that's OK. We will discuss this technique a little later in Section Four of this book. But for the purposes of this chapter, it's important to understand that this can take place.

What I am saying here is that if people have extremely negative or destructive feelings, urges, or unnatural compulsions that persist for many years, or even decades, and control their lives, it is possible that a demonic spirit may be the source. If this has occurred, these demons may create, through our emotions, all kinds of traumatic and unnatural lusts and cravings, or make one suffer great spiritual anguish, grief, and torment.

Certain self-tests can be done to determine if these feelings, urges, or compulsions are demonic in nature (quite often they are not). However, if this has taken place in your life, it can create a spiritual issue known as *spiritual bondage* (we will discuss later in Chapter Fourteen) that can persist for months, years, or even decades.

If you have a feeling that something is just not right in your life, or you have lived with severe grief, pain, uncontrollable compulsions, or anxiety, you can do a *self-test* to determine if the source of this compulsion *may be* demonic in nature. To do this, examine your past to see if you or your family members have potentially given the Enemy a "legal right" to your life in any of the areas previously mentioned.

I would suggest that most emotional issues are not demonic in nature and can be resolved through conventional means. However, if "legal access" has been given and a demonic spirit has taken up presence in the person's life, the emotional compulsions will be relentless and will not subside unless this person is delivered from this demonic spirit.

This book is not a book on demonic deliverance; however, in Section Three, "Our Defenses," as well as in Section Four, I outline a few generally recognized principles on this topic and some universally accepted steps for deliverance from such a condition.

The topic of emotions acting as a hiding place for demons is a foreign concept to most people. As you read through the remainder of this book, please keep in mind that our Enemy can and will use our emotions against us in his battle to gain control of our lives.

So how does Satan manipulate mankind so effectively that he can use our own emotions against us without our knowledge? For that, we need to look at what creates our emotions.

Thoughts—the Origin of
Our Emotions

If I asked you to name the most dangerous weapon in the world, what would you pick? A nuclear bomb, a biological weapon, a satellite with laser-strike capabilities? I believe the answer to this question will shock you. Many agree that the most dangerous weapon in the world is a thought. Quite a statement, huh? Let me explain.

Thoughts Create Emotions

No conscious action or deed ever takes place without first originating as a thought. This means that the genesis of every deed, whether good or evil, is a thought. The devil knows this. This is why he is so interested in our thought life and why we are told in Scripture to take every thought captive to obey Christ.[144]

The devil knows that if he can plant a self-destructive or evil thought into an untrained mind, he might get the person to latch on to this thought and begin to focus on it. Focusing on a negative or evil thought will normally generate an emotional response associated with that thought. For the Christian and non-Christian alike, this may create the temptation to sin.

But coupling this emotional response with an unrepentant and unforgiving heart, creates a good chance the unsuspecting person will eventually act out on this self-destructive or evil thought. Pretty slick, huh? And all of this goes on without our knowing it.

This is why it is critically important to understand that not every thought you have originates in your own mind. Although this might be hard for some of us to believe, as we pointed out earlier in Chapter Seven, Scripture makes it abundantly clear that our minds can be *sifted, incited, filled,* and *placed* by the Great Deceiver. If we aren't alert to the devil's technique and, therefore, fail to examine our thoughts that create our emotions, then we open ourselves up to the devil's trickery and giving him access to control us.

Although we may be unaware of it, most of the thoughts we have that produce actions in our lives go through four steps: 1. our thoughts create focus, 2. our focus dictates our emotions, 3. our emotions produce actions, and 4. our actions fuel our thoughts.

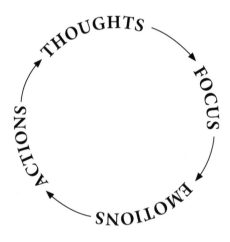

If the devil can trick you into developing a negative and unscriptural thought life, he knows these thoughts will ultimately control what you focus on, leading to destructive emotions; which, in turn, leads to destructive actions or habits that will rob us of God's intended blessings and purpose. Let me explain.

The National Science Foundation published an article in 2005 regarding their research about the number of thoughts the average human has per day. The report found that the average person has between 12,000 and 60,000 thoughts every single day. Even more interesting was their finding that up to 95% of these thoughts are repetitive thoughts (the exact same thoughts as the day before) and 80% of these thoughts are negative.[145] So it appears as if Satan has up to 60,000 opportunities per day to slip at least one of his destructive and self-defeating thoughts into our minds.

And, obviously, Satan has made great in-roads in this mental battle if 80% of our daily thoughts are negative. Scripture specifically tells us in Philippians 4:8 to think about, *whatever is true, whatever is honorable, whatever is just, whatever is pure, whatever is lovely,* [and] *whatever is commendable* (brackets added). I think this clearly exemplifies why we are told in Scripture to *take every thought captive to Christ*[146]—scriptural advice that I will discuss further below.

Take Every Thought Captive to Christ

Like all the other areas of our life, God did not leave us uninformed or unequipped about how to use our thoughts and emotions. He gives us His principles in Scripture for doing this. As stated above, we are told to *take every thought captive to obey Christ.*[147] Just what does this mean? It means comparing our thoughts to the Scriptures and taking our thoughts to Christ through prayer.

So how do we implement this command?

First, start by comparing your thoughts with the **Word of God**. This is accomplished by evaluating what you are thinking, and if it's not consistent with God's Word, throw it out. If you don't know the Bible, you can't pass this first test. It's easy to understand how people get off course emotionally if they don't have a map for where they should be. The best navigator in the world would get off course, too, without a map to keep him or her in check. You're no different. Your thought map is the Bible.

Next, take each thought **captive to obey Christ**—literally. That is, ask God for discernment to help you understand and walk in God's truth. Scripture tells us that the Holy Spirit will guide us into all truth (John 16:13).

Here are four specific steps to keep in mind when taking your thoughts captive to obey Christ:

1. As stated above, compare your thoughts to what the Bible says about what you are considering.[148]
2. See if your thoughts are consistent with God's Word or in opposition to His Word.[149]
3. Eliminate thoughts inconsistent with the Word of God.[150]
4. Seek discernment from God on your choice of action. [151]

So, how does this help us?

First, by following these steps, we are forced to examine our thoughts. That may be a completely new process for those of you who simply let your mind run unattended. It makes us develop accountability for how we deal with our thoughts. **Second,** it allows us to examine where each thought originates. And **third,** it puts us in a position to be led by God through prayer and by Scripture; to discern which thoughts we should discard and which thoughts we should keep.

Remember your thoughts are the seeds of your greatness or your destruction. Someone once said:

WATCH YOUR THOUGHTS . . . they become your words.
WATCH YOUR WORDS . . . they become your actions.
WATCH YOU ACTIONS . . . they become your habits
WATCH YOUR HABITS . . . they become your character.
WATCH YOUR CHARACTER . . . it becomes your destiny.

– Anonymous

So, it's true. Your thoughts are the GPS (global positioning system) of your mind. And wherever your mind goes, your life follows. If your GPS coordinates are fixed on God's Word, you will always be led in the right direction by the Holy Spirit because He lives inside every believer.[152] But if your GPS coordinates are set solely by feelings that change from minute to minute, hour to hour, or day to day, then you will constantly be changing course with no hope of arriving at your desired destination.

That being the case, don't expect to change a life-long pattern of thinking easily. Your pattern of thinking has formed a rut in your mind that your thoughts automatically follow every time a similar situation arises. Like driving on a worn dirt road, if you get into a rut, it's difficult to get out. As stated above, if 95% of our daily thoughts are repetitive, that's a huge rut to break out of. So, you have to make a deliberate effort. Making new ruts on a different path will take some time. Start by studying Scripture and getting to know God's instructions for your thought life. When considering all the pathways that look and feel like they're leading us in the right direction, remember: unless they are supported by Scripture, they're mismarked.[153] More of this topic will be discussed in Section Four of this book.

By knowing that thoughts ultimately create emotions, and by taking a closer look at our emotions and by comparing them to the fruit of the Spirit outlined in Galatians 5:22–23, you may discover that you have unknowingly succumbed to the devil's emotional deception in one or more areas of your life. This emotional deception, and the emotional ruts it may have created, may be the one thing you just couldn't put your finger on that has held you back and prevented you from experiencing the life God intended you to live.

So how do we get out of these emotional ruts and live the life God designed for us to live? It's literally a matter of the heart. Let's look at how our heart—the gatekeeper of our emotions—plays a lead role in this process.

12

The Heart—
Gatekeeper of Our Emotions

The heart is the center of our physical, mental, spiritual, and emotional makeup. We are told in Proverbs 4:23 (NIV), *Above all else, guard your heart, for everything you do flows from it.* Your heart is ground zero for your emotions. The heart is also known as the center of consciousness, and it's what God searches, along with one's mind, to reward each person according to their conduct and deeds.[154]

And the heart is the center of our emotional life. Emotions such as joy and love originate in the heart.[155] However, the heart is also capable of producing a host of unfavorable emotions such as sorrow, bitter jealousy, and even hate,[156] and our hearts can even condemn us.[157]

In fact, the Hebrew language has no word for conscience, so it uses the word heart to convey this concept (see Job 27:6 as an example). It is also used to reference a person's true nature. When somebody is a good person, we often say, *"He or she has a wonderful heart."* There are several Bible verses that talk about the heart of man. Let's look at a few.

The Bible tells us in Luke 8:15 that the **heart** is the garden where the seed of God, His Word, is sown and grows to maturity.[158] The apostle Paul tells us in Romans 10:9 that we must believe in our **heart** that Jesus rose from the dead to be saved, *For with the **heart** one believes and is justified . . .*[159] (emphasis added).

Jesus tells us in Mark 11:23 that our faith also springs from our heart. He said, *"Truly, I say to you, whoever says to this mountain, 'Be taken up and thrown into the sea,' and does not doubt in his **heart,** but believes that what he says will come to pass, it will be done for him"*[160] (emphasis added).

And, although the heart is but one little piece of our anatomy, Proverbs 4:23 says the *springs of life flow from it,* which is probably the reason it also tells us to keep our hearts with all vigilance.

Our hearts also determine how much God or Satan rule in our lives. Interestingly, it's also our hearts that determine how much God or Satan rule in the first and second heaven as we discussed in Chapter Three. We are also told in Matthew 6:21 *For where your treasure is, there your **heart** will be also* (emphasis added). So where is your treasure? Find what is the most important thing to you, and you will find your heart.

So as the thousands of daily thoughts pass through our minds, it is ultimately the gatekeeper—your heart—that determines how you process these thoughts, what you choose to dwell upon, and what emotions come forth. If the statistics are correct, and as we have stated, 85% of daily human thoughts are negative,[161] then it appears the Enemy has made great in-roads in penetrating the hearts of man. Don't let the Great Deceiver trick you into this deception. Recognize that he is at play in your thought life, and shut him out. As we previously discussed, choose to follow God's advice in Philippians 4:8 (NIV) and think about . . . *whatever is true, whatever is noble, whatever is right, whatever is pure, whatever is lovely, whatever is admirable—if anything is excellent or praiseworthy think about such things.*

So be on alert, because the Enemy continually tries to influence us, and bombard our hearts and minds daily with all sorts of negative thoughts, suggestions, and nudges intended to evoke negative and destructive emotions, hoping we will succumb to his suggestions.

So where does the devil concentrate his mental and emotional attacks against us to influence our hearts and minds? What areas of our lives are most vulnerable? What are our emotional "soft spots?" You can be sure our adversary, the devil, knows—but do we? Let's take a look at our three emotional vulnerabilities, where the devil levies his mental and emotional assaults against us.

13

Our Three Emotional Vulnerabilities
(*Temptation, Accusation, and Salvation*)

Man is made up of three parts: **body**, **soul**, and **spirit**. Our **body**, of course, is our physical makeup. Our **souls** are who we are. It's where our thoughts, emotions, and will reside. And our **spirit** is our eternal makeup that never dies. The devil attacks all three in different ways with different weapons.

The devil entices these three parts as follows:

- Our **bodies**, or what is commonly called the flesh, with all forms of deceptive temptations that promise satisfaction, but end up drawing us away from God.
- He bombards our **souls** with deceitful accusations intended to reduce our self-value and self-worth, making us unproductive for God's kingdom.
- And he attacks our **spirits** with doubts about our salvation.

Although most of us understand that we continuously make decisions that affect our body, spirit, and soul, very few of us fully understand the critical role our *emotions* play in this process. Let's look at the emotional tools the devil uses to attack us in our three emotional vulnerabilities.

The Body—Through Temptation

The devil's first area of attack is our body. For the body, he uses his tool of temptation (lust of the flesh, lust of the eyes, and the pride of life)—the same tool he has used for millennia, as we have previously discussed in Chapter Seven. He tempts us by enticing the emotions of *lust* of the flesh, *lust* of the eyes, and the *pride* of life.[162] Remember, the devil never tells us the whole truth about anything. He only tells us enough truth to lead us to his lie and to the consequences of his half-truths.

Interestingly, both Satan's temptations of **Adam and Eve in the Garden of Eden**, and **Jesus' temptations in the wilderness**, were based on the three specific *fleshly vulnerabilities* of man.

1. **Lust of the flesh** (physical desire)
   Eve: The fruit was good for food.[163]
   Jesus: The devil tempted Him to turn stones into bread, to satisfy Jesus' hunger, following His forty-day fast.[164]
2. **Lust of the eyes** (materialism)
   Eve: The fruit was pleasing to her eye.[165]
   Jesus: The devil offered Him all the authority and splendor of the kingdoms of the world.[166]
3. **The pride of life** (to be like God)
   Eve: The fruit was also desirable for gaining wisdom like God.[167]
   Jesus: The devil tempted Him to put God to the test.[168]

As we previously referenced, the apostle John refers to these three areas when he says, *For all that is in the world—the desires of the flesh and the desires of the eyes and pride of life—is not from the Father but is from the world.*[169] Even though the devil's temptations have remained unchanged throughout the years, they remain quite effective.

I think it is safe to say that all our thoughts and actions are motivated by two conflicting desires: striving to satisfy our *flesh* or striving to satisfy the *Spirit*. If we are striving to satisfy our *flesh*, we are driven by lust of the flesh, lust of the eyes, and pride of life. If we are striving to satisfy the *Spirit*, we are pursuing what the Bible calls *fruit of the Spirit*: love, joy, peace, patience, kindness, goodness, faithfulness, gentleness, and self-control.[170] I also think it's safe to say that the majority of us strive to satisfy both the *flesh* and the *Spirit*. As we mature in the Lord, hopefully striving to satisfy the *Spirit* outweighs striving for the *flesh*, but it is a lifelong process.

We are in essence built by God with a spiritual gap. And how we fill this gap defines our life. This spiritual gap is designed for the true love, joy, and peace that can only be obtained through a personal relationship with His Son, Jesus Christ, and the indwelling of the Holy Spirit. Our attempt to fill this spiritual gap with worldly indulgences or physical stimuli can only produce temporary emotional highs that quickly fade. And like any addiction, these indulgences or stimuli need to be repeated over and over to regain the emotional high.

No amount of fleshly satisfactions can provide the lasting internal love, joy, and peace we were designed to receive through the Holy Spirit. This is why Scripture tells us that we are complete in Christ,[171] and why Christ tells us to drink from His well, because the Holy Spirit is the *true source* of *love, joy, and peace*.[172] These blessings are continuous—never ending—and are available to us from the moment of our conversion.[173]

But most people never discover this. They understand we receive the Holy Spirit upon our salvation, but they miss the part of the Holy Spirit bringing love, joy, and peace into our lives. They search their whole lives for contentment from this world when it has already been placed inside of them by their Creator. I call this the "ruby slippers" syndrome, which I will explain further in Section Four of this book under Tool #8.

The Soul—Through Accusation

You may be saying to yourself, "I know my salvation is secure and I do my best to overcome temptation." If so, I applaud you. But you would be surprised to learn how many good Christian people unknowingly play right into the hands of the devil **by accepting and believing his lying accusations**. Those little thoughts pop into your mind at a time of weakness telling you you're not good enough, not loved, or not worthy.

If you recall, our souls are who we are–our thoughts, will, and emotions. The devil attacks our soul through accusation. His array of emotional tools used to accomplish this task consists of self-defeating fear, worry, guilt, regret, anger, negativity, anxiety, confusion, low self-esteem, resentment, indifference, hopelessness, and unforgiveness of ourselves and others.

Do any of these thoughts sound familiar? Have you fallen for any of these lines that Satan has placed in your mind?

- "You can never be forgiven for that."
- "You're just not good enough."
- "You're too ugly—no one will ever love you."
- "You'll never amount to anything."
- "You'll never measure up."
- "You're not smart enough."
- "You're a failure."
- "No one likes you."
- "What type of person would have such a terrible thought?"
- "You don't deserve a good life."
- "You don't deserve to be loved."
- "You don't deserve peace."
- "You don't deserve a sound mind."
- "You don't deserve to be happy."
- "You're a terrible person."
- "You're losing your mind."
- "This is unfixable. It's too late for you. No going back."
- "Forgiveness for you is not an option."

And what young child, adolescent, or adult who is unschooled regarding this deception will not only accept these thoughts as their own but believe them to be true? The Great Deceiver may even get you to question your natural born gender,[174] or even whether your life has value—all to make you more susceptible to his deception.[175]

As these thoughts swirl around in our minds, even in our adolescence, we begin to accuse ourselves. The Enemy bombards us over and over again with our past failures and our personal weaknesses, creating an ongoing high-light reel in our mind of our mistakes and the comments of those who have wronged us. These many small seeds of deception—planted into our minds even in our childhood and cultivated over the years by our adversary—grow into life-limiting beliefs and self-defeating emotional responses (known as spiritual strongholds) that hold us back from experiencing the full blessing God has intended for us.

Why are these accusations so effective? With salvation and temptation, our other two vulnerabilities, we normally make a conscious and deliberate decision to accept or reject God's Word. However, with accusation, it's quite different. Through ignorance of the devil's involvement in this area of our lives, most of us never make a conscious decision to accept or reject the subtle accusations and self-defeating thoughts planted in our minds by the Great Deceiver. That is, we never think of securitizing these self-defeating negative thoughts that just pop into our mind. They pass right under the radar, as one of our many thousands of negative thoughts each day.

We can't overlook the fact that Scripture calls the devil *the accuser* of the brethren, accusing us before God day and night.[176] In other words, if we don't know the devil can attack us through the many oppressive thoughts and accusations that he places into our minds, then we will most likely leave the door of our mind wide open to these attacks. If these false accusations are left unchecked, over time, they start to shape our belief system regarding the way we think and feel about ourselves and others. This distorted belief system then supports and justifies our self-defeating emotions that we accept as normal.

Remember, God did not place any emotion inside you or your character that would limit your potential to lead a happy and fruitful life. So do a self-examination to determine and eliminate any unhealthy emotions we have been deceived into carrying around by the Enemy, and open up into God's Spirit and walk fully in His power.

The Spirit—Through Salvation

The third area where the devil attacks us is our spirit, which he does by attempting to prevent us from obtaining our salvation. His tool to accomplish this task is by instilling *doubt* in the Word of God. If the devil can unsettle our sense of salvation, he can unsettle us at our very core.

Christ came to take the sting (or fear) out of death.[177] But the devil wants desperately to distort God's truth by placing doubts about the identity of God's Son, Jesus Christ, into the mind of every person. He knows that if he can mislead us in this important area, then he can separate us from our eternal glory with God and leave us hopeless. For the devil, attacking our salvation is his coveted brass ring.

He attempts to mislead us regarding our salvation in one of five basic ways.

First, he tries to convince us that Jesus Christ is not the Son of God. Satan contends that Jesus was just a prophet and no more. If we reject Christ as the Son of God, we also reject His inheritance, which is our only means of eternal salvation—and, our only means of spiritual protection.

Second, he attempts to lead us into a false sense of security. He plants the notion in our minds that a loving and merciful God would never condemn anybody and, therefore, will save everyone from eternal damnation regardless of our beliefs, even though His Word is clear that this is not true.

Third, he attempts to lead us to believe there isn't any Creator, there was no beginning, and there is no afterlife. That afterlife is a myth, and that when we die, we simply cease to exist. With all the complexities of the human body, nature, and the universe, it's hard to believe anyone would adopt this position. But sadly, some do.

Fourth, he wants us to believe that there are many paths to salvation, which is exactly the opposite of what Jesus told us when He said, *I am the way, and the truth, and the life. No one comes to the Father except through me.*[178] And Romans 10:9 says, . . . *if you confess with your mouth that Jesus is Lord and believe in your heart that God raised him from the dead, you will be saved.* Only through one's confession of Jesus Christ as one's personal Lord and Savior, and belief in His resurrection from the dead for their sins, is one saved.

And **fifth**, growing in popularity is Satan's attempts to convince us that someone other than God created us. There is an increasing belief by many in the Ufology community that an alien race or extra-terrestrials are really our creators. They argue that this alien race seeded us on earth millennia ago, have been observing us from afar, and will come to rescue us in our time of need. This directive is a commonly reported story passed along to those who claim to be abductees by these other world visitors and those who have reported having contact with these extra-terrestrials through channeling. A storyline that many believe is tied to the Great Deception that will come forth as an end time event[179]—a topic we will discuss in the second book of this series, Part Two of *In the Devil's Toolbox.*

The Seal of Salvation

When one is saved, it means we have legally become God's property. Satan loses his "legal right" to us. We are told that at the moment of our salvation, the Holy Spirit comes into our hearts (our spirit being) and seals us for the day of redemption.[180] Even though Satan can still harass us and hurtle his mental insults on us, even gaining temporary "legal access" to our lives, if we permit him, our salvation in God remains secure.

Throughout ancient history, kings often secured important documents with a wax seal embossed with a ring that bore their own unique symbol. This seal confirmed to anyone receiving the document that it was from the king himself and was his personal property. If you have confessed Jesus Christ as your personal Lord and Savior, and believe in your heart that God raised Him from the dead, you have been sealed by the Holy Spirit as the Lord's property, and your name has been written in the book of life in heaven (Luke 20:10, Revelation 20:15).[181] This is a position that not only evidences our salvation, but as we will see, it can provide great protection from the Enemy.

With this in mind, let's move on and discuss the three different levels of spiritual warfare that one may succumb to, and see how much ground—if any—you have surrendered to the Enemy.

14

The Three Levels
of Spiritual Warfare

As we have previously discussed, there are several ways to give the devil and his host of demons "legal access" to our lives. If we have allowed this access, we have in some way provided a means for them to inflict their spiritual warfare upon our lives. The level of spiritual warfare we encounter is often dependent on how much access we have given to the Enemy. Factors that can determine the level of spiritual warfare that we may be dealing with, among other things, includes, the type of spiritual door we have opened, and the length of time we allowed it to remain open.

Below, I have outlined three basic levels of spiritual warfare to which one may succumb. I will briefly describe each of these levels, and discuss some of the typical characteristics of each.

The First Level of this Spiritual Battle
(Spiritual Strongholds)

If someone has succumbed to this first level of spiritual attack, they have developed an incorrect pattern of thinking based on a lie from the Enemy. This is what's known as a *spiritual stronghold*. Strongholds can develop in a number of areas in our lives. This level of attack is directed at a person's mind. It most commonly originates by some demonic entity *outside* of that person.

The devil incites all of us, so we all experience this first level of spiritual warfare, whether we know it or not. Remember, the Bible warns us that the devil roams around like a roaring lion, looking for whom he can devour.[182] Also, we are told to put on the whole armor of God so that we may be able to stand against the schemes of the devil[183]—a command that would be completely unnecessary if we were not battling with the devil, fallen angels, and his host of demons.

As we previously covered, the devil can *sift, incite, fill,* and *place* thoughts in the mind of man. If we are unaware of the devil's ability to plant thoughts and suggestions into our mind, as we previously discussed in Chapter Seven, then we can easily allow the devil to influence our thoughts, emotions, and behavior. Simply understanding this truth and questioning any thoughts we know are unscriptural can go a long way toward stopping any demonic influence before it has a chance to take root.

Often, people suffering from these strongholds have poor self-image or self-worth. Thoughts of unworthiness or not believing they deserve good things in life are indications of this level of attack. Likewise, holding grudges or resentments for an extended period of time (several years, for example) is also a clear indication of this level of attack.

If someone is under constant attack in this level, they may demonstrate mental stress and suffer an inability to think clearly. Their dreams may be routinely unpleasant but not traumatic. Disruptions in daily life can include a general sense of unfulfillment or continuing to repeat patterns that keep them from obtaining the blessing the Lord intends.

A self-test you can conduct to see if you might be dealing with emotional strongholds, is to compare your thoughts and beliefs about yourself, others, and your life circumstances to what the Word of God says about these matters.

Common reactions to emotional strongholds include:

- "I just can't help it—that's just the way I am."
- "Why do I keep repeating the same mistakes over and over?"
- "I want to stop, but I can't seem to."
- "I can't quit thinking about this."
- "I feel like I'm in a fog."
- "Why do I keep repeating the same destructive patterns in my life?"

Fortunately, attacks at this level come from *outside of a person*, so resisting the devil is the **first** and most important defense in dealing with this type of warfare.[184] A **second** defense against these assaults, as we have discussed, is to take your thoughts captive by examining them to see if they are God-honoring. Doing so will expose any misdirected thinking the devil has placed in your mind. Our **third** defense is the sword of the Spirit[185]—knowing and applying the Word of God and His truth against Satan's lies. Scripture makes it clear we have power over this type of influence. Second Corinthians 10:4 says, *For the weapons of our warfare are not of the flesh but have divine power to **destroy strongholds*** (emphasis added). By knowing and doing these things, you can destroy these strongholds, and will leave very little room for the devil to attack you in this manner although he will continue to try.

The Second Level of this Spiritual Battle (Spiritual Bondage or Oppression)

People at this level of spiritual warfare have given the devil and his host a deeper level of access into their lives. Spiritual warfare attacks at this level are initiated from the *inside* of a person, making this level quite different from the first.

Contrary to the beliefs of many, this can happen to a Christian. Being a Christian prevents you from the threat of possession or being fully taken over by the Enemy because the Holy Spirit lives inside of us.[186] However, you can still surrender enough ground to the Enemy to allow "legal access" for demons to set up shop, so to speak, and to exist within your body or mind.[187] One could think of this as a spiritual infection. This level of spiritual bondage can create all sorts of traumatic, unnatural lusts and cravings and create severe grief and torment.

I believe denying the reality that this level of spiritual warfare can happen to a Christian leaves many believers with nowhere to turn for assistance when such spiritual bondage occurs in their life. When a church tells us this can't happen, the believer is left searching for answers through medicine, counseling, and other treatments that are wholly ineffective for ridding oneself of a demonic spirit. It should be understood, however, that this is in no way possession (being totally given over and in control of the devil, which this cannot happen to a true Christian).

As we discussed in Chapter Nine, there are several ways to give the devil "legal access" to inflict this level of spiritual warfare. The examples below are not a complete list of what opens the door to this level of spiritual bondage but provides a general idea of the type of conduct the may give the devil "legal access" to your life. I want to stress that just because someone has engaged in a specific type of conduct listed below *does not mean* they are automatically demonized or have become indwelt with a demonic spirit. What I am saying, is that by involving oneself in these activities, you *run the risk* of providing "legal access" to the Enemy in this level of spiritual warfare.

As previously discussed, we can give the Enemy access to our lives through our **actions**, **words**, and **thoughts**—attitudes and emotions. Some examples that may open one up to this level of spiritual warfare include:

- Continual and deliberate sin
- Drug use and taking other mind-altering substances
- Addictions
- Spiritualism
- Shamanism
- Voodoo
- Soliciting contact with demonic entities

- Channeling or soliciting contact with non-earthly entities
- Eastern and other false religions
- Witchcraft
- New Age
- Satanism
- Membership in an organization based on such practices
- Soliciting spirits through games
- Ouija
- Manifestations of power that derive their authority from the devil or demons
- Severe trauma
- Physical abuse
- Mental abuse
- Sexual abuse
- Living any lifestyle that the Lord says is sinful or is against His Word
- Extreme fears or phobias
- Engaging in unscriptural prayer (i.e. asking the Lord to be tried, tempted, or your weaknesses exploited)
- Generational curses
- Long-term unforgiveness

Demonic attacks disguised as emotional issues may develop at this second level of spiritual warfare. Constant feelings of agony, rejection, grieving in the spirit, and internal pain are all indicators of this type of spiritual warfare. One key indicator that you may be dealing with this level of spiritual warfare, is that these traumatic feelings won't go away over time. They can last for weeks, months, years, or decades. Additionally, when suffering under this type of spiritual warfare, one may suffer persistent and traumatic dreams that are very visual and delivered in the first person. A heightened sense of emotional trauma, pain, and rejection in the dreamed event, with the emotional impact of this dream carrying on long after you awake. If your daily symptoms include feeling severe emotional pain, anguish, deep rejection, and a continual grieving in your spirit, you may be dealing with demonic spirits.

As stated previously, many *demonic spirits* have emotional traits associated with their character such as the demonic spirits of fear, anger, rejection, unforgiveness, lust, and many of the other emotional tools listed in Section Four of this book. If you have provided "legal access" to one or more such demonic spirits in your life, they will attempt to exert their influence over you. You may experience this demon's emotional characteristics, as well as the compulsions and pain it creates. If you find yourself in this level of spiritual warfare, deliverance is required—either through self-deliverance through the power of the Holy Spirit or by one operating under authority of the Holy Spirit.

The Third Level of this Spiritual Battle
(Spiritual Possession)

This level is the worst of the three levels of spiritual warfare because when it occurs, a person is under the complete control of the devil. In other words, he or she is possessed (I am defining possession here as a complete surrender to the devil, with total control of mind, body, and spirit given over to the demonic). Scripture gives no example of this happening to a true Christian. It is my belief and understanding that a true Christian cannot fall into this level of influence because the Holy Spirit already dwells within us.

Besides, why would the devil want to visibly disclose such a display of his presence for all the world to see when he can do much more damage staying behind the scenes with his less visible level-one and level-two spiritual attacks?

If you are fearful that you have fallen into this third level of demonic influence, please talk to someone who is trained in the area of deliverance. You may only be dealing with a spirit of fear or deception that is intended to keep you under a fear of possession.

One additional note, if a person has succumbed to this level of spiritual warfare, there is still hope. Jesus' death on the cross triumphed over Satan. Christ was given all power and authority in heaven and earth by His Father, God. So, deliverance for someone *even possessed* by the Enemy is possible, but only achieved by and through the Lord Jesus Christ, and administered by someone who walks in His power and authority. Remember, the devil comes to steal, kill, and destroy, but Christ came so that we may have life and have it abundantly.[188] So if you believe you have fallen into the possession of the Enemy, there is still hope.

In the next section of this book, we will focus on steps we can take to protect ourselves from the many assaults of the Enemy, and how to free ourselves from any *strongholds* and *bondages* that may have occurred. For some, simply understanding that many self-defeating emotions may originate from the devil might help in breaking these strongholds. For others, learning for the first time that their torment may be caused by another (a demonic spirit), and not themselves, and that Jesus Christ (and true believers walking in His Spirit) have the power and authority to free those tormented by these spirits, may be just the news—and hope—they need to hear.

Let's look now at how true believers get this incredible *power* and *authority* to accomplish these formidable tasks.

SECTION 3

Our Defenses

Our Authority Over the Devil's Assaults

The good news for believers is that Jesus has been given all authority in heaven and on earth.[189] That should give us all a big sigh of relief. We start out knowing that our Lord is Lord of all and that He has the final say regarding our life here on earth, as well as our eternal destiny. Accordingly, for believers, I would suggest that this is the most important section of the book.

As followers of Jesus Christ, we have inherited the right to use His power and authority over all the wiles of the Enemy.[190] In the pages that follow, I will discuss how the Lord has passed down His power and authority to His church—something for which we should all be quite thankful.

To provide some clarity on this important topic, I will divide this section into three parts. **First**, since we derive all our power and authority from Jesus, we will look at the power and authority Jesus Himself demonstrated over this world before the cross. **Second**, we will look at the power and authority Jesus gave His disciples, while He was with them on the earth, and the power and authority they received through the Holy Spirit after His ascension into heaven. And **third**, we will look at Scripture verses which indicate that as true believers in Christ who are walking in the will of the Lord, we also possess this power and authority.

Jesus' Power and Authority

Below I will outline the six areas in which Jesus demonstrated His God-given authority over this world.

1. *Jesus' power over the elements.*[191]

   Mark 4:39 *And he awoke and rebuked the wind and said to the sea, 'Peace! Be still!' And* **the winds ceased, and there was great calm.** (emphasis added)

   Mark 6:38–42 *'How many loaves do you have? Go and see.' And when they had found out, they said, 'Five, and two fish.' Then he commanded them all to sit down in groups on the green grass.* **And Jesus fed the 5000 from these five loaves and two fish.** (emphasis added)

2. *Jesus' power over sickness, disease, and infirmity.*[192]

   John 5:8–9 *Jesus said to him, (the paralyzed man) 'Get up, pick up your bed, and walk.'* **And at once the man was healed, and he took up his bed and walked.** (parenthesis added)

3. *Jesus' power over evil spirits.*[193]

   Matthew 17:18 *And Jesus rebuked the demon,* **and it came out of him,** *and the boy was healed instantly.* (emphasis added)

4. *Jesus' power to forgive sin.*[194]

   Mark 2:5, 10–11 *And when Jesus saw their faith, he said to the paralytic,* **'Son, your sins are forgiven.'**. . . *'But* **that you may know that the Son of Man has authority on the earth to forgive sins'**—*he said to the paralytic—'I say to you, rise, pick up your bed, and go home.'* (emphasis added)

5. *Jesus power over death.*[195]

   John 11:43–44 *When he had said these things, he (Jesus) cried out with a loud voice, 'Lazarus, come out.'* **The man who had died came out** . . . (parenthesis and emphasis added).

6. *Jesus' power over our eternal destiny.*[196]

Luke 23:43 *And he (Jesus) said to him (one of the two criminals on the cross beside Christ), 'Truly, I say to you, **today you will be with me in paradise'** (parenthesis and emphasis added).

When doing these things, Jesus was operating under the authority of His Father.[197] However, after the cross, Jesus' authority changed. He was handed all authority in heaven and on earth by God the Father. How do we know this? Jesus told us so. After His crucifixion, Jesus physically appeared to the disciples before ascending into heaven and told them about His position of authority. Scripture tells us that Jesus came and spoke to them, saying, **"All authority has been given to Me in heaven and on earth"**[198] (emphasis added).

The Disciples' Power and Authority while Ministering with Jesus

In addition, Jesus gave the disciples great power and authority during His earthly ministry with them. Evidence can be found of this delegation of power and authority when Jesus sent the twelve disciples out to preach the kingdom of God and to heal the sick. He gave them **power and authority over all demons and to cure diseases . . .**[199] Likewise, when Jesus sent the seventy-two disciples ahead of Him. He gave them **authority to tread on serpents and scorpions, and over all the power of the Enemy**, *and nothing shall hurt you*[200] (emphasis added). And Luke 10:17 says, *The seventy-two returned with joy, saying,* **"Lord, even the demons are subject to us in your name!"** (emphasis added).

The Disciples' Power and Authority
after the Resurrection of Jesus

After Jesus' death and resurrection, the disciples were left with the incredible task of spreading what Jesus had started—sharing the good news of the gospel and building the kingdom of God here on this earth. But Jesus did not abandon His disciples in this task. Instead, He bestowed on them the power of the Holy Spirit and gave them His authority to act as agents on His behalf.

One of the last promises Jesus made to His disciples, during the forty day period after His resurrection from the grave—but before His ascension up into heaven—was that He would not leave them as orphans.[201] As confusing and as difficult to understand as this might have seemed to the disciples (since they understood Jesus would soon be leaving them and going to the Father in heaven) they waited patiently in the upper room where they were to stay for what Jesus called the Helper to arrive (what we now call the Holy Spirit).[202]

The Gift of the Holy Spirit

In fact, Jesus had told His disciples, *Nevertheless, I tell you the truth: it is to your advantage that I go away, for if I do not go away, the Helper will not come to you. But if I go, I will send him to you.*[203] Clearly an unusual statement, but one which the disciples would shortly come to understand.

Ten days after Christ's ascension into heaven, or fifty days from the date of His crucifixion[204]—the date known as Pentecost—the Helper or Holy Spirit whom Jesus had promised would come, did.[205] The Bible describes this event in Acts 2:2–4 (NIV) like this:

> *Suddenly a sound like the blowing of a violent wind came from heaven and filled the whole house where they were sitting. They saw what seemed to be tongues of fire that separated and came to rest on each of them. All of them were filled with the Holy Spirit and began to speak in other tongues as the Spirit enabled them.*

Neither the disciples nor the world would ever be the same. This Spirit, the Holy Spirit, which had been gifted by God only on the rarest of occasions in the Old Testament,[206] would now be available to all who accepted Jesus' sacrifice on the cross for his/her sins and professed Him as his/her Lord.

The Bible tells us that the apostle Peter, on the day of Pentecost after preaching the message of salvation to the masses, said to them, *". . . Repent and be baptized every one of you in the name of Jesus Christ for the forgiveness of your sins, and **you will receive the gift of the Holy Spirit"** (Acts 2:38, emphasis added).

This was the ultimate game-changer for mankind. This Spirit, whom Jesus sent for us, baptizes us,[207] regenerates our inner human spirit,[208] seals us for the day of redemption,[209] brings into our lives His fruit of love, joy, peace, etc.,[210] convicts us of our sins,[211] comforts us,[212] leads us in our daily walk free from the bondage of the Law,[213] intercedes for us,[214] teaches us all things, reminds us of God's Word,[215] empowers us with His spiritual gifts,[216] guides us into all truth,[217] and equips us for our witness.[218] In other words, through the relationship with Jesus and our indwelling of the Holy Spirit, we have been made one hundred percent complete.[219]

And we have the ability to walk fully empowered by the Holy Spirit as demonstrated by these first disciples of Christ. Peter demonstrated this power and authority when he healed a man who was lame from birth,[220] when he healed a man who was paralyzed,[221] and when he raised a woman named Tabitha from the dead.[222]

We also see this power and authority demonstrated by the apostle Paul when he healed a man crippled from birth,[223] raised a young man from the dead who had fallen from a third-story window,[224] and drove out a spirit of divination from a slave girl.[225]

Let's look at a few scriptural verses in which the apostles (Peter and Paul) demonstrated the power of the Holy Spirit. We are even told that Paul's anointing was so great that . . . *even handkerchiefs or aprons that had touched his skin were carried away to the sick, and their diseases left them and the evil spirits came out of them.*[226]

1. *The apostles' power over sickness, disease, and infirmity.*

Acts 3:6–7, *But Peter said, "I have no silver and gold, but what I do have I give to you. In the name of Jesus Christ of Nazareth, rise up and walk!" And he took him by the right hand and raised him up, and **immediately his feet and ankles were made strong**.* (emphasis added)

Acts 9:33–34, *There he found a man named Aeneas, bedridden for eight years, who was paralyzed. And Peter said to him, "Aeneas, Jesus Christ heals you; rise and make your bed." And **immediately he rose**.* (emphasis added)

Acts 14:8–10, *Now at Lystra there was a man sitting who could not use his feet. He was crippled from birth and had never walked. He listened to Paul speaking. And Paul, looking intently at him and seeing that he had faith to be made well, said in a loud voice, "Stand upright on your feet." And **he sprang up and began walking**.* (emphasis added)

2. *The apostles' power over evil spirits (deliverance).*

Acts 16:16–18, *As we were going to the place of prayer, we were met by a slave girl who had a spirit of divination and brought her owners much gain by fortune-telling. She followed Paul and us, crying out, "These men are servants of the Most High God, who proclaim to you the way of salvation." And this she kept doing for many days. Paul, having become greatly annoyed, turned and said to the spirit, "I command you in the name of Jesus Christ to come out of her." **And it came out that very hour**.* (emphasis added)

3. *The apostle's power over death*.

> Acts 9:40–41, *But Peter put them all outside, and knelt down and prayed; and turning to the body he said, "Tabitha, arise." And she opened her eyes, and when she saw Peter she sat up. And he gave her his hand and raised her up. Then, calling the saints and widows, **he presented her alive.*** (emphasis added)

> Acts 20:9–12, *And a young man named Eutychus, sitting at the window, sank into a deep sleep as Paul talked still longer. And being overcome by sleep, he fell down from the third story and was taken up dead. But Paul went down and bent over him, and taking him in his arms, said, "Do not be alarmed, for his life is in him." And when Paul had gone up and had broken bread and eaten, he conversed with them a long while, until daybreak, and so departed. **And they took the youth away alive**, and were not a little comforted.* (emphasis added)

The Believers' Power and Authority

But what about us? As receivers of this same Holy Spirit, do we have the same power and authority the early disciples operated under almost two thousand years ago? Yes, we do. But just like the apostles in Jesus' day, it is only by and through the power and authority of the Lord Jesus Christ that these miracles happen. And like the apostles, our ability to operate under the power and authority is based on *our position in Christ*.

I will outline two Scriptures that confirm we, as Christians, have this same inherited power and authority. I will also discuss how to know if we are correctly positioned in Christ to implement this authority.

In both of the Scriptures below, Jesus explains the power and authority He is giving to *believers*. One is found in the book of Mark when the resurrected Christ spoke with His eleven disciples prior to ascending into heaven. *And these signs will follow **those who believe: In My name they will cast out demons**; they will speak with new tongues; they will take up serpents; and if they drink anything deadly, it will by no means hurt them; **they will lay hands on the sick, and they will recover*** (emphasis added).[227]

The other verse is found in the book of John, in Jesus' conversation with His disciples before He was betrayed and crucified. *Most assuredly, I say to you, **he who believes in Me**, the works that I do he will do also; and greater works than these he will do, because I go to My Father. And whatever you ask in My name, that I will do, that the Father may be glorified in the Son. If you ask anything in My name, I will do it* (emphasis added).[228]

Some don't know we have this authority. Some don't believe we have this authority. And some want nothing to do with this authority. Which category do you fall into?

I find it both a wonder and a curiosity that God chose man to bring His eternal plans to fruition. We have been granted the incredible privilege of partnering with the Lord and doing His work here on earth. Can you think of a greater privilege? I cannot. And He supplied us with His power and authority to do just that.

Implementing This Power and Authority

The Greek word for **power** is *dunamis,* which means physical power, force, might, and ability, while the Greek word for **authority** is *exousia,* meaning control, authority, dominion—especially moral authority.[229] One may possess the **power** or the ability to act, **but not possess the authority to do so**. Our power comes from our legal standing as believers, as possessors of the Holy Spirit,[230] but our authority is based solely on our personal *relationship* and standing with God through Jesus Christ. This proper relationship with God enables us to walk in authority, similar to that of the disciples, with the Holy Spirit moving freely through us.

The greater our relationship or standing with God, the more effective this power will be. To walk in the full power and authority of the Lord, however, requires that we have fully surrendered ourselves to Christ and are living a surrendered life to Him. How do we know if we have surrendered ourselves to Christ? Jesus tells us in Matthew 16:24. *Then Jesus told his disciples, 'If anyone would come after me, let him deny himself and take up his cross and follow me.'* Christ again clarified His requirement for complete surrender to Him when He said, *For whoever would save his life will lose it, but whoever loses his life for my sake will find it.*[231]

The late John Paul Jackson did a wonderful job explaining how power and authority work through the life of a believer in his recorded teaching appropriately titled *Power and Authority* (available through Streams Ministry).[232] This series is well worth your time if you want to go more in-depth on this topic. His teachings on this topic may also be found on the Internet under the title *The Difference between Power and Authority*.[233]

How are we to exert this authority as believers? First and foremost, we are called as Christians to pray.[234] One of a Christian's greatest privileges, weapons, and responsibilities in this battle is prayer—to make our request be known to Almighty God.[235]

Although Christians commonly agree that we should pray for God to act on our behalf for protection, provision, healing, and deliverance from all sorts of evil, there is often a debate among Christians on whether we have the actual authority from Christ to act on His behalf in the areas of healing and deliverance. Some believe that our authority is limited to prayer. Others believe we have the power and authority from Christ to act on His behalf in these areas. Which is correct? I believe both. I believe there is biblical support for the requirement for us to *pray* for God to intervene on our behalf, as well as evidence to support the position that we possess the power and *authority to act* on Christ's behalf. Let's look at one scriptural passage that appears to support both of these positions.

In Mark 9:14–29, Jesus is called on to expel a demon from the body of a child. The disciples were unable to do it on their own, but Jesus did so with a command. The apostles were amazed and asked Jesus why they had been unable to expel that demon. Jesus replied, "*This kind cannot be driven out by anything but prayer.*" Some manuscripts say prayer and fasting.

I think this is an important passage in Scripture. Implicit in the statement is that while the majority of the demons were expelled by the disciples through the power and authority of Jesus' name,[236] this particular kind of demon required something more—prayer. I believe this demonstrates that while we may exert the power and authority Jesus has given us, we should also ask for the Lord's help in prayer.

We are Recruits of the Most High

Every year, thousands of police recruits around the country get sworn in as official police officers by their Chief of Police. Prior to their swearing in, the police recruits have no more authority than you or I would have to act on behalf of the police department. However, following the ceremony, they are duly authorized officers, able to act in the name of the Police Chief and the entire police department. No one would suggest that these duly authorized officers, after being sworn in, should call upon their Police Chief to come make the arrest—an arrest they have been authorized by the police department to make themselves. That would be absurd. Yet, this is exactly what many Christians believe we are required to do when confronting evil. Some Christians believe that instead of stepping up and confronting evil in the name of Jesus, we should instead step away and simply pray for the Lord to intervene—intervene in situations in which we have been *duly authorized* to act. I can only imagine that the Lord may be thinking, "Act! You have My authority—act!"

Those who don't believe we have this authority to act on the behalf of God's kingdom forget we are duly authorized officers of the Most-High. We have been given the authority to act in accordance with His will—in His name and with His power—if we are living within a personal relationship with the Lord. As stated previously in this chapter, immediately before the Lord's ascension into heaven, and in the same verse in which He gave the Great Commission to preach His gospel to the world, Jesus told His apostles *"And these signs will accompany those who believe: in my name **they will cast out demons;** they will speak in new tongues . . . **they will lay their hands on the sick, and they will recover"** (emphasis added).[237] That sounds like authority to me! And I see no statute of limitations on this delegation of power and authority.

Again, I would like to make it clear that I *do* suggest we are to call upon the name of the Lord in prayer for help, assistance, and to intervene in our daily lives. Prayer is one of our greatest weapons against the Enemy. But we should also act when confronted by evil, because the Lord has authorized us to do just that.[238] Failing to do so, I believe, is squandering the authority that has been given to us by the Lord to advance His Kingdom.

Why We Need this Power and Authority

I think our need for God's power and authority becomes very apparent when the apostle Paul tells us who we will be battling. *For we do not wrestle against flesh and blood, but against the rulers, against the authorities, against the cosmic powers over this present darkness, against the spiritual forces of evil in the heavenly places.*[239]

And in 2 Corinthians 10:3–4, Paul also talks about our weapons of divine power when he states, *For though we walk in the flesh, we are not waging war according to the flesh. For the weapons of our warfare are not of the flesh but have divine power to destroy strongholds.* So, to think God left us powerless and without authority to advance His kingdom in our cosmic battle against the forces of evil is unrealistic and not supported by Scripture.

And obviously, we have no power on our own to battle these spiritual forces. We must rely on the power and authority given to us by Christ for this formidable task.

So what weapons have we been given to implement this power and authority? We have been given . . .

1. The Weapon of **Prayer**
2. The Weapon of God's Word **(Promises)**
3. The Weapon of God's **Power and Authority** (Deliverance)

All are critically important weapons in defending ourselves, others, and reclaiming lost ground (strongholds and bondages) surrendered to the Enemy.

Let's look first at prayer, what most people believe is our most powerful and formidable weapon in this spiritual battle.

The Weapon of Prayer

As Christians, it's nice to know that we have been given what many believe is the greatest spiritual weapon of all: Prayer. It could easily be called the weapon of mass destruction in the spiritual realm. Through prayer, we have access to the very throne room of God with this promise, "... *Truly, truly, I say to you, **whatever you ask of the Father in my name, he will give it to you.***"[240]

Let's examine twelve recommended requirements for a *heart-filled* and *effective prayer*, and twelve potential *hindrances to prayer*. I will then discuss incredible scriptural evidence that our heart-filled and effective prayer is heard by God, and activates God's holy angels in the heavens.

Effective Prayer

Scriptural instructions for *effective prayer* include:

1. **Pray according to the will of God.** This is the confidence we have in approaching God: "that if we ask anything according to *His will*, He hears us."[241] *God's will* is that we live according to our faith in

Him and His words. Matthew 26:39 says, "And going a little farther he [Jesus] fell on his face and prayed, saying, 'My Father, if it be possible, let this cup pass from me; nevertheless, not as I will, but *as you will*'" (emphasis added).

2. **Pray in the name of Jesus.** Jesus tells us in John 14:13, 14, "Whatever you ask *in my name*, this I will do, that the Father may be glorified in the Son. If you ask me anything *in my name*, I will do it" (emphasis added).

3. **Pray in faith.** In Hebrews 11:1, the Bible defines faith as, "the assurance of things hoped for, the conviction of things not seen." Jesus said in Mark 11:24, "Therefore I tell you, whatever you ask in prayer, *believe that you have received it*, and it will be yours" (emphasis added).

4. **Pray with persistence.** We are instructed by Jesus that we are to take our prayers before the Lord without ceasing. In other words, be persistent in prayer. This is reflected in the parable of the persistent widow found in Luke 18:3–8a. "And there was a widow in that city who kept coming to him and saying, 'Give me justice against my adversary.' For a while he refused, but afterward he said to himself, 'Though I neither fear God nor respect man, yet because this widow *keeps bothering me*, I will give her justice, so that she will not beat me down by her *continual coming*.' And the Lord said, 'Hear what the unrighteous judge says. *And will not God give justice to his elect, who cry to him day and night?* Will he delay long over them? I tell you, he will give justice to them speedily'" (emphasis added).

5. **Pray from obedience.** Obedience means adhering to the Word of God. John tells us in 1 John 3:22, "And whatever we ask we receive from him, *because we keep his commandments* and do what pleases him" (emphasis added). Likewise, as we are told in James 5:16 (KJV), "... *The effectual fervent prayer of a righteous man availeth much.*"

6. **Pray specifically.** We are to bring all our cares and concerns, both large and small, to the Lord. In Philippians 4:6 Paul tells us, "Do not be anxious about anything, but in everything by prayer and

supplication with thanksgiving *let your requests be made known to God*" (emphasis added). He knows our request before we make it, but He still wants us to ask. James 4:2 (NIV) instructs, "You desire but do not have, so you kill. You covet but you cannot get what you want, so you quarrel and fight. *You do not have because you do not ask God*" (emphasis added).

7. **Pray in humility.** Christians are not to be proud but humble.[242] We are told in 2 Chronicles 7:14 (NIV), "If my people, who are called by my name, will *humble themselves* and pray and seek my face and turn from their wicked ways, then I will hear from heaven, and I will forgive their sin and will heal their land" (emphasis added). In addition, an angel gave Daniel two important criteria for his prayers to be heard—a heart set on understanding and humility. The angel said in Daniel 10:12, "Fear not, Daniel, for from the first day that you set your heart *to understand and humbled yourself before your God*, your words have been heard, and I have come because of your words" (emphasis added).

8. **Pray to seek understanding.** Likewise, we should all strive to understand God and His words. The above verse in Daniel 10:12 makes it clear that from the first day Daniel set his heart to *understand* God and humbled himself before the Lord, his words were heard, and an angel was dispatched with an answer to his prayer. Again, as cited above, Daniel 10:12 says, "Fear not, Daniel, for from the first day that you set your *heart to understand* and humbled yourself before your God, your words have been heard, and I have come because of your words" (emphasis added).

9. **Pray in the Spirit.** When the Holy Spirit, who resides within every believer,[243] connects us (our mind and spirit) to the Lord Jesus in the throne room of heaven, we pray in the Spirit.[244] That requires that we put aside our fleshly thoughts and emotions, and uninhibitedly approach our Lord God in thanksgiving and prayer. The apostle Paul tells us in Ephesians 6:18 that we should be "praying

at all times *in the Spirit*, with all prayer and supplication. To that end, keep alert with all perseverance, making supplication for all the saints" (emphasis added).

10. **Pray with praise and thanksgiving.** Scripture tells us in 1 Thessalonians 5:18 (KJV), "In everything *give thanks*: for this is the will of God in Christ Jesus concerning you." Furthermore, Paul tells us in Philippians 4:6, "Do not be anxious about anything, but in everything by prayer and supplication with *thanksgiving* let your requests be made known to God" (emphasis added).

11. **Abide in Christ.** Abiding means to remain or dwell in something or someone. Jesus tells us in John 15:7, "If you *abide in me*, and my words abide in you, ask whatever you wish, and it will be done for you" (emphasis added).

12. **Pray in agreement.** Although it is a mystery, we are told that there is great power when we pray in agreement with others. The Bible says that because the Lord your God fights for you, one will put a thousand to flight but two will put 10,000 to flight.[245] Many underestimate the power of prayer—that one Christian in agreement with God can put a thousand to flight should be quite sobering. And two in agreement can do ten times as much. Consider what a multitude could do. In Matthew 18:19 Jesus tells us, "Again I say to you, *if two of you agree* on earth about anything they ask, it will be done for them by my Father in heaven" (emphasis added). That should eliminate any doubt in the believer's mind of the power of prayer.

Hindrances to Prayer

Scripture also gives us hindrances to prayer, including:

1. **Lack of Knowledge of God's Word.** I think most Christians understand that it is very difficult to follow God's Word without knowing

it. The solution to this problem is to read and meditate on God's Word. Hosea 4:6 says, "My people are destroyed for *lack of knowledge*" (emphasis added). And Isaiah 5:13 says, "Therefore my people go into exile for *lack of knowledge*" (emphasis added).

2. **Selfish prayers.** Scripture tells us in Philippians 2:3, "Do nothing from *selfish ambition* or conceit, but in humility count others more significant than yourselves" (emphasis added). James 4:3 also says, "You ask and do not receive, *because you ask wrongly, to spend it on your passions*" (emphasis added). These verses make it clear that selfish prayers go unanswered.

3. **Unconfessed sin.** Sin leads to separation from God. If we hold onto unconfessed sin, we create a gap between ourselves and the Lord. Prayers in this state fall into that gap, not reaching the throne room of heaven. That is also pointed out in Psalm 66:18: "If I had cherished *iniquity in my heart*, the Lord would not have listened" (emphasis added). Likewise, we read in Isaiah 59:2: "Your *iniquities* have made a separation between you and your God, and *your sins* have hidden his face from you *so that he does not hear*." We are also told in Proverbs 28:13 (NIV), "Whoever *conceals their sins* does not prosper, but the one who *confesses and renounces* them finds mercy" (emphasis added).

4. **Unforgiveness.** In the Lord's Prayer, we ask God to forgive us our debts *as we also have forgiven our debtors*.[246] And, we are told that if we forgive other people when they sin against us, our heavenly Father will also forgive us.[247] Forgiving others is not an option—it is mandatory for our own forgiveness. Mark 11:25 says, "Whenever you stand praying, *forgive*, if you have anything against anyone, so that your Father also who is in heaven may forgive you your trespasses" (emphasis added).

5. **Ungodly pride.** Ungodly pride is much different than self-confidence. While self-confidence focuses on one's abilities, ungodly pride focuses on the praise of one's abilities. Confidence is good. Ungodly

pride is not. James 4:6 says, "God opposes the *proud* but gives grace to the humble" (emphasis added).

6. **Improper marital relationship.** The Bible tells us that a proper marital relationship is necessary for a proper relationship with our heavenly Father. Physical or mental abuse, infidelity, or abandonment of one's spouse are all examples of an improper marital relationship. We know this because we are told in 1 Peter 3:7, "Likewise, husbands, live with your wives in an understanding way, showing honor to the woman as the weaker vessel, since they are heirs with you of the grace of life, *so that your prayers may not be hindered*" (emphasis added).

7. **Disbelief.** Disbelief is the refusal to accept the Word of God. The Bible tells us in James 1:5–8, "If any of you lacks wisdom, let him ask God, who gives generously to all without reproach, and it will be given him. But let him ask in faith, *with no doubting*, for the one who doubts is like a wave of the sea that is driven and tossed by the wind. For that person must not suppose that he will receive anything from the Lord; he is a double-minded man, unstable in all his ways" (emphasis added).

8. **Unreconciled brother.** We are to mend unreconciled issues with our brothers. If we have an unreconciled brother whom we have wronged or offended, then we need to reconcile with that brother. The Lord tells us in Matthew 5:23–24 (NIV), "Therefore, if you are offering your gift at the altar and there remember that your brother or sister has something against you, leave your gift there in front of the altar. First go and *be reconciled to them*; then come and offer your gift" (emphasis added).

9. **Anti-Semitism.** "Anti-Semitism is hostility toward or discrimination against Jews as a religious, ethnic, or racial group."[248] Psalm 122:6 says, "Pray for the peace of Jerusalem! 'May they be secure who love you!'" And Genesis 12:3 (NIV) says, "I will *bless those who bless* you, and *whoever curses you I will curse*; and all peoples on earth will be blessed through you" (emphasis added).

10. **Cherishing evil in our hearts.** Similar to unconfessed sin, actively pursuing evil in our heart separates us from God. Psalm 66:18 says, "If I had *cherished iniquity in my heart, the Lord would not have listened*" (emphasis added).

11. **Willfully refusing to obey God's laws.** Doing so places one in opposition to God. Proverbs 28:9 says, "If one *turns away his ear from hearing the law, even his prayer is an abomination*" (emphasis added).

12. **Refusing knowledge.** Not fearing the Lord and rejecting His knowledge means God will turn a deaf ear to your requests. Proverbs 1:24–26, 28–29 says, "Because I have called and *you refused to listen*, have stretched out my hand and no one has heeded, because you have *ignored all my counsel* and would have none of my reproof, I also will laugh at your calamity; I will mock when terror strikes you . . . *Then they will call upon me, but I will not answer; they will seek me diligently but will not find me.* Because they *hated knowledge* and did not choose the fear of the LORD" (emphasis added).

Prayer Activates God's Holy Angels

If you have ever wanted a look behind the curtain at what actually takes place in the spiritual world when you pray, you will enjoy this next Bible passage. This incredible passage that we previously discussed in Chapter Three, not only reveals how our heart-filled prayers can activate God's angels, but also give us evidence of the battle that rages in the second heaven between God's angels and the devil's evil angels. The passage described in Daniel 10:12–14 states,

*Then he said to me, 'Fear not, Daniel, for **from the first day that you set your heart to understand and humbled yourself before your God, your words have been heard, and I have come because of your words**.*

The prince of the kingdom of Persia withstood me twenty-one days, but Michael, one of the chief princes, came to help me, for I was left there with the kings of Persia, and came to make you understand what is to happen to your people in the latter days. For the vision is for days yet to come.' (emphasis added)

The above passage in Daniel makes it perfectly clear that God hears our heart-filled prayers, and that He dispatches His angels for our assistance. (Remember, most biblical scholars understand Revelation 12:4 to mean that one-third of the angels in heaven defected with Satan, leaving two-thirds that remained faithful to God, so Satan is outnumbered two to one.)

This passage also reveals the battle that rages in the heavenlies—heaven number two. It also describes how one of Satan's fallen angels (the prince of Persia) prevented God's messenger angel from getting to Daniel for twenty-one days. After giving his message to Daniel, and before departing, God's angel informed Daniel . . . *now I will return to fight against the prince of Persia . . .*[249] indicating this continual spiritual battle in the second heaven.

And how do we know the prince of Persia was not a human prince? Because angels don't have trouble getting past human princes. As we mentioned in Chapter Three, Isaiah 37:36 chronicles a time in which the angel of the Lord went out, and in one night, struck down 185,000 men in the camp of the Assyrians. Clearly, angels are immensely more powerful than man. This verse also tells us that God's archangel, Michael, came to assist in the battle. Again, none of God's archangels need assistance when dealing with a human. This was spiritual warfare in the heavens, and it was activated by Daniel's prayer.

Let's move on and look next at our second mighty weapon in this spiritual battle, the weapon of God's promises.

17

The Weapon of God's Word
(God's Promises)

W e all want guarantees in life. A guarantee on our new car, a guarantee on our new computer, or a guarantee on our recent home repair. But how about the big stuff? I mean the really big stuff, like life itself? We are often told life doesn't come with a guarantee. But is that true?

I would like to challenge that thinking. There *are* some guarantees in life. But none of them are manmade. Let's face it; if they were manmade, you'd know they'd fail eventually anyway. So, let's take a look at the only guarantees we have in this life that will not fail—the *Promises of God*. We can call these promises the greatest guarantees ever issued. And they are found throughout God's Word.

While teaching His disciples at the Mount of Olives regarding the end of the age, Jesus gave His disciples this guarantee about His words; *Heaven and earth will pass away, but my words will not pass away*.[250] So we know without a shadow of a doubt that Jesus' words (promises) will remain true.

So, just how many of God's promises are there in the Bible? Honestly, I'm not sure. Some estimate over three thousand.[251] I don't know about you but that gives me great peace. Most believers can recite a favorite verse or two that they rely upon, live by, and provide guidance in their time of need. I certainly have my favorite verses as well. But if truth be known, these verses, for the true believer, are more than words to rely on; they are life itself. Matthew 4:4 (NIV) tells us . . . *'Man shall not live on bread alone, but on every word that comes from the mouth of God.'"* So these words are the means by which we claim our salvation, provide protection for ourselves and our families, achieve the life God has designed for us, and ensure us that God will provide for our needs. They are in essence, our life.

I have provided for you a list of twenty-four promises of God for our **instruction**, our **protection**, our **provision**, and our **salvation**. These promises are a living and powerful weapon, sharper than any two-edged sword, defeating any doubt that might creep into your mind when the *world*, the *flesh*, and the *devil* all tell you that what you are about to read is not true.

Promises for Our Instruction

1. **Jeremiah 29:11–13** " For I know the plans I have for you, declares the LORD, plans for welfare and not for evil, to give you a future and a hope. Then you will call upon me and come and pray to me, and I will hear you. *You will seek me and find me, when you seek me with all your heart."* (emphasis added)
2. **Romans 8:28** "And we know that for those who love God *all things work together for good, for those who are called according to his purpose."* (emphasis added)
3. **Proverbs 3:5–6** *"Trust in the LORD with all your heart, and do not lean on your own understanding. In all your ways acknowledge him, and he will make straight your paths."* (emphasis added)
4. **Mark 12:30–31** "And you shall *love the Lord your God with all your heart and with all your soul and with all your mind and with all your strength.'* The second is this: 'You shall *love your neighbor as yourself.'* There is no other commandment greater than these." (emphasis added)

5. **James 1:5–8** "If any of you lacks wisdom, *let him ask God, who gives generously to all without reproach, and it will be given him.* But let him ask in faith, with no doubting, for the one who doubts is like a wave of the sea that is driven and tossed by the wind. For that person must not suppose that he will receive anything from the Lord; he is a double-minded man, unstable in all his ways." (emphasis added)

6. **James 5:13–16** "Is anyone among you suffering? Let him pray. Is anyone cheerful? Let him sing praise. Is anyone among you sick? Let him call for the elders of the church and let them pray over him, anointing him with oil in the name of the Lord. *And the prayer of faith will save the one who is sick*, and the Lord will raise him up. And if he has committed sins, he will be forgiven. Therefore, confess your sins to one another and pray for one another, that you may be healed. The prayer of a righteous person has great power as it is working." (emphasis added)

7. **Isaiah 55:11** ". . . so shall my word be that goes out from my mouth; *it shall not return to me empty*, but it shall accomplish that which I purpose, and shall succeed in the thing for which I sent it." (emphasis added)

Promises for Our Protection

8. **Psalm 91:1–16** "He who dwells in the shelter of the Most High will abide in the shadow of the Almighty. I will say to the LORD, 'My refuge and my fortress, my God, in whom I trust.' For he will deliver you from the snare of the fowler and from the deadly pestilence. He will cover you with his pinions, and under his wings you will find refuge; his faithfulness is a shield and buckler. You will not fear the terror of the night, nor the arrow that flies by day, nor the pestilence that stalks in darkness, nor the destruction that

wastes at noonday. A thousand may fall at your side, ten thousand at your right hand, but it will not come near you. You will only look with your eyes and see the recompense of the wicked. *Because you have made the* LORD *your dwelling place—the Most High, who is my refuge—no evil shall be allowed to befall you, no plague come near your tent.* For he will command his angels concerning you to guard you in all your ways. *On their hands they will bear you up, lest you strike your foot against a stone.* You will tread on the lion and the adder; the young lion and the serpent you will trample underfoot. 'Because he holds fast to me in love, I will deliver him; I will protect him, because he knows my name. When he calls to me, I will answer him; I will be with him in trouble; I will rescue him and honor him. *With long life I will satisfy him and show him my salvation.*'" (emphasis added)

9. **Ephesians 6:11** "Put on the whole armor of God, *that you may be able to stand against the schemes of the devil.*" (emphasis added)

10. **Deuteronomy 31:6** "Be strong and courageous. Do not fear or be in dread of them, *for it is the Lord your God who goes with you. He will not leave you or forsake you.*" (emphasis added)

11. **Isaiah 54:17** "*No weapon that is fashioned against you shall succeed,* and you shall refute every tongue that rises against you in judgment. This is the heritage of the servants of the Lord and their vindication from me, declares the Lord." (emphasis added)

12. **Proverbs 30:5** "Every word of God proves true; *he is a shield to those who take refuge in him.*" (emphasis added)

13. **Ephesians 6:2–3** "'Honor your father and mother' (this is the first commandment with a promise), '*that it may go well with you and that you may live long in the land.*'" (emphasis added)

14. **1 John 5:18** "We know that everyone who has been born of God does not keep on sinning, but *he who was born of God protects him, and the evil one does not touch him.*" (emphasis added)

Promises for Our Provision

15. **Matthew 7:7–10** *"Ask, and it will be given to you; seek, and you will find; knock, and it will be opened to you.* For everyone who asks receives, and the one who seeks finds, and to the one who knocks it will be opened. Or which one of you, if his son asks him for bread, will give him a stone? Or if he asks for a fish, will give him a serpent?" (emphasis added)

16. **John 16:24** "Until now you have asked nothing in my name. *Ask, and you will receive, that your joy may be full."* (emphasis added)

17. **Matthew 6:33** "But seek first the kingdom of God and his righteousness, *and all these things will be added to you."* (emphasis added)

18. **Matthew 6:19–21** "Do not lay up for yourselves treasures on earth, where moth and rust destroy and where thieves break in and steal, but lay up for yourselves treasures in heaven, where neither moth nor rust destroys and where thieves do not break in and steal. *For where your treasure is, there your heart will be also."* (emphasis added)

19. **Malachi 3:10** "Bring the full tithe into the storehouse, that there may be food in my house. *And thereby put me to the test, says the LORD of hosts, if I will not open the windows of heaven for you and pour down for you a blessing until there is no more need"* (emphasis added). [This is the one and only time we are told in the Bible to test God.]

Promises for Our Salvation

20. **Romans 10:9–10** *". . . because, if you confess with your mouth that Jesus is Lord and believe in your heart that God raised him from the dead, you will be saved.* For with the heart one believes and is justified, and with the mouth one confesses and is saved." (emphasis added)

21. **John 14:6** "Jesus said to him, "*I am the way, and the truth, and the life. No one comes to the Father except through me.*" (emphasis added)

22. **Psalm 34:22** "The Lord redeems the life of his servants; *none of those who take refuge in him will be condemned.*" (emphasis added)

23. **Romans 10:13** "*...everyone who calls on the name of the Lord will be saved.*" (emphasis added)

24. **John 3:16** "For God so loved the world, that he gave his only Son, *that whoever believes in him should not perish but have eternal life.*" (emphasis added)

These twenty-four weapons have been given to us by God for our instruction, our protection, our provision, and our salvation. The enemy has no defense against the Word of God. In fact, the devil and his host of demons *know* these words are true and do everything in their power to convince you otherwise. Stand firm, and know that the Lord in which you serve has provided us these mighty words that have divine power to destroy strongholds, and to tear down arguments and every presumption that sets itself up against the knowledge of God.[252]

So, with this second weapon of God's Word in mind, let's move on to the third mighty weapon in this spiritual battle—the weapon of God's power and authority (deliverance).

18

The Weapon of God's Power and Authority (Deliverance)

Deliverance is defined in Webster's Dictionary as "Release from captivity, slavery, oppression or any restraint, or rescue from danger or any evil."[253]

Jesus tells us in Luke 4:18 that He came to do just that: *The Spirit of the Lord is upon me, because he has anointed me to proclaim good news to the poor. He has sent me to* **proclaim liberty to the captives** *and recovering of sight to the blind,* **to set at liberty** *those who are oppressed* (emphasis added).

So, in essence, we have all been delivered. Those who love the Lord and have responded to His call upon their life have been delivered from death to life. Be thankful for that. But deliverance can also mean deliverance from *mental strongholds* and *spiritual oppression* or *bondage*—two other areas that are important in the life of every believer that are oftentimes overlooked in the ministry of the mainstream church. I will use this chapter to discuss these two other areas of deliverance since they are greatly misunderstood, and again are oftentimes overlooked as part of our Christian ministry.

I will start out by clarifying that all deliverance comes by and through the authority of our Lord Jesus Christ. We are told in Zechariah 4:6 "... *Not by might, nor by power, but by my Spirit, says the LORD of hosts.*" All the power and authority exerted by believers in doing the will of God comes to us through the Holy Spirit, as originally given to believers on the day of Pentecost.

Second, I would argue that other than the power of prayer, the power of God's Holy Word, and the gift of our salvation (which is the Holy Spirit's calling upon our life and our acceptance of Jesus Christ as our personal Lord and Savior),[254] no other Christian ministry validates the power and authority of the gospel of Jesus Christ more than deliverance. Being delivered to freedom from the bonds of the demonic is tangible proof of the truth, power, and authority of the deity of Jesus Christ over the entire earth and all of the powers of darkness.

Some may argue that healing ministries would provide a better example of Jesus' dominion over this earth, but I would disagree. If we look back at Scripture, we see that on almost every occasion where Jesus delivers someone from a demonic spirit, their gratitude was expressed in obedience to what Jesus instructed them to do—an obedience that was rarely followed with Jesus' miraculous physical healings. Deliverance from a demonic spirit changes a person. Ask those who have been delivered and set free from a demonic spirit, and they will confirm to you it was the power and authority of Jesus alone that *set them free*. An experience from which all whom have been set free from this bondage are truly humbled and quite thankful.

Scripture tells us in Joel 2:32 (KJV) *And it shall come to pass, that whosoever shall call on the name of the LORD shall be **delivered** . . .* (emphasis added). It is the Lord, and only the Lord, that can bind Satan, cancel his "legal right" against us, break his chains of bondage over our life, and rescue us from the grasp of his evil host of demons.

Did Jesus not tell His apostles after His resurrection on the cross—"*And these signs will accompany those who believe: In my name **they will drive out demons**; they will speak in new tongues*"[255] (emphasis added)? As I have previously stated, I have yet to see an expiration date on Jesus' statement. And yet, deliverance is a topic that is rarely discussed today.

So, are we to believe that the demons Jesus dealt with here on earth—that are repeatedly referred to in the New Testament and that the Lord gave believers the inherited authority to cast out—simply cease to exist after the first century? Are these evil entities no longer interested in inhabiting the bodies of men and tormenting them with their compulsions? To think so would be foolhardy and would certainly not be in line with the Scriptures. It's simply a topic that the mainstream church rarely talks about today. But these evil entities remain one of the invisible yet dominant driving forces in our fallen culture. With this in mind, let's discuss this somewhat controversial area of Christian ministry: Deliverance.

First off, I hope by now you understand that we live in a spiritual battlefield. A battlefield so fierce that, as we stated earlier, the late Billy Graham once commented that "the wars among nations on earth are mere popgun affairs compared to the fierceness of battle in the spiritual unseen world."[256] A battle in which mankind is "both the pawns—and the prize."[257]

And as previously discussed in Chapter Fourteen, we are all engaged in this spiritual battle at different levels depending upon how much ground we have surrendered to the Enemy. As we have previously discussed, the two most common spiritual conditions we succumb to in this battle are spiritual *strongholds* and spiritual *bondages*. Although I will discuss both, I will focus the majority of this chapter on the topic of spiritual bondage, the more serious of the two.

Spiritual strongholds, by definition, are improper mindsets. We previously classified this condition in Chapter Fourteen as level one spiritual warfare. Although this condition is unfortunately quite common among believers, spiritual strongholds can normally be corrected through self–examination (to discover and rid oneself of incorrect beliefs that are not supported by Scripture), by repentance of this mindset, by re-focusing and accepting God's Word, and by taking all of our thoughts captive to obey Christ.

Spiritual bondage (also referred to as spiritual oppression), the more severe of the two, is quite a different and more serious matter. We also previously classified this condition in Chapter Fourteen as level two spiritual warfare. Spiritual bondage normally occurs when someone has given up a "legal right" to the Enemy (the devil or his host of demons) to enter into their life or the lives of their family members. This spiritual state normally requires deliverance and a severance of this "legal right" from these demonic entities to be set free.

Can a Christian Fall into Spiritual Bondage?

This brings us to the more controversial area of this topic of deliverance ministry. Can true Christians fall into spiritual bondage or become spiritually oppressed to a level that requires spiritual deliverance to set them free? Contrary to the belief of many within the Christian community (as we have stated previously in Chapter Fourteen), the answer to this question is "yes." Christians are not immune from the harassment of demons and can become demonized (dealing with a demonic spirit from inside their bodies and minds) and suffer spiritual bondage.[258] While being a Christian prevents you from the threat of possession (being owned by the Devil or demon with a loss of free will),[259] Christians *can* surrender enough legal ground to provide a "legal right" to the Enemy for a demon(s) to enter their life causing all types of mental anguish, internal pain, sexual perversions, and spiritual oppression.

I am well aware that this topic has been debated by Christians for years and that many in the Christian community are opposed to this position. The major objection to the belief that a Christian can become demonized is based on the biblical truth that the Holy Spirit lives within the believer, and that the Holy Spirit cannot exist or dwell in the same place as an evil spirit. I would certainly concur with this statement. But we all sin. And we continue to do so after we have received the Holy Spirit of God. So a similar and even more basic question could be presented: How can we possibly sin with our bodies and minds when the Holy Spirit of God is within us since the Holy Spirit cannot dwell with evil? So I believe there must be a logical answer to this question.

As we discussed previously in Chapter Thirteen, man, as designed by God, is made up of three parts: *body, soul,* and *spirit.*[260] Our **bodies** are our physical makeup (or what is commonly referred to as the flesh), our **soul** (sometimes referred to as our heart) is our mind, will, and emotions, and our **spirit** is our eternal spiritual being that lives forever.[261]

When Jesus Christ comes into a person's life, they receive the Holy Spirit of God. But where does the Holy Spirit of God actually reside within us? Some believe that it's only man's regenerated spirit that is an adequate place for the Holy Spirit to dwell. John 3:6 tells us, *Flesh gives birth to flesh, but the Spirit gives birth to spirit.* As pointed out by Watchman Nee, in his writing below, "The Holy Spirit and the Human Spirit," he supports the position that man's regenerative spirit is the adequate place for the Holy Spirit to reside.

"The Holy Spirit and the Human Spirit" (by Watchman Nee)

Since we have seen that the Holy Spirit indwells the believer at the time of their regeneration, we should see in more detail where the Holy Spirit dwells so that we can understand His work within us.

We must remember that the real meaning of regeneration is not an outward change or the soul of the body being stimulated, but it is the spirit receiving life. Regeneration is a new event that takes place within the human spirit. It is the enlivening of the deadened spirit. The reason the deadened spirit can be made alive is due to receiving a new life. But the most important point is that when we receive a new spirit, we also receive the Holy Spirit of God to dwell within us. The phrase "put within you" occurs twice in Ezekial 36:26–27 and indicates that the place where the Holy Spirit dwells in the human spirit.

We have seen that our whole being is just like the holy temple. "Do you not know that you are the temple of God, and that the Spirit of God dwells in you?" (1 Corinthians 3:16). What the apostle means is that because believers are the temple of God, the Holy Spirit dwelling in us is just like God dwelling in the holy temple of the old days.

Although the entire temple signifies the presence of God and is the dwelling place of God, the actual place of God's dwelling is the Holy of Holies. The Holy Place and outer court are only places for God to work and move according to His presence in the Holy of Holies. After man's regeneration, only man's regenerated spirit is an adequate dwelling place of the Holy Spirit—not his mind, emotion, will, and body.[262]

The apostle Paul makes the reference that the Holy Spirit dwells in the believer as God did in the old temple. The apostle Paul stated, *Do you not know that you are God's temple and that God's Spirit dwells in you?*[263]

As referenced by Watchman Nee above, the entire temple that existed in Jesus' day symbolized the place of God's presence and served as a general picture of God's habitation; it was, nevertheless, the Holy of Holies where God actually dwelt. The other two areas of the temple, the Holy Place and the outer court, were for divine activity—not the actual dwelling place of God.

Similarly, while all three parts of man evidence the design and glory of God, it would appear that only man's regenerated spirit, and not man's soul nor man's body, is fit to be God's dwelling place. Why? Because even after conversion, our bodies still battle with our fleshly desires, and our souls—or our heart, mind, and emotions—can fall into temptation and corruption.[264]

Let me briefly explain.

Our Body

We know from personal experience that we are always at war with our body (or flesh). Scripture tells us *For the flesh desires what is contrary to the Spirit, and the Spirit what is contrary to the flesh. They are in conflict with each other, so that you are not to do whatever you want.*[265] The apostle Paul also tells us, *For I know that nothing good lives in me, that is, in my flesh.*[266] If the Spirit is contrary to the body, why would the body be the dwelling place for the Holy Spirit? I don't believe it would.

Our Soul

Second, as we have previously covered in Chapter Thirteen, most scholars also agree that our soul consists primarily of the *mind, will,* and *emotions*. Let's briefly examine all three. As we discussed earlier, I believe Scripture makes it clear that Satan has access to, and can and does plant thoughts and suggestions into our *mind*. If our mind is the dwelling place of the Holy Spirit, then Satan would be able to access the Holy Place of God, similar to the Holy of Holies—an access which he certainly does not have.[267]

Our *will* is who we are—our personalities, our beliefs, our desires, and our decisions. As previously stated, our *will* is often referred to as our heart. But we are told in Scripture, *The heart is deceitful above all things and beyond cure. Who can understand it?*[268] If the heart is deceitful beyond cure, would this be the proper dwelling place for the Holy Spirit? I certainly don't believe so.

Lastly, let's look at our *emotions*. As we have discussed earlier, and again I believe Scripture makes clear,[269] our emotions can be and are used against us by the Great Deceiver. I believe Satan's ability to access our emotions would also rule out this being the Holy Spirit's dwelling place in man.

Our Spirit

Almost by the process of elimination, it would appear that only our spirit would be a fit place for the dwelling place of the Holy Spirit. This conclusion also appears to be consistent with the following Scripture:

- "The Lord be with your *spirit*..." (2 Timothy 4:22, emphasis added)
- "The *spirit* of man is the lamp of the LORD, searching all his innermost parts." (Proverbs 20:27, emphasis added)
- *"But whoever is united with the Lord is one with him in spirit."* (1 Corinthians 6:17 NIV, emphasis added)

- "For his Spirit joins with our *spirit* to affirm that we are God's children." (Romans 8:16 NLT, emphasis added)
- "And I will give you a new heart, and a new *spirit* I will put within you. And I will remove the heart of stone from your flesh and give you a heart of flesh. *And I will put my Spirit within you, and cause you to walk in my statutes and be careful to obey my rules.*" (Ezekial 36:26–27, emphasis added)

All verses above indicate a relationship between the spirit of man and the Holy Spirit. In The Holy Bible Recovery Version (discussing Genesis 2:7), it states: *Man's spirit is his inward organ for him to contact God, receive God, contain God, and assimilate God into his entire being as his life and everything.*[270] In fact, it's the act of the Holy Spirit of God coming into the spirit of man that regenerates us, brings us new life, and ensures us eternal life with God. Our spiritual regeneration takes place, and is fully complete, at the minute of our conversion. Our body and our souls on the other hand, although affected by and evidencing our regeneration, require a life-long process of sanctification to bring them closer into compliance with our new spirit. So again, neither body or soul would appear fit to be the proper dwelling place of the Holy Spirit.

Although opinions may differ, it appears that our spirit would be a proper dwelling place of the Holy Spirit. And where the Holy Spirit resides, no demon can dwell. Therefore, when we say that a Christian is demonized, we are not saying he has a demon in his spirit. We are saying that he has a demon in one of these other areas, within his body or soul (our mind, will, and emotions). And it's these two areas, body and soul, that are the targets of demonic attack and are among a demon's greatest accomplishments to inhabit.[271]

And even if a believer inadvertently gives Satan and his demonic host "legal access" to their bodies or souls (mind or emotion), the third part of their makeup—our spirit, where some believe that Holy Spirit resides—is inaccessible to the enemy, and remains securely in God's possession.

Similar to Watchman Nee's discussion above regarding the location of the Holy Spirit within the believer, I believe when Jesus confronted the money changers in the outer courts of Solomon's (Herod's) temple,[272] likewise reinforces the concept that, although these evildoers had full access to the temple outer courts, they were not allowed to approach or enter the Holy of Holies where the Spirit of God resided. As with man, I would argue that while Satan may gain access to, and maintain his presence in the outer temple (that is our body and mind, emotions, and will), he is not permitted to enter our regenerated spirit—with whom the Holy Spirit of God now dwells if we are a believer in Christ.

Hopefully this provides some clarification on why some believe a demon may be able to gain access to and operate from within the body or soul of a believer, while not inhabiting or co-existing with the Holy Spirit.

Deliverance is for the Believer

And one final point. Those who argue and believe that the ministry of deliverance is not for believers, in my opinion, should rethink their position. In reality, deliverance *is not* for the *unbeliever*. For a person to remain free from demonic strongholds or oppressions, they need to submit their life to Jesus Christ. If they refuse to ask Jesus Christ (and in effect the Holy Spirit) into their life, and have received deliverance, they will likely end up in worse shape than before the deliverance. This will occur because they have no protection from a similar, if not worse, re-occurrence of such evil spirits since they refuse to fill their life with the Word of God.[273]

As stated by John Eckhardt in "Why a Christian Can Have a Demon," the ministry of deliverance is a **covenant right of believers**. Like every other blessing from God—healing, prosperity, miracles, and so on—it is promised only to His covenant people, those who believe in Jesus and have come to God through Christ's blood. God, in His mercy, **will bless people outside the covenant because He is merciful**; but primarily, His blessings are based on covenant.[274]

The late Derek Prince clarified the essence of the deliverance ministry when he stated, *"Deliverance from evil spirits is the one miracle that has no counterpart in the Old Testament. It is, therefore, the one distinctive sign that the Kingdom of God has come."*[275] (emphasis added)

I will not attempt to discuss any further my position on this topic nor the many arguments made in defense of this position, but will suggest that you do your own homework on this topic. For those who are interested in this topic, and would like more information on the spiritual weapon of deliverance, or feel they may be a victim of this level of spiritual warfare, an excellent starting reference on this topic is *They Expel Demons* by Derek Prince,[276] and *Pigs in a Parlor: A Practical Guide to Deliverance*, by Frank and Ida Mae Hammond,[277] or for the more advanced, *The Handbook for Spiritual Warfare* by Dr. Ed Murphy.[278]

At the risk of being repetitive, I want to restate one thing: Denying the reality of Christians dealing with internal demons leaves many with nowhere to turn for assistance when such spiritual bondage occurs in their life. If their church says, "This can't happen," they are left searching for answers through medicine, counseling, and other treatments that are wholly ineffective for ridding oneself of a demonic spirit. Those who are suffering in this area fully understand this dilemma.

As we discussed in Section One of this book, there are several ways to give the devil "legal access" to inflict this level of spiritual warfare. We will not repeat those here, but I will simply restate that many demonic spirits have emotional traits associated with their character. At this level of spiritual warfare, these spirits can cause constant feelings of fear, agony, rejection, thoughts of suicide, grieving in the spirit, and internal pain, as well as unnatural compulsions. As we have previously indicated, if these symptoms do not subside over time, lasting for months, years, or even decades, this is a strong indication you may be dealing with demonic spirits.

Again, unlike level one spiritual warfare, in which we can overcome by accepting God's truths, along with changing our thoughts and mindsets, as I have stated, level two spiritual warfare is more like an infection—it's inside the body and requires deliverance from the demonic entity to set the person free. For those dealing with such bondage, your hope comes from the Lord.

The Four Basic Steps to Deliverance

This book is not intended to be a step-by-step guide, nor a reference manual on spiritual deliverance. There are many books and references on this topic. However, to provide some very general guidelines for spiritual deliverance and freedom from spiritual bondage, here are four basic steps universally accepted by the deliverance ministry.

Step 1: Surrender Your Life to Jesus

The first step to rid yourself of this level of spiritual warfare is to surrender your life to Jesus Christ completely. If you do not want to wholly and wholeheartedly rid yourself from these demonic entities, or if you secretly wish to maintain some level of sin in your life, then you will never sever the "legal right" these demons have obtained. Jesus would oftentimes ask those who were requesting deliverance or healing what they wanted. I believe He was soliciting from them their desire to be made whole. A desire that all must possess who wish to be completely delivered from evil.[279]

Step 2: Identify the Conduct that Provided the "Legal Right" to Satan

Second, it is critically important to identify the belief or conduct that opened the door, giving the "legal right" to this demon or evil spirit to come into your life in the first place. Without identifying the conduct that provided the "legal right" to the Enemy, any deliverance will most likely be short-lived because the Enemy's access point will remain open. Your Enemy will again have access to you because you have unknowingly left yourself exposed by not identifying and closing the conduct that gave the devil his "legal right" to your life. Not knowing how you opened the spiritual door to the Enemy will probably prevent you from ever completely freeing yourself from his bondage. It's like locking your doors to keep all the intruders out but leaving a window wide open. Despite your efforts, you still remain exposed to the Enemy and are subject to his return.

Only through your identifying the entry point(s) that created this "legal right" for the Enemy to access your life, followed by complete and full confession, repentance, and renunciation (an outwardly verbal declaration of disassociation)[280] of the action(s) that created this access, can you break yourself free with the deliverance only Christ provides.

Step 3: Deliverance from these Demons

Step three in the deliverance process is the step that tends to make those unfamiliar with this process quite uneasy. However, deliverance certainly does not need to be a traumatic event. It requires someone who is walking in the power and authority of Jesus Christ, *a Holy Spirit-filled Christian*, to verbally command these demonic entities to depart from your body and mind and not return.[281] Only true Christians, walking in both the power and the authority of the Lord, will have any effect over these demonic spirits. If one is without such authority to act on behalf of the Lord, their command of these spiritual entities to leave one's life is like a convicted prisoner standing before a judge and commanding he be set free. His command has no authority and has absolutely no effect.

Demons only respond to the Lord Jesus and one who walks in His power and authority. As we have discussed, Jesus demonstrated His power over demons while on this earth, as did His apostles and those He appointed to assert this power. As believers, Scripture tells us we have been given access to this power and authority.[282] But *only* if we are walking in a proper relationship and standing with the Lord do we have this authority.

I should note that although self-deliverance from this level of spiritual warfare is certainly possible, it oftentimes requires the help of someone who has experience in the area of deliverance. If you find yourself in this level of spiritual warfare and are dealing with demonic entities, seeking someone with training in the area of deliverance ministry is probably a good idea.

You can find Christian deliverance ministries in almost every state. With some research and a few phone calls, you should be able to find someone with specific training in this area. Also, as previously discussed, we are provided a particular story in the Bible where the apostles could not cast out a demon, and Jesus told them some demons require prayer to expel.[283] Accordingly, I believe it is also wise in every situation to always ask the Lord Jesus for deliverance in prayer.

Step 4: Fill Your Heart and Mind with the Word of God

And last, to remain free from such bondage, you must *fill the house*, so to speak, by filling your heart and mind with the Word of the Lord and living for Him daily in a holy manner.[284] Keeping your life *swept and in order* will leave no place for demonic spirits to dwell should they try to return because you are filled with God's holiness.

Some within deliverance ministry believe the formula for deliverance is normally a 40-20-40 process. Forty percent of one's deliverance time is spent determining how the Enemy initially gained "legal access" to one's life. This may require some painful digging into your past by someone trained in the area of deliverance. Twenty percent of this process is the actual deliverance of the demonic spirit(s). The remaining forty percent consists of "filling the house" (so to speak) with the Spirit of God and immersing oneself in the Holy Word of God on a daily basis.

Again, we are specifically warned by Scripture about those who are delivered, **whose hearts and minds are not filled with the Word of God.** Luke 11:24–26 gives us this warning: *When the unclean spirit has gone out of a person, it passes through waterless places seeking rest, and finding none it says, 'I will return to my house from which I came.' And when it comes, it finds the house swept and put in order. Then it goes and brings seven other spirits more evil than itself, and they enter and dwell there. And the last state of that person is worse than the first.*

A Final Thought on Deliverance

Deliverance was a vital part of the early Christian church. They were continually setting Christians free from their prior bondages and ties with Satan—an important and vital ministry that I believe is woefully lacking in the mainstream church today. Many assume that because we are Christians, we should have no fear of the Enemy. This is true if we are living a fully submitted life and walking in the power and authority of God. Scripture tells us that if we are, then the gates of hell will not prevail over us.[285] However, if we are just "playing Christian," we have a lot to be worried about.

People who suffer from strongholds and bondages such as oppression, depression, addictions, anguish, grief, pain, and compulsions (often associated with the mental and emotional torment of demonic spirits) are being set free today in Jesus' name—just as they were two thousand years ago. All the power and authority of Jesus is alive and as powerful today as it was back in the days of the original disciples—because Jesus Christ is the same yesterday and today and forever.[286]

To suffer such strongholds and bondages is not shameful. To remain in them *is* when we have been given the power by Jesus Christ to rid ourselves of such strongholds and bondages.

With the understanding of the mighty weapons we have been given for our warfare, which includes **prayer**, God's **promises**, and our **power and authority (deliverance)** over the Enemy—let's take a look at what the Bible outlines as the armor He gives us to wear as we fight this spiritual battle with the Enemy.

19

The Whole Armor of God

In addition to giving Christians everything we need to prevail over all the wiles of the Enemy and to free ourselves from his demonic strongholds and bondages, God has also given us His armor to wear while we are engaged in this cosmic battle with the spiritual forces of evil. The book of Ephesians lays out the game plan for wearing this armor in this continual battle with the Enemy.

> *Finally, be strong in the Lord and in the strength of his might. Put on the whole armor of God, that you may be able to stand against the schemes of the devil. For we do not wrestle against flesh and blood, but against the rulers, against the authorities, against the cosmic powers over this present darkness, against the spiritual forces of evil in the heavenly places. Therefore, take up the whole armor of God, that you may be able to withstand in the evil day, and having done all, to stand firm. Stand therefore, having fastened on the belt of truth, and having put on the breastplate of righteousness, and, as shoes for your feet, having put on the readiness given by the gospel of peace. In all circumstances take up the shield of faith, with which you can extinguish all the flaming darts of the evil one; and take the helmet of salvation, and the sword of the*

Spirit, which is the word of God, praying at all times in the Spirit, with all prayer and supplication . . .[287]

Without God's spiritual armor, we are naked and fully exposed to all the deceit and deception of the Enemy. I know how that feels; it's not a good thing—especially when you're unaware that you're unprotected. And of course, the devil doesn't want you to know that you are exposed until it's too late—when his hooks are set firmly into your mind, emotions or heart—or both.

With God's armor, the Bible says we will be able to resist on the evil day and hold our ground. So let's take a closer look at all of this armor and what it was meant to accomplish for us.

The Belt of Truth

Jesus said, *I am the way, and the truth, and the life. No one comes to the Father except through me.*[288] He also said, *If you abide in my word, you are truly my disciples, and you will know the truth, and the truth will set you free.*[289] Free from what? The power of sin over us.[290]

Without absolute truth, there is no truth.[291] And if the devil can keep us from understanding and accepting the Word of God as truth, he knows we will have no true reference point from which we can judge his clever lies. So he lies to us to keep us from believing the Word of God. But God's truth, His Holy Word, is our defense against this assault.

Let me give you a brief example. The devil may try to convince you that God's promise to forgive our sins just doesn't apply to you. The most common battle cries uttered by victims of this assault include, "It's just too late for me," or "There is no way God can forgive me for that." Little do people remember that both Moses and even the apostle Paul (who is responsible for writing thirteen New Testament books and was called by God to carry the gospel to the Gentiles)[292] took another person's life at one point.[293] What if these two heroes of the faith would have cried, "It's just too late for me?"

Or the devil may even go so far as to make you fearful that if you truly repent of your sins, you may die—either physically or spiritually. That may sound odd, but for those who have experienced this emotional scare tactic, it is no laughing matter.

Satan's lies are always grounded in deception to keep you in bondage and to keep you from experiencing the total freedom that is offered through the acceptance of Jesus Christ as your Lord. The apostle Paul understood and warned us of this type of deception when he instructed us that even if we are told something by an angel,[294] if it is contrary to the Word of God, then we should ignore it. Likewise, we are told to *test all who claim to speak by the Spirit*.[295]

So, know God's Word, and then stand firm on His truth.

The Breastplate of Righteousness

This breastplate is God's righteousness, not our own. Our own righteousness will never stand up to the assaults of the Evil One. It is only the inherited righteousness of God, through our acceptance of His Son, Jesus Christ, that enables us to stand firm and withstand the direct assaults of the devil. We know that the devil's accusations against us can never pierce the protective breastplate of righteousness that we receive as Christians through Christ's redemptive sacrifice on the cross.[296]

When the great accuser continually reminds us of our past failures, current weaknesses, and sinful state, we can rely on the righteousness of Christ as our defense—righteousness purchased by the blood of the Lamb that we now wear as our own.

The Gospel of Peace

The gospel of peace is the Word of God. Scripture tells us we are to let this peace control our hearts.[297] Have you ever noticed that when you are having a good day and you're calm, it is much more difficult to get angry or rattled? Our emotions are steadier, and we are much less likely to be influenced by outside assaults.

If we let the peace of Christ penetrate our hearts, we are like a boat with a deep keel. Although the turbulent winds of life will hit our sail, they will barely tip our boat and will have much less effect on us. However, without God's true peace, we will be at the mercy of our environment, with our lives and emotions completely controlled by each new gust of wind that comes along. And guess who is driving the winds.

The Shield of Faith

The Bible says that it is impossible to please God without faith.[298] Based on faith, we inherit our salvation,[299] receive our justification,[300] and live out our sanctification.[301] Faith is the assurance of things hoped for, the conviction of things not seen.[302] The shield of faith halts all the flaming arrows of the Evil One. None of the devil's assaults can penetrate this God-given shield. It is the only piece of armor that protects us *from all the flaming arrows* of the Enemy. How does one establish his or her faith? By reading God's Word and spending time in prayer with God. Scripture tells us that faith comes by hearing and hearing by the Word of God.[303]

The Helmet of Salvation

Christ came to take the sting out of death by giving us the opportunity for eternal life with our Creator. Scripture tells us, *For God so loved the world, that he gave his only Son, that whoever believes in him should not perish but have eternal life.*[304] Our Creator planned this from the beginning.

Our salvation assures us of life everlasting in paradise with Christ—and with our Christian loved ones—a stark alternative to death and eternal separation from God. As a result, our salvation is critical to our mental and emotional well-being. A stable mind is much less vulnerable to all the other schemes of the devil and his demons. As we have seen, if the devil can get you to question your salvation as a believer in Christ, then he has a much greater opportunity to gain control of your mind and make you unstable. By understanding the assurance of our salvation, we can stand with a stable-minded defense against the devil and his deception.

The Sword of the Spirit

With this weapon, we switch from defense to offense. A sword is for offense and for advancing our position. And that's exactly what we are told to do with the sword of the Spirit, or God's Word. As we have discussed in Chapter Seventeen, God didn't put us in this world to just hold our ground and survive. He put us here to win by advancing His kingdom. And He has given us this tool to do just that.

Truth is a two-edged sword—a sword that will cut in both directions.[305] Even a brief attempt at using God's Word will reveal this dynamic. Generally speaking, you can share any theory, belief, or opinion on religion with any given group of people and experience very little resistance. But try citing God's Word in the same discussion and see what happens. The dead arise because you just pierced the darkness in their spirit with God's truth. And if they have been harboring the devil's deception, you'll see an immediate resistance to truth. Why? Because all the false theories in this world advance the devil's kingdom. God's truth exposes this deception. And the devil will execute all the fury at his disposal within the deceived person to resist this truth. It's his last defense.

So there you have it, the armor of God. If you are a Christian, you have all of these tools ready at your disposal to live abundantly and to advance God's kingdom. And that's very, very good news indeed.

20

The Good News about
the Toolbox

If you get nothing else out of this book, I hope you walk away with the understanding that if you are a redeemed child of God and have placed your trust in Jesus Christ as your personal Lord and Savior, then God has given you everything you need to live an abundant and fulfilling life in this world, along with the privilege to spend eternity in heaven with Him.

But the devil desperately wants to keep these truths hidden from us. As we have discussed, he will hurl an onslaught of half-truths, deception, and outright lies our way to keep us from understanding these truths and from living the life God intended us to live.

I believe the following three short stories may provide some insight on how Jesus' death and resurrection on the cross completely changed the game plan for all of mankind.

The Swimmers (Our Problem)

The contest was on. Three athletes had taken on the challenge—an open-water swim to a distant island; a challenge all three swimmers expected to complete.

The first was a weekend athlete. Although not a great seasoned swimmer, he thought he might have what it took. Since this was an ocean swim, his crew covered his body with oil, designed to protect him from the bitter ocean water, and he eagerly began the attempt. After three hours and nearly two and a half miles into the swim, his crew pulled him aboard the boat, nearly lifeless. It was simply a challenge he was unprepared to meet.

The second swimmer approached the shoreline. He was well-conditioned and well-trained. He had competed in several swimming events in his lifetime, and prided himself on being in very good shape for his late twenties. Ever confident that he would succeed, his crew applied his swimming oil, and off he went. After some twenty-two miles and eleven hours into the swim, he succumbed to total exhaustion and fatigue. His crew likewise pulled his beaten and battered body into the boat.

Watching emotionless from a distance was the third swimmer. He was accustomed to seeing failure, but only from a distance. He, himself, had never failed. As a professional triathlete, he considered no challenge too big. His self-confident demeanor had served him well, bringing him awards, honor, and successes throughout his life. Failure to reach this goal was not only unthinkable; it was unimaginable. Confidently, he prepared himself with a special swimmer's oil, designed by his personal crew. He had planned well, prepared well, and knew exactly what he needed to do, down to the last detail to complete the swim.

After some twenty-four long hours and almost forty-nine miles into the competition, the swimmer's strokes began to lag. His crew could no longer see the stream of water from his kicks. His once perfect stroke now only looked ordinary. At fifty-seven miles, three out of every four strokes he took were barely recognizable. He struggled to stay above water as he continued to swim. At sixty-two miles and thirty-plus hours into the swim, he barely remained above the water, listing first to his right, then to his left, as if he were looking for the shore. Exhausted, broken, and nearly dead, his despondent crew pulled their once hailed hero into the boat—sixty-five miles out from the shore where he had started.

Ironically, the island they were attempting to reach was 2,000 miles away. So, the best of the best, the fittest and the most prepared, *only* missed the mark by some 1,900 miles. It made absolutely no difference if the swimmer was an overweight couch potato or a world-class triathlete—it was humanly impossible to make it even a fraction of the way to the island.

To make it to heaven—the place Jesus has prepared for us—we must be perfect. None of us are. No matter how good we are, we still fail miserably. Even under our best attempts, like the swimmers, we only display a fraction of a percent of the holiness required by God to be with Him in heaven. Even Billy Graham, in all his goodness, could only make it a fraction of the way to heaven on his own merit. So then how can *we* possibly make it?

The Judge (Our Solution)

He was simply known as The Judge. A man of impeccable integrity. No one knew for sure how long he had been on the bench. He was an older man, but not elderly—a combination of compassion, concern, and consideration. His judgments were always just, fair, and proper. His righteousness on the bench preceded him. It seemed he always issued the exact, proper ruling for each and every case.

He always had an audience in his courtroom, from the elderly to school children on field trips. People just wanted to see this righteous judge in action.

The Judge had never been accused of partiality. None of his rulings had ever been overturned. Because of this, virtually none of his decisions were ever challenged. Both lawyers and defendants were always in a bit of awe in his presence. They presented their case, answered the Judge's questions, and waited for the ruling—one that was always fair, impartial, and accurate. He was simply the most righteous judge anyone had known.

Then it happened. The Judge had a son who had been in trouble with the law. The case had been decided in another court. His son, his only son, was convicted of a serious crime. Due to a conflict with the other court, his son's case was transferred to The Judge's own courtroom for sentencing. All parties, both the plaintiff and the defendant, knew The Judge was his father, but no one asked the judge to recuse himself. All parties simply remained silent on the issue. Because The Judge was known for his great fairness and integrity, they let the case proceed in his court.

His son was led into the courtroom with a conviction for a serious crime hanging over his head—one that carried a potential for several years in prison. Rugged and thirty-something, he shuffled in with shackles on both his feet and wrists. Neither the Judge nor his son made eye contact. The Judge's son kept his head down and was led to the defendant's table, where he took a seat. The Judge called the court to order and read the caption of the case before him. The defendant stood. As he did, his son made eye contact for the first time with his father. The man behind the bench would now decide his fate. This situation was as personal as it gets.

The courtroom was standing room only. Old and young alike waited in anticipation. How would The Judge rule? He had always been righteous and fair in the past, but this was different. He had skin in the game here. Would he hold to his character, giving his son the deserved punishment, or would he hedge ever so slightly?

The Judge read the crime that his son had committed. He asked if his son wanted to say anything before sentencing, but the courtroom remained silent. With that, The Judge pronounced his son's sentence: "Ten years in the federal prison." Not a word was whispered. A few glanced back and forth in the gallery. The sentence was—well, just—exactly what one should receive for the crime committed. But he gave it to his own son. Everyone was surprised, but not shocked. The Judge had rendered a *just sentence*.

Breaking the silence, and in an unusual act of candor, The Judge rose to his feet. He looked intently at his son and slowly removed his robe. In a quiet, continuous motion, he folded the robe twice and placed it on his chair. The Judge stepped down from his bench, approached the bailiff, and said, "Place my son's shackles on me. I will be serving his ten-year sentence."

The courtroom was silent. No one dared speak. The bailiff's look of bewilderment captured the confusion in the room. What had just happened? Had the Judge just sacrificed his life for that of his son?

His son stood speechless, trying to comprehend what just happened. One minute he had been sentenced to ten years in prison, only to be freed from his sentence in the next. All in attendance had just witnessed an incredible display of self-sacrifice. One life surrendered to redeem another. The ultimate sacrifice.

This is exactly what the Lord Jesus Christ did for us.

God created man in His likeness,[306] for His pleasure,[307] for His praise,[308] and for His glory.[309] But God's fellowship with man required that man be in His presence. Adam and Eve enjoyed this sacred fellowship with God in the Garden of Eden. That was up until the point of their sin. Once sin entered their lives, God, being righteous, had to execute His just sentence for their sin, which was death—or separation from Himself.

However, this caused a problem. God had created man for His pleasure, praise, and glory, and to enjoy fellowship with Him. But through man's sin, man had separated himself from God, breaking this fellowship. For the punishment of sin is death,[310] and true death is separation from God.[311]

But God's great love for us never fails. Jesus, just like the righteous Judge, got up from His seat of glory in heaven, voluntarily came down to earth, and took the penalty of sin that was ours rightfully—separation from God.

Jesus suffered not only a physical death on the cross but a spiritual death as well. In taking our sin, Jesus—on the cross—for the first time in eternity, was separated from His Father. Remember His words from Matthew 27:46: *"My God, my God, why have you forsaken me?"* The Father abandoned His Son for *our* sins—yours and mine.

In doing so, Jesus separated Himself from God, so we never have to. All we need to do is accept His payment in full for our sins. If we accept this offer, we are reunited with the Lord, and our access to God is no longer denied.

How do we know this is true? When Jesus spoke His final words from the cross *"It is finished,"*[312] the veil of the temple that separated the Holy place from the Holy of Holies was torn in two from top to bottom.[313] This tearing of the veil signified that, through Jesus' sacrifice, mankind now once again had access to a personal fellowship with God the Father in heaven—a privilege only previously experienced by Adam and Eve before the fall and a select few of God's anointed.[314] How could anyone reject such a gift?

So, Jesus' sacrifice on the cross for our sins is how we make it to heaven—that island 2,000 miles away that no one could ever reach. Our acceptance of His (Jesus') substitutional sacrifice on the cross pardons us for our sins, cleanses us, and reunites us with our heavenly Father. We are no longer separated from God or His Spirit, and never need to be again.

Knowing this, you might be saying, "Okay, I've got it. I understand. I know that I need the Lord Jesus for the forgiveness of my sins, and I have accepted this atoning gift. I have been reunited with God and have received His Spirit, the Holy Spirit, and am thankful for that. But why do I feel so unfulfilled? I honestly don't feel all the love, joy, and peace in my life that God tells me I possess." Does that sound familiar? If you have ever felt like this, there may be a reason you're not experiencing all that God has given you for this life. Let's look at the third and final story.

The Light (Our Application)

Two friends were arguing one day about who was the wisest. After some debate, one friend said to the other, "I will tell you a riddle. If you can tell me what it means, you are the wisest. If you can't solve it, then I am the wisest." His buddy, always up for a challenge, agreed on one condition: that he be given a clue.

"Done," replied the friend. "Here's the riddle: What is light but not bright, visible but not seen, present but not found, and powerful but subdued?"

"That's impossible," his buddy said. "No one can guess this riddle."

"Alright," the friend said. "I will give you your clue."

He left the room and pulled out an old quartz lamp from his bedroom closet. The light stood on a tall, skinny pole, about five feet high, and had a swivel switch for its brightness—and boy, did the lamp get bright. The glass part on top of the lamp looked like a glass basketball.

Then he took a dark-colored bed sheet and ripped it into strips about six inches wide. He took out a marker and wrote something on each piece. After fifteen minutes of writing, he took the strips and wound them around the glass ball at the top of the lamp—so much so that it covered the round, glass part of the lamp with about three inches thick of dark cloth. He took the lamp and placed it into a pitch-dark room, then turned it on. Then he went to get his buddy in the other room.

"Ok, come with me and I'll give you your clue."

They headed into the pitch-dark room.

Both friends stepped inside the room and closed the door behind them. It was pitch black.

"Ok, where's the clue?"

"First, find the lamp," the friend replied.

Feeling his way around the room, his buddy came to what felt like a pole with a cloth top. He grabbed it and began to remove the cloth off the glass portion of the lamp. As he started to unwind the cloth, a bit of light escaped. Just enough light reached his eyes for him to be able to read a word written on the cloth: *fear. Hmm.* He continued. After removing another strip of cloth, he found the word *worry* then *regret*. As he continued unwrapping the lamp, he saw the words *guilt, anger, unforgiveness,* and *resentment.*

The more he unwrapped the cloth, the more the words dropped off the lamp until the fabric had been completely removed, and the glass on the lamp was uncovered. At that point, the pitch-dark room became brilliantly bright.

His buddy said, "Ok, what's the clue?"

The friend said, "Was the light on when you stepped into the pitch-dark room?"

His buddy pondered for a moment. "No. it wasn't…" After a few more seconds, he responded, "Oh, wait a minute! Yes, it was, but I couldn't see it."

"That's right, but why?"

"Because we had all of this dark cloth surrounding the light."

"You're exactly right, and that's your clue."

All that, his buddy thought about it. He knew what he had seen but could only wonder what it meant. After pondering several minutes, he said, "Okay—I give up. What's your riddle mean?"

The friend smiled. "The bright light represents the Holy Spirit. The dark cloth represents all the emotional baggage we accumulate throughout our lives. And what you did in uncovering the light is what we must do to release the Holy Spirit's power within us. Even though the bright light (the Holy Spirit) goes on at the moment of our salvation, and is always burning brilliantly in our spirit, to experience and feel His fruit is largely dependent on our not quenching the Holy Spirit.[315] In other words, only by eliminating the emotional baggage that Jesus told us to resist, and by submitting ourselves to the Spirit of God, can we free God's Spirit within our lives and begin to feel the presence of the Holy Spirit—love, joy, and peace—within us. Get it?" he said with a smile. "Light, but not bright; visible, but not seen; present, but not found; and powerful, but subdued."

His buddy grinned. "You are wiser than me. How did you learn such a thing?"

The friend just smiled. "It was a gift."

We know that, according to the Bible, the fruit of the Spirit is love, joy, peace, patience, kindness, goodness, faithfulness, gentleness, and self-control.[316] The Holy Spirit provides for us every spiritual blessing we need to live the life God intended us to live from the moment of conversion.[317] That's why Scripture tells us we are complete in Christ.[318] This is a topic we previously discussed in Chapter Thirteen.

I'll bet if you really examine the motive behind many of the things you do (lust of the flesh, lust of the eyes, pride of life), you'll find the objective is to bring more love, joy, peace, and happiness into your life. But the good news for you is this: As a Christian, you don't need to *bring* these spiritual blessings into your life—love, joy, peace, etc.—they are *already in* your life. You already have it! As stated above, you received this at the moment of your salvation, compliments of the Holy Spirit. You only need to surrender to the Lord and let these spiritual blessings manifest themselves.

As previously discussed in Chapter Thirteen, God, in His wisdom, created within us this spiritual gap that can only be fulfilled by the Holy Spirit. That is a truth the devil desperately doesn't want you to know. The devil wants you to believe that your spiritual cravings for love, joy, peace, and happiness can only be obtained through physical things like sex, drugs, money, power, praise, etc. But physical things can never fill the spiritual gap that God created inside of us. That's why physical stimulus may give a temporary high, but they do nothing for lasting contentment. Christ tells us, *But whoever drinks of the water that I will give him will never be thirsty again.*[319] The fulfillment of the Holy Spirit comes at no expense to us and is permanent.

And that's the good news about the toolbox: **As a child of the risen Lord, you are fully and completely equipped for this life and the next.** But this doesn't mean we can't be deceived into adopting emotional and spiritual strongholds and bondages that can keep us from living abundantly. As you read through "The Devil's 15 Emotional Tools of Attack" in the next section, ask yourself: "How many of these emotional and spiritual strongholds have I unknowingly succumbed to that may be blocking the Holy Spirit's presence of love, joy, and peace in my life?"

So, let's crack open The Devil's Toolbox and look at a few.

In The Devil's Toolbox

The Devil's 15 Emotional Tools of Attack
Life-limiting Mindsets

We all have certain mindsets that form our beliefs about ourselves, others, and the world in which we live. But what is the basis for these mindsets, and how did we develop them? I believe that most of our mindsets about ourselves and others are developed at a young age, and over time they become the foundation of our lives.

If these mindsets are based on truth, as taught in the Scripture, then we're fine. But if they are based on some other source, such as our own emotions, someone else's opinion of us, or rooted in some criticism or insult that was hurled our way at some point in our life, then these mindsets can be false, misleading, and life-limiting.

Interestingly, for some, criticism throughout one's life can be turned into the fuel that propels them to great heights to prove their doubters wrong. But for others, criticism can create false truths that become so deeply rooted in their belief system that they destroy self-worth, discolor their worldview, and hamper their personal relationships—even destroying their future marriages.

What is the driving force behind these false mindsets? It's part of the Enemy's master plan to kill, steal, and destroy,[320] and in many cases, it can include the involvement of demons and/or lying, evil spirits. The Bible says that the devil prowls around looking for someone to devour.[321] That includes not only the devil but also his host of demons, also known as lying spirits. A *lying spirit* is exemplified in the Bible as an evil entity whose job it is to bear "false witness."[322] When someone is emotionally damaged or abused, these demons—or lying spirits—do their best to harass and accuse this person with mental accusations to accept the devil's lies as truth. Likewise, when someone is subject to a false doctrine that is contrary to God's Word, these lying spirits immediately get busy trying to snatch away God's truth from them and substitute it with this new false doctrine.[323] What a detrimental exchange.

Of course, these lying spirits have no truth in them other than what we give them. But if we succumb to their lying accusations and allow them to take hold in our lives as truth, they can develop into lifelong strongholds. These false accusations can develop into mindsets that we come to believe about ourselves and others. And of course, these mindsets are set up by our Enemy to destroy our lives and rob us of God's intended blessing for us[324]—and they can do just that. In many cases, we actually build our life views around them. If this has occurred, as we have discussed, it's said that someone has developed a "spiritual stronghold" based on this deception and deceit of the Enemy.

Probably the most deceptive aspect of this unholy exchange is that we often unknowingly become the *sole guardians* of this defective view. What I mean by this, is that we sometimes end up guarding and defending this improper mindset as our "own view." We can, of course, surrender these false views, but often we don't want to. These false views become like our favorite pair of jeans, they just feel comfortable to us, and we never want to throw them out. These lies actually become the excuses we use to support our moderate happiness and fulfillment. This is not what God designed us for but what Satan hoped we would become. The good news is, of course, we don't have to remain this way. But we must be brutally honest with ourselves and be willing to do a thorough self-evaluation to determine how and where our mindsets developed.

As stated by Roy Sauzek in his booklet *The Death of a Pet – for Christians:*[325]

In certain cases when the pet who has been a life-long partner dies, there is a feeling that a part of the person dies too, because the pet really was a part of the person's life. A person goes through grief, mourning, spiritual death, and sometimes anger. They don't know how to act because something was taken from their life. They feel differently. **All these things are also true of the death of false doctrines or false ideas we don't want to part with**. Anytime one goes through a real death of **false thinking**, pet style, they go through these things (emphasis added).

I think this is a very good analogy of the process that is sometimes required to change one's thinking. For a while, this new way of thinking just doesn't seem normal. And it's not normal for the one who has been living under false doctrine.

So ask yourself, "Do I believe what God says about me, or do I have some critical belief about my appearance, my self-worth, or my character that I might have developed in my youth?"

If you have developed a defeated or poor self-image, try to think back to when you first received that tainted picture. Usually, there is an event that triggers these false views. Such a self-examination may take some time and may even be painful, but it can be well worth the effort to find the genesis of these life-limiting strongholds. Then ask yourself this question, "Do I defend these false beliefs or even make excuses for my life based on these lies?" Now do this with every part of your life, physically, mentally, spiritually, emotionally, socially, and financially.

After you have performed this truth check, which again, may be somewhat painful and uncomfortable, renounce (an outwardly verbal declaration) any and all beliefs that are not based on God's Word, and start to build new views based on what God says about you and others.

Demons Posing as Emotions

An even more sinister side to this spiritual warfare is that emotions themselves can become a hiding place for demons. The demonic spirit can, and sometimes will, mask itself as an emotion. By doing so, it can remain hidden, often for many years, or even decades, with its host simply believing their pain, anguish, or inappropriate and lustful desires are their own, when it may be, in fact, a demonic spirit. Quite a cover.

At this level of spiritual warfare, the demon has actually taken up residence in a person's body. As indicated earlier, contrary to the beliefs of many in the Christian community, this can happen to a Christian. Again, it is important to remember that this is in no way *possession*, but more an *infection* with a demonic spirit. These are two totally different things. The person will function normally, but this demon spirit will be prompting, urging, and compelling this person to work out its lustful cravings and desires through their body—or causing great emotional anguish, torment, grief, and pain in one's spirit. Although this might sound crazy to some, for those who have suffered through this torment, it is not. Even though it is rarely discussed in many Christian churches, this is a fairly common occurrence.

Few have been taught the fact that the Enemy can—and sometimes does—use emotions as a hiding place for demons. So be aware that prolonged periods of mental anguish, torment, grief, or internal urges that prompt us to harm ourselves or others, are all red flags that there may be a hidden spiritual component at work.

With that said, let's look at the fifteen emotional tools of attack the devil uses to infiltrate our lives, to accomplish his task to kill, steal, and destroy.

Tool #1: Fear
Tool #2: Worry
Tool #3: Regret / Abortion
Tool #4: Guilt

Tool #5: Anger / Rage

Tool #6: Doubt

Tool #7: Negativity

Tool #8: Anxiety / PTSD

Tool #9: Pride

Tool #10: Lust / Sexual Sins / Pornography

Tool #11: Insecurity / Lack of Self-Worth

Tool #12: Hopelessness / Despair / Depression / Suicide

Tool #13: Jealousy / Envy

Tool #14: Unforgiveness / Resentment

Tool #15: Rejection

TOOL #1
Fear

Bible Text

- "There is no *fear* in love, but perfect love casts out *fear*. For *fear* has to do with punishment, and whoever *fears* has not been perfected in love." (1 John 4:18, emphasis added)
- "For God gave us a spirit not of *fear* but of power and love and sound mind." (2 Timothy 1:7 KJV, emphasis added)
- "And do not *fear* those who kill the body but cannot kill the soul. Rather *fear* him who can destroy both soul and body in hell." (Matthew 10:28, emphasis added)
- "Have I not commanded you? Be strong and courageous. Do not be *afraid*; do not be discouraged, for the Lord your God will be with you wherever you go." (Joshua 1:9 NIV, emphasis added)
- "Peace I leave with you; my peace I give to you. Not as the world gives do I give to you. Let not your hearts be troubled, neither let them be *afraid*." (John 14:27, emphasis added)

Self-Test

Do you have a hard time loving others, do you feel as if you are distant from God, do you suffer from anxiety, anger, resentment, or feel insecure or unconfident in your daily life, if so, you may have succumbed to the spirit of fear and are being duped by the enemy!

Emotional Partners with . . .

Anger, Worry, Regret, Guilt, Indecision, Procrastination, Anxiety, Hate, Insecurity, Confusion, Perfectionism, Lack of Confidence

God's Opposite Emotion

Love, Power, Sound Mind

To start this discussion on how greatly influential fear can be, we should first understand there are two types of fear discussed in the Bible. One is a healthy type of fear that actually brings us into closer relationship with God; the other is a destructive type of fear that actually can separate us from God and can wreak havoc into our lives. Let's look first at just a few of the many Bible verses that discuss the healthy type of fear that can bring us closer to God.[326]

The most quoted of these verses is Proverbs 1:7, which states, *The fear of the LORD is the beginning of knowledge; fools despise wisdom and instruction.* This one is relatively easy to unpack. If the Lord is Lord of all, and if He has the ultimate say in our eternal destiny, then wouldn't it be logical, if we are to fear anyone, it should be the one who holds our eternal destiny in His hands? Clearly, only the foolhardy would spurn such a fear. This reasoning is stated in Matthew 10:28, which tells us *And do not fear those who kill the body but cannot kill the soul. Rather fear him who can destroy both soul and body in hell.*

We are likewise told in Proverbs 14:27, *The fear of the LORD is a fountain of life, that one may turn away from the snares of death.* Proverbs 19:23 says, *The fear of the LORD leads to life, and whoever has it rests satisfied; he will not be visited by harm.* In addition, Luke 1:50 explains, *And his mercy is for those who fear him from generation to generation.* Clearly, *fear of the Lord* is a healthy emotion and is the mental state we expect to experience as we marvel at the majesty and wonder of the Lord.

However, contrary to the healthy emotion of fear of the Lord, is fear *not* of the Lord, but of the Enemy. This opposite ungodly fear is designed to strip us of our God-given power, separate us from functioning in the love of God, and make us mentally unstable in all our ways. How do we know this? Scripture tells us, *For God hath not given us the spirit of fear; but of power, and of love, and of a sound mind.* (2 Timothy 1:7 KJV) So, fear refuses to let love, joy, and peace run free.

In fact, if I ask you to tell me what the opposite of love is, I bet you would respond that it's hate. Surprisingly, you would be wrong. The opposite of love is fear. Look again at the above referenced Scripture. There are two sides to this verse about fear. Laid out in an equation form, it would look something like this:

If we have **no** Fear = we have Power, Love, and a Sound Mind

Or

If we **have** Fear = we lack Power, Love, and a Sound Mind

To further clarify the distinction between these two opposites—love and fear—1 John 4:18 also tells us, *There is no fear in love, but perfect love casts out fear. For fear has to do with punishment, and whoever fears has not been perfected in love.* So perfect love and fear are opposites; one cannot fully exist when the other is present. They are wholly incompatible and exact opposites. Furthermore, our sound mental state, our ability to properly love, and our power and authority to act as agents of the Most High may suffer when fear is present.

In fact, some even argue that man in his basic form only has two controlling emotional states: love and fear. And that all of our other positive emotions such as joy, peace, happiness, and contentment flow through love. While all of our negative emotions such as anger, worry, regret, anxiety, and guilt find their root in fear. I will not argue this position, but only pose it as a thought to consider. Irrespective of whether this is correct or not, we can be sure of one thing: negative fear is from the Enemy and is designed to keep us from functioning in the fullness that the Lord God has designed.

So, fear is one of the devil's most destructive tools.

It allows the devil to have his way with us. It paralyzes us. It makes us afraid to move. And once trapped in this cycle, the devil will chisel away at our self-confidence and self-worth.

Fear can take on many forms. Fear of failure, fear of people, fear of illness, fear of the unknown, fear of harm, fear of rejection, fear of making a wrong decision, and phobias of all types—the list goes on.

Brief moments of fear are natural. But problems arise when we live in a constant state of fear. Fear, like its cousin worry, works like fertilizer, enhancing the effectiveness in all of the devil's other areas of attack. Fear also allows the devil and his legion to plant seeds of doubt in our minds to make us less effective for the Kingdom of God.

Jesus told His disciples not to be fearful, anxious, or troubled because He was with them. Fear and anxiety are opposite to faith and trust in God. Fear, like worry and anxiety, deal with the future. The Bible says God knows what we want and need and will supply it for us.[327] Being fearful, or in a constant state of worry can be indicators that we are not trusting God. Fear and worry assume we're in control, and that God isn't.

The apostle Paul tells us *we walk by faith, not by sight.*[328] If we could put faith into a formula, it would look something like this:

If faith > fear—then we **have** faith

If faith < fear—then we **lack** faith

You must have faith in God's Word before it can free you from fear, and by faith, we can have the mind of Christ.[329]

The Interesting Relationship between Fear and Legalism

There appears to be a very interesting relationship between two separate spiritual principles found in Scripture. Each principle on its own gives us guidance on how we are to live as a believer in Christ. But when examined together, these two spiritual principles give us an interesting formula which helps us understand if we are living a life of freedom or a life of bondage.

The two separate spiritual principles are found in the following two scripture verses. The first, which we have talked about, is living in love and power and not living with fear.

Fear

"For God has not given us a spirit of **fear**, but of **power** and of **love** and of a **sound mind**." (2 Timothy 1:7 NKJV, emphasis added)

Works / Legalism

And the second verse explains that we are justified (saved and made right with God) by **faith**, not **works** (another name for "works" is legalism).

"For it is by grace you have been saved, through faith—and this is not from yourselves, it is the gift of God—**not by works, so that no one can boast**." (Ephesians 2:8–9, emphasis added)

So, you might ask, "Just how are these two verses related?" I believe these two spiritual principles are by-products of one another. You see, legalism (the doctrine that salvation is gained through good works)[330] creates fear. If we are forever trying to earn our salvation, then we are always in fear that we haven't obtained it. Whereas, when we are living with the understanding that we are saved through our faith in Jesus Christ, and nothing else is required, fear is removed, allowing God's Spirit of *love*, *power*, and *sound mind* to flow through us. These principles are as follows:

Salvation through Faith (Grace)

Faith in Jesus Christ	→	**Power, Love, Sound Mind**	→	We experience **Freedom**

- "For in Christ Jesus neither circumcision nor uncircumcision counts for anything, but only *faith working through love*." (Galatians 5:6, emphasis added)
- "Now the Lord is the Spirit, and where the Spirit of the Lord is, there is *freedom*." (2 Corinthians 3:17, emphasis added)
- "*But if you are led by the Spirit, you are not under the law*." (Galatians 5:18, emphasis added)

As opposed to . . .

Salvation through Works (Legalism)

Salvation by **Works** (or Legalism)	→	Creates spirit of **Fear**	→	We experience **Bondage** (are under a curse)

- "For all who rely on *works* of the law *are under a curse*; for it is written, 'Cursed be everyone who does not abide by all things written in the Book of the Law, and do them.' But the Law is not of faith, rather 'The one who does them shall live by them.' Christ redeemed us from the curse of the law by becoming a curse for us—for it is written, 'Cursed is everyone who is hanged on a tree.'" (Galatians 3:10, emphasis added)

- "For you did not receive the spirit of slavery **to fall back into fear**, but you have received the Spirit of adoption as sons, by whom we cry, 'Abba! Father!'"(Romans 8:15, emphasis added)
- "Now before faith came, we were held captive under the law, **imprisoned** until the coming faith would be revealed." (Galatians 3:23, emphasis added)

To sum this principle up, the spirit of *legalism* and the spirit of *fear* are brothers. These two spirits create a lifetime of bondage and unhappiness. Opposite of this, the spirit of *faith* and the spirit of *power, love,* and *sound mind* also appear to be brothers. These spirits generate a feeling of freedom, love, joy, and peace.

So, even if you are not a fear-filled person, but you're living a life of legalism—always trying to earn your way into heaven by good works—you are probably living a life of fear and may have cut yourself off from the freedom and abundance that Jesus offers us through His Spirit.

If you are dealing with fear, I suggest you re-read the promises in Chapter Seventeen and spend time in prayer, claiming these promises given to us by the Lord over your life.

TOOL #2
Worry

Bible Text

- "Therefore I tell you, do not **worry** about your life, what you will eat
or drink; or about your body, what you will wear. Is not life more
than food, and the body more than clothes? Look at the birds of
the air; they do not sow or reap or store away in barns, and yet your
heavenly Father feeds them. Are you not much more valuable than
they? Can any one of you by **worrying** add a single hour to your
life? And why do you **worry** about clothes? See how the flowers
of the field grow. They do not labor or spin. Yet I tell you that not
even Solomon in all his splendor was dressed like one of these. If
that is how God clothes the grass of the field, which is here today
and tomorrow is thrown into the fire, will he not much more clothe
you—you of little faith? So do not **worry**, saying, 'What shall we
eat?' or 'What shall we drink?' or 'What shall we wear?' For the
pagans run after all these things, and your heavenly Father knows
that you need them. But seek first his kingdom and his righteousness, and all these things will be given to you as well. Therefore do
not **worry** about tomorrow, for tomorrow will worry about itself.

Each day has enough trouble of its own." (Matthew 6:25–34 NIV, emphasis added)

- "Do not be *anxious* about anything, but in everything by prayer and supplication with thanksgiving let your requests be made known to God." (Philippians 4:6, emphasis added)
- "*Anxiety* in a man's heart weighs him down, but a good word makes him glad." (Proverbs 12:25, emphasis added)

Self-Test

Is worry your default mindset? And is new worry the only thing that takes you away from previous worry? If so, you are being duped!

Emotional Partners with . . .

Fear, Guilt, Regret, Anxiety

God's Opposite Emotion

Faith, Trust, Hope

Worry is a sin. Worrying says we don't trust God. God knows what we want and need before we ask it.[331] Like fear, worry lives in the future. Worry is concentrating on what we don't want to happen later today, tomorrow, or next year. Not only does worry destroy our peace of mind, but it also can make us unusable for God. Let me share a short story.

Two football teams took the field. The red team kicked off to the blue team. The blue team went into their huddle to call the first play, but the quarterback called a play nobody knew. Confused, they went to the line, snapped the ball, and the blue team lost ten yards. They huddled again, and the quarterback called another play nobody knew. When the ball was snapped, the blue team lost ten more yards. The same thing happened on third down. The coach, who was furious at this point, sent in the kicking team, and they punted. To everyone's surprise, the blue team's quarterback took off his blue jersey, exposing a red jersey, and walked into the huddle for the red team. Calling the next play, the red team rushed to the line, ran, and gained twenty yards.

If the wrong quarterback is calling your plays, you don't have a chance to win. If the devil and his legion are prompting you to worry, he is calling your plays, and you don't stand a chance.

Worrying keeps you from living in the moment and enjoying the peace and love our Lord provides. Handle things when they come up. It will make your life so much easier and fulfilling.

TOOL #3
Regret / Abortion

Bible Text

- "For godly grief produces a repentance that leads to salvation without *regret*, whereas worldly grief produces death. (2 Corinthians 7:10, emphasis added)
- "Brothers, I do not consider that I have made it on my own. But one thing I do: *forgetting what lies behind* and straining forward to what lies ahead, I press on toward the goal for prize of the upward call of God in Christ Jesus." (Philippians 3:13–14, emphasis added)
- "And we know that for those who love God all things work together for good, for those who are called according to his purpose." (Romans 8:28)

Self-Test

Do you constantly relive past failures, disappointments and unrealized hopes and dreams in your mind? Are the majority of your daily thoughts looking backward in time, and not forward to the future? If so, you are being duped!

Emotional Partners with . . .

Fear, Worry, Guilt, Anxiety

God's Opposite Emotion

Faith, Hope, Love, Forgiveness

Let's look at the book of Matthew and parallel two worst-case scenarios regarding regret that we can imagine.

In scenario number one, Judas, one of Christ's original twelve disciples, betrayed Jesus and turned Him over to Roman authorities, where He was tried and put to death. The morning after he betrayed Christ, and the same day the chief priests in Jerusalem put Christ to death, Judas was overcome with regret for what he had done. Matthew 27:3–4 tells us his story:

> *Then when Judas, his betrayer, saw that Jesus was condemned, he changed his mind and brought back the thirty pieces of silver to the chief priests and the elders, saying, 'I have sinned by betraying innocent blood.' They said, '"What is that to us? See to it yourself.' And throwing down the pieces of silver in to the temple, he departed, and he went and hanged himself.*[332]

In the next example, scenario number two, the apostle Peter betrayed Jesus on the very same evening as Judas. Matthew 26:69–75 says:

> *Now Peter was sitting outside in the courtyard. And a servant girl came up to him and said, 'You also were with Jesus the Galilean.' But*

he denied it before them all, saying, 'I do not know what you mean.'
And when he went out to the entrance, another servant girl saw him,
and she said to the bystanders, 'This man was with Jesus of Nazareth.'
And again he denied it with an oath: 'I do not know the man.' After
a little while the bystanders came up and said to Peter, 'Certainly you
too are one of them, for your accent betrays you.' Then he began to
invoke a curse on himself and to swear, 'I do not know the man.' And
immediately the rooster crowed. And Peter remembered the saying of
Jesus, 'Before the rooster crows, you will deny me three times.' And he
went out and wept bitterly. (emphasis added)

For most people, denying that you even know a person is probably the deepest form of rejection you can demonstrate. Imagine this happening in your younger days. One of your parents comes to pick you up from school. You're surrounded by friends. They show up after a long day at work, not looking their best, and driving your family's rundown car. Not knowing it's your parent, your friends begin to joke about the car and the person inside. Because you feel embarrassed, you tell them you don't even know who that is.

How bad would you feel about denying your parent? That's what Peter did to our living God, denying he even knew Jesus; and not just once, but three times.

Judas killed himself after betraying Christ. Peter, on the other hand, went out and wept bitterly. Peter repented for his sins, and through the prayers of the Lord, went on to live a powerful life for Christ. In fact, Peter became a prominent spokesperson for the Christian community,[333] and was the one Jesus gave the keys to the "kingdom of heaven" in Matthew 16:19. He also became a miracle worker, like Jesus,[334] was divinely protected from harm by angels[335] and was the one who started the Christian community among the Gentiles.[336] All this from a man who denied he even knew Christ.

Regrets come in many forms: a perceived missed opportunity, a personal failure a relationship blunder, a regretful act, a mistake we've made, a past decision, or any of a thousand courses of conduct that cause regret. No matter the regret, we have the same two options:

1. Let it ruin our lives (notice that Judas never sought Jesus' forgiveness), or
2. Accept God's forgiveness for our sin or failure and move on, living the life God intended us to live.

Remember the powerful words from Philippians 3:13–14 that give us our lifelong GPS heading: *But one thing I do: forgetting what lies behind and straining forward to what lies ahead, I press on toward the goal for the prize of the upward call of God in Christ Jesus.*

You can bet the devil is hoping you choose the first option. A defeated and grief-stricken Christian does little for God's kingdom while he/she remains in such a state. The devil will do everything in his power to sell you on why you can't, or shouldn't be forgiven. Or, more importantly, why you shouldn't forgive yourself. And let's face it, it doesn't matter that you have been promised forgiveness, if you believe you don't deserve to be forgiven, you'll never take steps to forgive yourself and move on.

Suffering from the Regret of Abortion

Many who have experienced the trauma of an abortion carry around a feeling of regret, self-hatred, self-condemnation, guilt, shame, unworthiness, discouragement, despair, hopelessness, and often thoughts of suicide. In fact, according to a study done by the University of Minnesota Extension Service, "a teenage girl is six times more likely to attempt suicide if she has had an abortion in the last six months than is a comparable teenage girl who has not had an abortion."[337]

And an even broader study conducted by the University of Minnesota revealed that 28% of all women who have had an abortion attempted suicide at some point in their life.[338] Clearly, there is a lingering spirit of regret, guilt, shame, and despair that persists long after the abortion occurs. In addition, some suggest that this act of abortion provides a "legal right" or spiritual opening for evil to enter into one's life. One can only imagine that if this has occurred, the continual grief and torment caused by abortion, coupled with the "lying spirits" that keep telling the person they can never be forgiven (nor deserve to be forgiven) for such an offense, so engulfs the mind and emotions of the victim that sometimes it leads to complete despair and even suicide.

Please remember: The devil is a liar. *You can be forgiven* and released from this sin and the guilt that accompanies an abortion, as well as any tormenting spirits that may have entered your life through this act. We (on our own) do not deserve to be forgiven for this—*or any other sin*—which we have committed in our lives.

The Bible tells us that *For whoever keeps the whole law but fails in one point has become guilty of all of it.*[339] So we all have failed miserably. But through our personal relationship with Jesus and acceptance of His atonement on the Cross for our sins, we **can be forgiven** and washed clean **for all of our sins** upon our personal confession and repentance.[340]

In addition, once this sin has been confessed and repented of by a believer, any "legal right" that may have been given to the Enemy, which may have allowed demons to harass, torment, or enter into one's life, is extinguished. And as we previously discussed in Chapter Fourteen and Chapter Eighteen, if any (spiritual bondage) has occurred as a result of this act, deliverance can set you free from this tormenting spirit and its spiritual yoke.

So what's in your backpack? Are you struggling through life? Is your load of past mistakes and their guilt too heavy for you to bear? If so, you have been duped. Jesus will empty your emotional backpack, free you from this burden, and give you His yoke of forgiveness and peace.

TOOL #4
Guilt

Bible Text

- "If we confess our sins, he is faithful and just to forgive us our sins and to *cleanse us from all unrighteousness*." (1 John 1:9, emphasis added)
- "For I will be merciful toward their iniquities, and I *will remember their sins no more*." (Hebrews 8:12, emphasis added)
- "As far as the east is from the west, so far does he *remove our transgressions* from us." (Psalm 103:12, emphasis added)
- "Therefore, *there is now no condemnation* for those who are in union with the Messiah Jesus." (Romans 8:1 NIV, emphasis added)
- "My little children, I am writing these things to you so that you may not sin. But if anyone does sin, we have an advocate with the Father, Jesus Christ the righteous. *He is the propitiation for our sins*, and not for ours only but also for the sins of the whole world." (1 John 2:1–2)
- "And I heard a loud voice in heaven saying, 'Now the salvation and the power and the kingdom of our God and the authority of his Christ have come, **for the accuser of our brothers** has been thrown down, who accuses them day and night before our God.'" (Revelation 12:10 emphasis added)

Self-Test

Do you believe you can't be forgiven or that you don't deserve to be forgiven? Or do you find yourself constantly scanning your past to see if there is something you should feel guilty about?

If so, you are being duped!

Emotional Partners with . . .

Fear, Worry, Regret, Anxiety, Unworthiness

God's Opposite Emotion

Forgiveness, Faith, Love, Peace

Guilt, like its brother *regret,* looks backward at past conduct. It keeps us stuck in the past—chained to something or some feeling we don't enjoy, and it prevents us from enjoying the present moment or the future.

Similar to the emotion of fear, there are two types of guilt:

1. True guilt, which is what we feel from the Holy Spirit when we transgress God's Word.
2. False guilt, which feels very similar to true guilt but originates from the devil.

True guilt helps move us to repentance and a right relationship with the Lord. While false guilt is Satan's accusation used to make us feel unworthy, seek forgiveness for the same thing again and again, or compel us to confess something that is not even a sin. This false guilt can be destructive and controlling. It actually uses our desire to be holy and right with God against us, leading to over-confession and the bondage that creates. So how can you determine when you are feeling true guilt or false guilt? And more importantly, what can you do to rid yourself of these feelings?

True Guilt

True guilt is what we experience when we violate God's laws and precepts—when we have entertained some sinful thought or performed some sinful deed against God or another person. Romans 3:23 tells us, that *all have sinned and fall short of the glory of God.* Although I don't think we ever quite understand the full consequences of our sins, God understands, and through the work of Holy Spirit He makes us aware that our conduct is not in line with the will of our Father. The Holy Spirit is designed to be the guiding force in our lives. The Bible tells us that we are to be led by the Spirit,[341] and that the Spirit will lead us into all truth.[342] This guiding force can be described as a soft hand on our shoulder, leading us back into correct relationship with our Creator.

God does not want us to remain in a state of guilt. Instead, He tells us to repent and move on. Contrary to popular belief, this does not necessarily require agonizing grief on our part, but it may certainly come with a feeling of remorse or great sorrow. Repentance is simply a decision to discontinue sinful conduct.

As a Christian, the moment we turn our heart away from some act and ask for forgiveness in the name of Jesus Christ, God promises us that our transgressions will be forgiven. Jesus Christ is the only one with the power to bring you back into perfect union with your Creator.[343] And Jesus demonstrated His power to forgive sins during His ministry on earth.[344]

The devil doesn't want you to know this or believe this. He does everything in his power to try to persuade you to doubt Jesus' promise of forgiveness. But again, the devil is the father of lies.

False Guilt

False guilt may manifest itself in one of several ways:

- As lingering guilt felt after true repentance.
- As a feeling of unworthiness.
- As a continual state of conviction that you don't have the right to be forgiven.
- As a belief that constant confession is required to keep yourself pure from any passing impure thought.
- As a conviction that you need to repent about conduct God doesn't specify as sin.
- As a constant need to re-examine the past and repent again and again over improper conduct.

Repenting of conduct that isn't sinful helps the devil paralyze you and steals your joy. If you are questioning whether your guilt is true or false guilt, ask God to reveal this to you. Ask Him to make His thoughts known to you and ask for discernment.[345]

Unlike the Holy Spirit's soft touch that leads us back to righteousness, there's nothing soft about the devil's condemnation. His accusations push you toward destruction and separation from God instead of unification with Him. His accusations tell you there is no way out, no hope for forgiveness, that you are done. He tries to take away your only hope, peace, and joy. But Jesus has paid your bill. There is no reason you can't leave your sins behind. Walk forward and be free.

The Story of the Backpackers

Two hikers went on a trip to the mountains. They had enough food and drink in their backpacks for the day. Along the way, the younger of the two kept tripping on rocks along the trail. Each time he did so, he would pick up the rock and put it into his pack so he wouldn't trip on it again when they returned. Toward the middle of the afternoon, the older hiker was quite fresh, while the younger was exhausted. After some time, the younger hiker told his friend he couldn't go on. The older backpacker noticed the large size of the other hiker's backpack and his condition, so he asked him why his backpack was so large.

"I've been carrying all the rocks that we stumbled on throughout the day," the other backpacker answered.

"Why?" asked the older backpacker.

"So I won't stumble on them on our return trip back down the trail."

After chuckling a bit, the older backpacker told him they would not be following the same trail back, the younger hiker realized that the load he carried had been a great waste of time and energy, and by carrying this extra weight, he had significantly shortened the distance they were able to travel. A bit embarrassed by his youthful ignorance, but relieved of the unnecessary burden, the two removed this useless load from the younger hiker's pack and enjoyed the rest of the day.

It may be a silly example, but the absurdity of carrying past stumbles or mistakes (sins) throughout our life is equally absurd.

So, how does this example apply to our guilt?

If you have professed your faith in Jesus Christ as your personal Lord and Savior, believing in your heart that God raised Him from the dead, then you have been forgiven of your sins.[346] Your backpack should be empty. However, if you have *not* accepted Jesus Christ as your personal Lord and Savior, and have *not* accepted His atonement on the cross for your sins, then you have *not* been forgiven of your sins. What this means is that every sin that you have ever committed in your life, going back to your youth, you carry around with you in your spiritual backpack—just like the young hiker's backpack of rocks. (Not to mention the natural-born sin we possess). The psalmist understood the weight of carrying our own transgressions when he wrote, *If you, LORD, kept a record of sins, Lord, who could stand?* (Psalms 130:3, NIV).

Jesus tells us, *"Come to me, all who labor and are heavy laden, and I will give you rest. Take my yoke upon you, and learn from me, for I am gentle and lowly in heart, and you will find rest for your souls. For my yoke is easy, and my burden is light."* (Matthew 11:28–30.). Jesus took **our** punishment for **our** sin when He took **our** place on the cross. He died so we can be forgiven. So, what's in your backpack?

TOOL #5
Anger / Rage

Bible Text

- "Be ***angry*** and do not sin; do not let the sun go down on your ***anger***, and give no opportunity to the devil." (Ephesians 4:26–27, emphasis added)
- "A man ***without self-control*** is like a city broken into and left without walls." (Proverbs 25:28, emphasis added)
- "Whoever is slow to ***anger*** has great understanding, but he who has a hasty ***temper*** exalts folly." (Proverbs 14:29, emphasis added)
- "Good sense makes one slow to ***anger***, and it is his glory to overlook an offense." (Proverbs 19:11, emphasis added)
- "Know this, my beloved brothers: let every person be quick to hear, slow to speak, slow to ***anger***." (James 1:19, emphasis added)

Self-Test

Do you get raging mad in an instant? Do you vent your anger in such a manner that you're left apologizing to everyone after it subsides? Does your anger burn for days, weeks, or years on end? When you get angry, do you start to run a highlight reel in your mind, recalling everyone who has ever wronged you in the past? If so, you are being duped!

Emotional Partners with . . .

Guilt, Negativity, Worry, Fear, Anxiety, Unworthiness

God's Opposite Emotion

Peace, Love, Self-Control

Have you ever noticed that when you are in a great mood, you are much more tolerant of people and situations that offend you in some way? And that you become much less forgiving and tolerant of those that offend when your mood is not so good? We all have this characteristic in common.

It's our internal peace that makes all the difference. Anger is always the outward manifestation of internal discontent, with its root cause oftentimes in fear. When we are well-centered in the Word of God, we develop peace. Peace stabilizes our emotions like the keel stabilizes a boat. The greater our peace, the deeper our keel. The deeper our keel, the less emotional winds will whip our boat.

Let's examine the three biblical components of anger—the *speed* with which we get angry, the *intensity* of our anger, and the *duration* of our anger—and then see what the Scripture says about each.

The Speed of Our Anger

God gives us many guidelines for dealing with anger. Here are just a few:

- Proverbs 12:18: *Fools **show their annoyance at once**, but the prudent overlook an insult.* (emphasis added)
- Proverbs 14:17: *A man of **quick temper** acts foolishly, and a man of evil devices is hated.* (emphasis added)
- Proverbs 16:32: *Whoever is **slow to anger** is better than the mighty, and he who rules his spirit than he who takes a city.* (emphasis added)

Our anger should be slow in coming, short in duration, and mild in intensity. Anger is a big deal to God. His Word even goes so far as to say, *Make no friendship with a man given to anger, nor go with a wrathful man, lest you learn his ways and entangle yourself in a snare.*[347]

If we don't follow God's formula on anger, we may give the devil a foothold into our mind and emotions.[348] Proverbs 14:29 goes on to say that, *Whoever is slow to anger has great understanding, but he who has a hasty temper exalts folly.* In other words, the smart man angers slowly and shows his training and intelligence by doing so in all situations.

The Intensity of Our Anger

- Proverbs 19:19 says, *A man **of great wrath** will pay the penalty, for if you deliver him, you will only have to do it again* (emphasis added).
- Proverbs 29:11 says, *Fools give **full bent** to their rage, but the wise bring calm in the end* (NIV, emphasis added).

The person who allows his or her anger to go unchecked will suffer many consequences. Remember we are told, *A man without self-control is like a city broken in two and left without walls.*[349] In other words, his conduct will cause him to be defenseless and subject to self-destruction and sin. Why? Because the closer the devil can get you to a state of rage, the further you are from your God-given emotions of love, joy, and peace.

The devil also knows that when he gets you into a state of rage, you are more susceptible to listening to his voice, telling you that your anger is justified and that others deserve your wrath. The more justified you feel in your rage, the more you will use it, and the more sin or damage you will inflict on others and yourself.

The Duration of Our Anger

Righteous anger, when we have a true right to be angry, is to be slow in coming[350] and brief in duration. However, Ephesians 4:26–27 exposes the consequences of prolonged anger when it tells us,

> *Be angry and do not sin;* ***do not let the sun go down on your anger,*** *and give no opportunity to the devil* (emphasis added).

Prolonged anger gives the devil an entrance into our minds and, therefore, our emotions, and when dwelt upon can turn into resentment, and over-time into hatred. It also has the potential to develop into a stronghold and even spiritual bondage if we allow it. Don't fall into this trap of the Enemy. Part of the Lord's Prayer is that we ask God to forgive our trespasses as we forgive those who trespass against us.[351] So forgive others and move on.

TOOL #6
Doubt

Bible Text

- "But let him ask in faith, with no ***doubting***, for the one who ***doubts*** is like a wave of the sea that is driven and tossed by the wind. For that person must not suppose that he will receive anything from the Lord; he is a double-minded man, unstable in all his ways." (James 1:6–8, emphasis added)
- "Truly, I say to you, whoever says to this mountain, 'Be taken up and thrown into the sea,' and does not ***doubt*** in his heart, but believes that what he says will come to pass, it will be done for him." (Mark 11:23, emphasis added)
- "Then he said to Thomas, 'Put your finger here, and see my hands; and put out your hand, and place it in my side. Do ***not disbelieve***, but believe.'" (John 20:27, emphasis added)

Self-Test

Do you ever doubt that Jesus Christ is the Son of God, or doubt His assurance of forgiveness, eternal salvation, and answered prayer? Satan, at some point in our lives, normally assaults each one of us with these probing thoughts. But you can be assured that if you pause too long and give root to these doubts placed into your mind by the Enemy, you are being duped!

Emotional Partners with . . .

Guilt, Regret, Worry, Fear, Anxiety

God's Opposite Emotion

Belief, Faith, Hope

Doubt and disbelief. These two well-camouflaged tricks of the devil bring havoc into the lives of believers. I believe doubt requires at least some level of belief. You must first have some level of faith before you can doubt your beliefs. So if you have doubt, you have some level of faith. Disbelief, on the other hand, is a faithless mental state where little if any belief exists.

Ways the Devil Attacks our Belief

I will address four areas in which the devil attacks our belief.

Doubt in Jesus' Resurrection

Doubt in Jesus' resurrection is the devil's ultimate objective. All other objectives are subordinate to this. It is his goal for you to reject the belief that Jesus Christ came into this world as God's Son, lived a sinless life, died for our sins, was raised from the dead on the third day in bodily form, and was taken into heaven by His Father.

All the schemes and tricks of the devil are tied into this one deception: If he can get you to reject Jesus as the risen Son of God, he will get you to spend eternity with him in hell. But, other than the Scriptures, what proof is there for the non-believer that Jesus is who He says?

Josh McDowell provides powerful proof of Jesus' deity in his book, *More Than a Carpenter*.[352] His proof, based on human nature, is as follows: If you had a group of eleven friends that all believed in and promoted some cause, how many of those eleven do you think would be willing to die for that cause? Most people answer maybe one or two. Now, let's say that all eleven discovered that the cause they were promoting was a lie. How many would still die for that cause? Almost all think that no one would be foolish enough to die for a lie.

Now let's take a look at Jesus' disciples both before and after the cross. Before the cross, I would call these disciples less than bold. Remember, most of Jesus' disciples followed at a distance for their own safety after Christ's arrest in the Garden of Gethsemane. Also remember, Peter, fearful for his well-being, denied Christ three times. But something happened to these disciples after the cross.

After the cross, the disciples were all willing to lay down their lives for their faith in the Lord Jesus and His testimony. So, what happened that changed these eleven men so dramatically—from cowardly to courageous? Human nature leaves us with no explanation other than a personal appearance by Jesus Himself—after His crucifixion—confirming the truth of His resurrection and the testimony of His Word, with the assurance of eternal life in heaven with Him. Only a personal appearance by the risen Lord would generate such a drastic change.

And yes, if you read the scriptures, ten of the eleven *were tortured and put to death for their belief and testimony in Jesus Christ as the Son of God and the risen Lord.*[353] Human nature tells us such a result would never happen without Christ's resurrection and appearance to the eleven disciples after the cross.

Doubt in Our Forgiveness

It seems so difficult, at times, for us to believe that God can forgive us, especially for some of our actions. Yet, Scripture tells us that if we repent of our sins, God is faithful and will cleanse us from all unrighteousness.[354] That almost sounds too good to be true, but it is true. To take it even a step further, God didn't put limitations on His forgiveness. Christ told us that He came not to help the righteous but to help the unrighteous, the lost. We certainly fit that bill, don't we?

My favorite passage on Jesus' forgiveness is in Luke 7:37–50, and it states in part, *And behold, a woman of the city, who was a sinner, when she learned that he* [Jesus] *was reclining at table in the Pharisee's house, brought an alabaster flask of ointment, and standing behind him at his feet, weeping, she began to wet his feet with her tears and wiped them with the hair of her head and kissed his feet and anointed them with the ointment*[355] (brackets added). The rest of the dinner guests were surprised that Jesus did not send her away due to her reputation for living a life of sin. He knew what they were thinking, so Jesus said to Simon, a Pharisee, '*Simon, I have something to say to you.' And he answered, 'Say it, Teacher.' 'A certain moneylender had two debtors. One owed five hundred denarii, and the other fifty. When they could not pay, he cancelled the debt of both. Now which of them will love him more?' Simon answered, 'The one, I suppose, for whom he cancelled the larger debt.' And he said to him,' 'You have judged rightly.'*[356]

Jesus then went on to say, *Therefore I tell you,* **her sins, which are many, are forgiven***—for she loved much.* **But he who is forgiven little, loves little**[357] (emphasis added). The more we are forgiven, the more we are apt to love the forgiver. Jesus knows this about mankind, but do we?

Forgiveness, according to our human knowledge, seems impossible. But to God, whose thoughts are higher than ours, nothing is impossible. Do not accept the devil's counterfeit propaganda when he plants the thought in your mind that Jesus won't forgive you! He will. You just might love Him a little more than your neighbor.

Doubt in Eternal Salvation

One of the most difficult things in the Bible for us to understand is eternal salvation. Jesus told us in His Word that one of the reasons He came to earth was to defeat death and to take the sting out of it.[358] He also said He came to take us out of our bondage from fear of death.[359] In fact, the entire gospel message is based on the promise of eternal salvation for those who confess Him as their Lord, and believe in His resurrection. The apostle Paul tells us, *because, if you confess with your mouth that Jesus is Lord and believe in your heart that God raised him from the dead, you will be saved.*[360]

If the devil can get you to doubt the truth of your eternal salvation, then he has a much better chance of also robbing you of a fruitful and joyful life.

Our belief in the promise of Christ, to spend eternity with Him in heaven, should give us joy and peace in this life, and a sense of stability and future hope, if we truly have faith in His Word.

Doubt in the Assurance of Answered Prayer

We all want our prayers to be answered, so let's see what Jesus says in Matthew 21:18–22 about that topic:

In the morning, as he [Jesus] was returning to the city, he became hungry.

*And seeing a fig tree by the wayside, he went to it and found nothing on it but only leaves. And he said to it, "May no fruit ever come from you again!" And the fig tree withered at once. When the disciples saw it, they marveled, saying, "How did the fig tree wither at once?" And Jesus answered them, "Truly, I say to you, if you have faith and do not **doubt**, you will not only do what has been done to the fig tree, but even if you say to this mountain, 'Be taken up and thrown into the sea,' it will happen. And whatever you ask in prayer, you will receive, if you have faith."* (brackets and emphasis added)

In John 16:24, Jesus also said, *"Until now you have asked nothing in my name. Ask, and you will receive, that your joy may be full."* In Matthew 7:7, In addition Jesus said, *"Ask, and it will be given to you; seek, and you will find; knock, and it will be opened to you."* And in Matthew 18:20, Jesus said, *"For where two or three are gathered in my name, there am I among them."*

Jesus made it clear that whatever we ask of Him that is in line with the will of the Father, it will be done for us, as long as we believe. What a promise. The devil knows that if he can wedge doubt between our petition to God and our belief that God will answer our prayer, then he can affect the outcome of that prayer. The more we believe, the greater the ability for God to move within our lives.

Our faith in the Word of God, coupled with prayer, is the most powerful resource we have in our walk with Christ. And it is the one thing, next to our faith in the risen Lord, that the devil would love to take from us. So hold on to your faith, and leave no room for the Enemy to plant his seeds of doubt.

TOOL #7
Negativity

Bible Text

- "Finally, brothers, whatever is true, whatever is honorable, whatever is just, whatever is pure, whatever is lovely, whatever is commendable, if there is any excellence, ***if there is anything worthy of praise, think about these things***." (Philippians 4:8, emphasis added)
- "For as he thinks in his heart, so is he." (Proverbs 23:7 NKJV)
- "Death and life are in the power of the tongue, and those who love it will eat its fruits." (Proverbs 18:21)

Self-Test

Are you constantly finding fault in others or always thinking of the worst possible outcome or scenario in every situation you encounter? If so, you are being duped!

Emotional Partners with . . .

Guilt, Regret, Worry, Fear, Anxiety, Unworthiness

God's Opposite Emotion

Faith, Hope, Love

History tells us of an extremely wealthy man named Joe. At one time, his estate was among the wealthiest in the East, well-diversified in warehouses, real estate, banks, and stocks. Anybody would have loved to own a fraction of what he had. And Joe was also blessed with a big family by today's standards—seven sons and three daughters.

Life had been easy for him. Everything he touched turned to money, and his large family even got along well, if you can believe that. But one day, everything changed. The real estate market crashed, causing runs on his banks as they quickly became insolvent. That same day, Joe found out that his stocks and bonds, which had been worth millions, were now virtually worthless. With the market crash and a failing economy, most of his remaining manufacturers went out of business, leaving him with empty warehouses and no income. He lost every asset he owned. And then, it got worse.

Joe's children boarded a plane to attend his fiftieth birthday party, but it ran into stormy weather shortly after takeoff and crashed leaving no survivors.

Then Joe's health started to deteriorate. Some thought it was because of the markets. Some thought it was because he lost his family. And others wondered if he was harboring some secret sin.

Joe's three business partners were speechless, at least at first. How could he have been so blessed for the misfortune to lose it all in such a short time? They questioned him about his faith in God since it seemed to them that God had abandoned Joe. They even hinted that maybe Joe was being paid back by God for some hidden sin. Maybe he had swindled people to make his fortunes. Even his wife suggested that he curse God and die.

Being an honest man, probably one of the few in his day, Joe rejected all this talk and never lost faith in God. Joe's belief in God gave him the power to remain positive when to the rest of the world, it looked like Joe was finished.

But, not only did Joe survive. When conditions improved, he managed to borrow enough to buy back his banks and real estate, and even invest in his prior stocks at depressed prices. When prices rose again, Joe's financial holdings returned to their pre-crash value; then, over time, they even doubled in value. And Joe, even though he was now older, his wife still bore him exactly ten more children.

And although this example sounds extreme, it's actually a modern-day retelling of an ancient true story of one who suffered great hardship but retained his faith, hope, and love for God. Just ask Joe . . . I mean Job. You can read his actual story in the book of Job in the Old Testament.

TOOL #8
Anxiety / PTSD

Bible Text

- "Peace I leave with you; my peace I give you. Not as the world gives do I give to you. Let not your ***hearts be troubled***, neither let them be afraid." (John 14:27, emphasis added)
- "***Do not be anxious about anything***, but in everything by prayer and supplication with thanksgiving let your requests be made known to God. And the peace of God, which surpasses all understanding, will guard your hearts and your minds in Christ Jesus." (Philippians 4:6–7, emphasis added)
- "Cast all your ***anxieties*** on him, because he cares for you." (1 Peter 5:7, emphasis added)
- "***Anxiety*** in a man's heart weighs him down, but a good word makes him glad." (Proverbs 12:25, emphasis added)
- "The LORD gives strength to his people; the LORD blesses his people with ***peace***." (Psalm 29:11 NIV, emphasis added)
- "I have said these things to you, that in me you may have ***peace***. In the world you will have tribulation. But take heart; I have overcome the world." (John 16:33, emphasis added)

- "You keep him in *perfect peace* whose mind is stayed on you, because he trusts in you." (Isaiah 26:3, emphasis added)
- "For God has not given us a *spirit of fear*, but of power and of love and of a sound mind." (2 Timothy 1:7 NKJV, emphasis added)

Self-Test

Do you find it hard to focus? Are you always jittery and anxious about many things? Are you fearful of failure, success, rejection, or the unknown? Are you constantly unsure of yourself, trying to find enough strength to cope for another day and just function in the world? If so, you're being duped!

Emotional Partners with . . .

Fear, Worry, Guilt, Shame, Regret, Rejection, Resentment, Unworthiness, Anger

God's Opposite Emotion

Love, Joy, Peace

Anxiety is a terrible thing. It robs one of the pleasures of life. Anxiety is, in essence a thief. It has no value, no substance, and no solution within itself. Anxiety is a self-fulling emotion. It is not from God, but in reality, it is a combination of many other negative emotions fueled by the Enemy. Anxiety is one of our most destructive emotions, and can be comprised of fear, guilt, resentment, worry, shame, unworthiness, and a host of other negative emotions. It feeds upon itself in a never-ending cycle, paralyzing the victim from ever accomplishing what God has designed him to do. Some believe the largest emotional component in anxiety is fear. This may be true. Anxiety, like fear, paralyzes its victims and prevents them from ever moving forward.

Needless to say, anxiety is the exact opposite of God's spiritual emotion of peace. Peace is a fruit, or attribute of the Holy Spirit, which God has placed inside of every believer as the first deposit of glories to come[361] upon our acceptance and profession of Jesus Christ as our personal Lord and Savior. We are told that the fruit of the Holy Spirit is love, joy, peace, patience, kindness, goodness, faithfulness, gentleness, and self-control.[362] But the full measure of this fruit is only realized when our own spirit aligns with God's. So peace—true peace—for the Christian, is already within us. If we lack peace, then we are in some way blocking or masking the fruit of the Spirit.

As we have previously discussed in Chapters Thirteen and Twenty, we have within ourselves a spiritual gap. And as stated in these chapters, even though as believers the Lord has filled this spiritual gap with His Holy Spirit, the devil still tries to convince us that we need his remedy to fill this gap. These emotional quick fixes, which promise satisfaction and fulfillment, such as drugs, sex, money, and power, quickly fade and leave us yearning for more. They always require another deposit for another temporary high of emotional fulfillment, and once they are gone, we're left more anxious, unhappy, and unfulfilled than we were before. That is the opposite of peace.

The "Ruby Slipper" Syndrome

As we have stated previously, God's solution for our spiritual gap is the indwelling of His Holy Spirit and His fruit—something we obtained when we accepted Christ as our personal Lord and Savior. And through the Holy Spirit, we have everything we need to live this life as God intended. Sadly, many never realize this. I call it the "ruby slippers" syndrome that I refer to earlier in Chapter Thirteen. Let me explain.

In the old movie *The Wizard of Oz*, the character of Dorothy found herself in a new world where her only objective was to get back home to Kansas. And although she was given a pair of red, ruby slippers to wear soon after arriving in the land of Oz, she failed to realize these ruby slippers gave her the ability to get back home at any time. Dorothy spent her entire time in Oz, desperately looking for a way to get back home, when she had *the ability to do so the whole time.*

Sometimes Christians have the same problem; they don't understand they were given all they need and were designed for in this life from the moment of salvation.[363] They spend their whole life trying to find love, joy, and peace when, in reality, all of these things have already been placed inside of them through the Holy Spirit. They only need to humble themselves to the Lord's will and let these fruits (which they already possess) manifest in their lives. The devil desperately tries to hide this "ruby slippers" truth from every believer.

Post-Traumatic Stress Disorder

PTSD appears to be closely related to, if not an actual, anxiety disorder. The debilitating effects of PTSD are felt by many within the first responder community: military, EMS, police, fire, as well as many other professions. It's a disorder that appears not to discriminate and tends to debilitate all who fall in its grasp. It can last weeks, months, years, or a lifetime. And although it would be appropriate to simply classify this disorder under the emotional tool of *anxiety*, I believe there may be an altogether different aspect of PTSD that is not often discussed. It is my belief there may be a spiritual component for some who suffer from this disorder.

I would like to point out that I have seen, what appears to me, many similarities between the symptoms of PTSD and the symptoms of second-level spiritual warfare. The theological scholars who write on this topic and those who work in deliverance ministry agree that trauma opens doors to the demonic—and war is nothing but trauma.

Emotional trauma may occur from constant *emotive pressure* **or** from a *single traumatic event*. Those who serve in the military or as emergency responders are subject to *both*. This may not be fair, but our adversary is not concerned about being fair.

Most of us deal with emotional deception from the Enemy one emotion at a time. With trauma, that is not the case. It appears that trauma may overload multiple emotions simultaneously, making us more vulnerable to the Enemy. I am not qualified to explain *how* the devil obtains his "legal right" to us in this time of weakness, but he apparently does just that.

In addition, we know that some demonic spirits and demons are territorial in nature.[364] Many of these wars are fought in regions of the world that have been under demonic rule for centuries. Accordingly, it would appear the probability of encountering demonic influence while in combat in such regions is undoubtedly higher than in other less demonic areas of the world.

I have never heard "spiritual warfare" mentioned when PTSD is discussed, but I think it would be a mistake to overlook the possibility of a demonic element to this issue—due to the problems those with this disorder suffer and the similarity of symptoms to those dealing with spiritual bondage. With nearly twenty veterans taking their lives every day,[365] clearly, the heart of the PTSD epidemic has not been addressed.

But please understand me here: *I am not suggesting, nor do I think that all PTSD cases are demonic in nature. I certainly do not.* There can be multiple reasons for such symptoms, including physical injury, concussive issues, mental issues, unrelated emotional issues, and many others. But I do believe that demonic spirits may be one reason for such symptoms, and I believe it would be a mistake to overlook this as a possibility. It has been estimated that only about forty percent of those suffering from PTSD find adequate relief of their symptoms.[366] It seems like the inability to get better over time, and patients remaining in a state of internal pain and anguish, indicates that PTSD treatments may not be addressing the source of the problem.

As previously stated, receiving physical, psychological, and pharmaceutical treatment will have little or no effect if someone is dealing with a demonic issue. Demonic spirits only obey and respond to the One who has authority over them: Jesus Christ, and those who are operating under His power and authority.

I believe looking for demonic presence as a source of, or a contributing factor to, PTSD is normally not a consideration, but should be considered when dealing with this issue. Hopefully, understanding that this condition may be spiritual in nature can become a talking point and may be helpful to some when seeking treatment. For others, it might even provide them an avenue to freedom.

TOOL #9
Pride

Bible Text

- "'God opposes the **proud**, but gives grace to the humble.'" (James 4:6b, Berean Study Bible, emphasis added)
- "Everyone who is **arrogant in heart** is an abomination to the LORD; be assured, he will not go unpunished." (Proverbs 16:5, emphasis added)
- "*Pride* goes before destruction, and a **haughty spirit** before a fall." (Proverbs 16:18, emphasis added)
- "Do not love the world or the things in the world. If anyone loves the world, the love of the Father is not in him. For all that is in the world—the desires of the flesh and the desires of the eyes and **pride of life**—is not from the Father but is from the world." (1 John 2:15–16, emphasis added)
- "I tell you, this man went down to his house justified, rather than the other. For everyone who **exalts himself** will be humbled, but the one who humbles himself will be exalted." (Luke 18:14, emphasis added)

Self-Test

Do you have a difficult time apologizing to people? Do you have a hard time admitting that you are wrong? Is it difficult for you to ask God for help? Do you believe you can handle everything on your own? If so, you are being duped!

Emotional Partners with . . .

Arrogance, Self-Righteousness, Haughtiness, Rebellion, Witchcraft

God's Opposite Emotion

Humility, Love, Grace

Unlike the other tools in the devil's toolbox that work by ingraining *destructive emotions* into our minds, this tool actually functions by our relying on too much of a *constructive emotion*: confidence. Too much of this becomes toxic and creates what I like to call "blind confidence" or pride. Pride is misplaced confidence in oneself rather than God, without recognizing a distinction between the two.

Remember, pride was the original sin. The devil was cast out of heaven because of his pride.[367] Likewise, we are told, *Pride goes before destruction, and a haughty spirit before a fall.*[368]

Pride says you, not God, are responsible for your successes. And pride can take many forms—pride of accomplishment, pride of position, spiritual pride, pride of wealth, and pride of prestige. Pride leaves no room for God. Pride has a hard time admitting defeat or weakness. It has a hard time apologizing, or admitting it's wrong. It places the prideful person above all others, and it steals the glory from God.

Some consider pride to be the root of all sins since it was the original sin. Because of pride, the devil refused to kneel and praise God rather, he wanted to be like God himself. Pride was the cause of the great battle in heaven between the devil and God's great archangel, Michael. And pride led to the devil and his legion being cast out of heaven for all eternity. It shouldn't surprise us, then, that God talks about pride in the same breath that He talks about the evils of theft, murder, adultery, slander, and deceit.[369]

Pride can prevent the unregenerate from humbly calling on the name of the Lord, which is necessary for salvation. It can prevent Christians from having a proper relationship with Jesus Christ by failing to humble themselves before God. And prideful people can often have a difficult time praying to the Lord, instead opting for self-sufficiency. As a result, they miss out on the blessing God has in store for them. Let's look at three areas where pride might arise in a person's life.

Pride Can Encourage Us to Rely on Works for Salvation

Believing we can accomplish everything we want in this world without God, goes hand-in-hand with the belief we can earn our way to heaven. Both are wrong.

The following two Bible verses clarify that pride has no part in our salvation. Ephesians 2:8–9 states: *For by grace you have been saved through faith. And this is not your own doing; it is the gift of God, not as a result of works, so that no one may boast.*

Galatians 2:16 also tells us: *Yet we know that a person is not justified by works of the Law but through faith in Jesus Christ, so we also have believed in Christ Jesus, in order to be justified by faith in Christ and not by the works of the Law, because by the works of the Law no one will be justified.*

We receive salvation only from our faith in and acceptance of Jesus Christ as Lord and not by our works or observance of the Law.[370]

Pride Can Prevent Us from Seeking God's Justification

Two people attended a well-known church for Sunday service. One was a well-respected senator, and the other was a homeless man just looking for relief from the cold weather. As the homeless man made his way into the church, he passed the senator before taking his seat in a corner pew.

During the service, the senator prayed, "O God, I thank you that I am not like the rest of this congregation—greedy, dishonest, adulterous, or even like this homeless man who has no self-respect. You know I am righteous, going to church once a week, and that I always tithe as I should."

The homeless man, on the other hand, could barely bring himself to pray when he heard the preaching from the pastor. He whispered, "O God, be merciful to me a sinner."

My question to you is, which of these two men went home justified? The homeless man! The Bible tells us, *For everyone who exalts himself will be humbled, but the one who humbles himself will be exalted.*[371] This story is the updated version of the Parable of the Pharisee and the Tax Collector, found in Luke 18:9–14, and what was true of pride then is true of pride now. We can never be justified with God through our works. Pride tries to convince us otherwise.

Pride Can Keep Us from Having Effective Prayer

Prideful people often refuse to humble themselves in prayer. Not only is this prayerful humility required for salvation, and to have a proper relationship with Jesus Christ, but as we have previously discussed, it's also required for effective prayer.

However, the Bible tells us what we can expect from God when we do humble ourselves before Him in prayer. Daniel 10:12 tells us, *"Fear not, Daniel, for from the first day that you **set your heart to understand and humbled yourself before your God, your words have been hard**, and I have come because of your words"* (emphasis added). Clearly, Daniel humbling himself before the Lord was a critical component to his prayer being heard.

Prideful people sometimes seem to have it all. But on closer examination, they also many times seem to lack peace, love, happiness, and joy. All these attributes originate with God, and he mercifully distributes them to us through our confession of faith in Christ.[372]

As ironic as it may seem, when you see someone pounding their chest, boasting about their accomplishments, and claiming to have the world by the tail, they're usually in for a fall.[373] And while the devil sometimes uses success and prosperity to keep us away from God, God Himself sometimes uses adversity to bring us back into reliance on Him. Never forget, God is in control—not us.

TOOL #10
Lust / Sexual Sins / Pornography

Bible Text

- "For all that is in the world—the ***desires of the flesh*** and the ***desires of the eyes*** and pride of life—is not from the Father but is from the world." (1 John 2:16, emphasis added)
- "Food is meant for the stomach and the stomach for food—and God will destroy both one and the other. The body is not meant for ***sexual immorality***, but for the Lord, and the Lord for the body." (1 Corinthians 6:13, emphasis added)
- "So flee ***youthful passions*** and pursue righteousness, faith, love, and peace, along with those who call on the Lord from a pure heart." (2 Timothy 2:22, emphasis added)
- "But each person is tempted when he is lured and ***enticed by his own desire***. Then ***desire*** when it has conceived gives birth to sin, and sin when it is fully grown brings forth death." (James 1:14–15, emphasis added)

Self-Test

Do you let your sexual passions dominate your thoughts or actions? Are your thoughts and passions for someone, or something, uncontrollable? Do you feel excessively compelled to have what you desire . . . and have it right now? If so, you are being duped!

Emotional Partners with . . .

Obsession, Insecurity, Guilt, Regret, Anxiety

God's Opposite Emotion

Love, Peace, Self-Control

Let's take a minute to define the difference between lust and love, and then we will examine both.

1 Corinthians 13:4–8 provides God's definition of love: *Love is patient and kind; love does not envy or boast; it is not arrogant or rude. It does not insist on its own way; it is not irritable or resentful; it does not rejoice at wrongdoing, but rejoices with the truth. Love bears all things, believes all things, hopes all things, endures all things. Love never ends.*

Christianity is the only religion that directs its followers to focus outside of themselves, putting others first. In fact, that is exactly how Jesus defines the greatest kind of love when He says, *Greater love has no one than this, that someone lay down his life for his friends.*[374]

The Bible lists four different types of love—agape, storge, phileo—and you won't be surprised to learn that the last of them is *eros*, romantic love. But, as he always does, the devil offers a counterfeit: lust. Lust is defined in *Webster's Dictionary* as an intense desire or need; to have an unbridled sexual desire.[375] And lust may feel like love, but there is a difference. Love wants to give. Lust wants to take. If you absolutely must have something, and have it now, then it's probably lust.

The word for lust is *epithumos*. The prefix *epi* means "to add to." In other words, it is something beyond our normal state. This kind of desire should be an alert that you are being duped. Remember Proverbs 16:25 says, *There is a way that seems right to man, but its end is the way to death*. That is why it is so critical for us to compare our thoughts to God's Word. To ensure we are experiencing God's life-building emotions and the feelings they produce, and not the devil's counterfeit, destructive emotions.

Sexual Sins

I acknowledge that lust is a broad term that can apply to just about anything. However, generally speaking, I will discuss the term here in its most common form and usage, applying it to sexual sins. These sins include, but are not excluded to, the act of lust,[376] adultery,[377] fornication,[378] incest,[379] homosexuality,[380] pedophilia,[381] and bestiality.[382]

All these sexual sins are sins against the body. And if you are a Christian, your body is the temple of the Holy Spirit.[383] As we discussed previously in Chapter Eight, if these sins are practiced, especially if done habitually, one runs the risk of providing "legal access" to the demonic spirits of that sin. In fact, according to the late Derek Prince of Derek Prince Ministries and the late Frank Hammond of Frank Hammond Ministries, many of the sexual sins listed above have demonic spirits behind them.[384] These demonic spirits, if given a "legal right," can come into one's body to manifest their character.

Are all those who practice such sexual sins filled with a demonic spirit? I don't believe so, but it certainly has the ability to provide a "legal right" for that to occur. And if one has opened up to, and acquired, a demonic spirit in a particular area of sexual sin, compulsions and bondage of this demonic spirit will follow. At this level of spiritual bondage, the person is no longer in control of these compulsions. The evil entities may have taken up residence in the person's body and are manifesting their demonic sexual perversions and lusts through the person. Refusal to act on these compulsions is still within the control of the person, but the ability to suppress these compulsive feelings is not.

A Spiritual Link between Homosexuality and Suicide

We know from Scripture that demons (unclean spirits) desire to dwell in human bodies.[385] As we have stated earlier, demons rarely travel alone.[386] They normally group with other demons and can manifest their compulsions in more than one area of a person's life.

With the disturbing statistics between homosexuality and suicide, one must wonder if such a spiritual link exists between the gay, lesbian, and transgender lifestyle, and the spirit of suicide (a topic that we will discuss later in Tool #12 in this section). According to statistics compiled in various studies, and reported on in the fall of 2016, by the New Atlantis, ". . . the authors estimated that the lesbian, gay, and bisexual individuals had a 2.47 times higher lifetime risk than heterosexuals for suicide attempts . . ."[387] While a second study reported on by the New Atlantis indicated ". . . that population-based surveys of U.S. adolescents since the 1990s indicate that suicide attempts are two to seven times more likely in high school students who identify as LGB, with sexual orientation being a stronger predictor in male than females."[388] And a third study, also reported on by the New Atlantis, found in an older 1984 study, ". . . a clinical sample of transgender individuals requesting sex-reassignment surgery showed suicide attempt rates between 19% and 25%."[389] Other such studies have also shown similar statistics.[390] These are disheartening statistics to say the least.

Clearly, there appears to be some type of link between living these lifestyles and suicide.[391] While there could be, and surely are, many external reasons for these incredibly high suicide numbers, such as discrimination, harassment, and rejection by family members, one cannot rule out the possibility of a spiritual link between this conduct and the spirit of suicide.[392]

If one is dealing with such demonic entities, this can become a terrible internal battle. If you feel as if you are no longer in control of your emotions, or feel a persistent luring or compulsion to end your life, you may be in the grasp of the Enemy. Please seek help by one who understands and is trained in such things. True freedom is found in Jesus Christ and Him alone.

When Jesus said He came to set the captives free, I believe it included this type of bondage. Those who have been freed from such bondage need not have anyone explain to them the reality of Christ's power and what freedom in Christ means, for they have experienced the bondage of Satan followed by their full freedom through Jesus Christ.

Incubus and Succubus

A topic not easily discussed, but a reality in the spiritual realm—with those whom (or whose family lineage) have given great ground to the Enemy in the areas of sexual sins or involvement in the occult[393]—is the topic of the demonic entities known as Incubus and Succubus. These demonic entities get their names based on their activity with those whom they assault. Incubus arrives its name from the Latin word *incubare* (meaning to lie upon) and is an evil male demon. Whereas the word Succubus arrives its name from the Latin word *succubare* (meaning to lie under) and is an evil female demon. These demonic spirits, which have been haunting mankind for millennia,[394] are known for their sexual assaults against both men and women. These entities are known for manifesting to the degree that they cause physical trauma to their victims by sexually assaulting them (having sexual intercourse with them).

Although this seems hard to believe, it's no laughing matter to those who have experienced such assaults. But as with any assault of the devil and his host of evil spirits, by surrendering one's life to the Lord, by confessing Jesus as their personal Savior, by renouncing any spiritual ties that may have been opened by oneself or one's lineage, one may command these spirits out of their life in the name of Jesus Christ—thus terminating the assaults, terminating Satan's "legal right" to their life, and forever preventing them from reoccurring.

The Coveting Sin of Pornography

You shall not covet . . .[395]

We are told in Exodus 20:17 that, among other things, we are not to covet our neighbor's wife. The Merriam Dictionary defines covet as: *to wish for earnestly* or *to desire (what belongs to another) inordinately or culpably.*[396] In essence, to covet is to desire something or someone that does not belong to us. For those who are married, this raises an additional question. How does "coveting another" affect the one that we are married to?

I was once told when a man looks covetously at a woman other than his wife, he robs his wife of her glory. Men, *that* comment should stop you in your tracks. Think about it: coveting another robs your own wife of her glory—a glory God dedicated to husbands to foster and nurture. So coveting (looking lustfully at another or watching pornography) does not affect just oneself; it also affects your spouse.

Staggeringly, statistics tell us 68% of Christians watch pornography.[397] So, what would these statistics be with the general (non-Christian) public? I would hate to guess.

So why is pornography such a problem? First, I believe it has to do in part with the biological process that takes place *within our brain* when we look at images designed to arouse us. As we discussed in Chapter Seven, "The Science behind God's Word," there are those within the medical community who understand how images that arouse our sexual desires generate the chemical known as dopamine in the brain. This euphoric feeling urges us to pursue more stimuli. Interestingly, as we gratify our lustful desires, our brain actually reduces the number of receptors available to be stimulated by this chemical, requiring more of the stimulus to get the same high. This creates a vicious circle of becoming more and more dependent on stimulation (pornography) to get the same erotic feeling, often resulting in what we call addiction.

Second, I believe the pornography problem has quite a lot to do with *ease of access*. Men and women no longer have to leave the comfort of home, car, or office to become immersed in this addiction. It's simply served up to any (oftentimes without solicitation) in the form of online advertisements, pop-ups, or side links. Since this pornography is free of charge and can be viewed within the privacy of your home, with nobody else watching, many are convinced this type of sin is harmless!

As with many of the other sexual sins, pornography can create a spiritual opening in your life that gives the devil and his host of demons "legal access" to your heart and mind. As we have discussed in previous chapters, this can create all kinds of mental strongholds and may even create a spiritual bondage that may require deliverance to resolve.

Pornography is neither holy, harmless, nor helpful. As with all of Satan's lures, it promises to satisfy but instead leaves its victims with a craving for more and more—a solution that is incapable of providing the true satisfaction only God can supply.

TOOL #11
Insecurity / Lack of Self-Worth

Bible Text

- *"Are not two sparrows sold for a penny? And not one of them will fall to the ground apart from your Father. But even the hairs of your head are all numbered. Fear not, therefore; you are of more value than many sparrows."* (Matthew 10:29–31, emphasis added)
- "For he chose us in him before the creation of the world to be holy and blameless in his sight. In love he **predestined us for adoption** to sonship through Jesus Christ, in accordance with his pleasure and will to the praise of his glorious grace, which he has freely given us in the One he loves." (Ephesians 1:4–6 NIV, emphasis added)
- *"I praise you, because I am fearfully and wonderfully made.* How precious to me are your thoughts, God! How vast is the sum of them!"* (Psalm 139:14, 17 NIV, emphasis added)
- "I can do all things through him who strengthens me." (Philippians 4:13)

Self-Test

When you consider taking action, do you first think about how others will respond and judge you? Or, do you ever find yourself sabotaging your own efforts because you don't believe you deserve a favorable outcome or deserve to be truly happy?

If so, you are being duped!

Emotional Partners with . . .

Guilt, Regret, Worry, Fear, Anxiety, Indecisiveness, Procrastination, Suicide

God's Opposite Emotion

Hope, Faith, Love

A sense of insecurity is probably one of the least talked about, but one of the most destructive tools of the devil. People will often let you see their anger, fears, and doubts, but they will rarely let you see their insecurities. They hold them close. We all have insecurities in one form or another, but when they become the dominant force in our life, we have been duped by the devil.

Insecurity can manifest itself in several ways: through a feeling of low self-esteem, worthlessness, inferiority, unworthiness, hopelessness, help-lessness, etc. It is not a coincidence that depressed people suffer similar emotions. If we look closely behind these destructive emotions, they reveal three basic areas of attack by the devil: our personal value, our personal expectations, and our personal power.

Our Personal Value

Low self-esteem, worthlessness, and unworthiness all come from the misconception that we have little or no personal value. As children of God, that is the opposite of what the Bible teaches us. Luke 12:7 says, *Why, even the hairs of your head are all numbered. Fear not; you are of more value than many sparrows.*

There was a man whose son got into serious trouble with the law. His father, a hard-working laborer, had spent the last several years of his life saving to buy a nice home for his wife and family. But if they were going to provide the proper type of legal defense their son needed, they would have to pay tens of thousands dollars. Without flinching, the father withdrew all his savings and gave it to the legal team representing his son. The house was his goal, his son was his family.

We are not a goal to God. We are His family. He wanted each one of us so much that He created us and gave His Son to die for us so we could live with Him in eternity. Would you do that for someone you didn't love or value?

If the devil can make you believe you just don't measure up, your life has little or not value, or that you don't deserve a rich and fulfilling life then you will be a bench warmer in life and will fail to fulfill the call God has upon you. Don't allow that to happen. You are God's family and He loves you greatly.

Our Personal Expectations

Hopelessness comes from a lack of expectation, particularly when referring to the fulfillment of God's promises. But that is the opposite of what the Bible teaches about *hope*. Biblical hope is the anticipation of a favorable outcome under God's guidance. In Galatians 5:5 we are told, *For through the Spirit, by faith, we ourselves eagerly wait for the hope of righteousness.* So, hope and faith are closely related, only faith is in the present, and hope is in the future.

Faith's primary meaning in Scripture is trust or confidence in God and His Word. We know that faith comes through hearing the words of Christ.[398] Its most literal definition can be found in Hebrews 11:1, which defines faith as, *The assurance of things hoped for, the conviction of things not seen.*

Faith is the main ingredient in salvation,[399] justification,[400] purification and sanctification,[401] adoption as children of God,[402] and yes, the assurance of things hoped for.[403]

And Paul tells us in Ephesians 6:16 that *faith* is a shield against all the fiery arrows of the devil. Paul knew that God gives us faith not only to receive our blessings, but to protect us from the deceit of the devil.

Our faith is based on our knowledge that Jesus was crucified, has risen, is seated at the right hand of His Father, and has been granted *all authority in heaven and on earth.*[404] Now, does that sound like someone with whom you can place your hope? It sure does to me.

Our Personal Power

Most people associate power with the ability to dominate others, but that is just the opposite of how God demonstrates His power. Isn't it interesting that God chose Christ's greatest hour of weakness—His death on the cross—to demonstrate His greatest power? Jesus conquered sin and death through submission to the will of the Father.

The apostle Paul tells us, *For when I am weak, then I am strong.*[405] So, while God uses our weakness to work His strength through us, the Enemy uses our weaknesses to try to work his lies of lack of self-worth and self-value against us. Insecurity and helplessness are nothing more than propaganda placed in our minds by the Great Deceiver.

Most people at some point have been responsible for young children? Would you have ever left them alone for an extended period of time? The answer is obvious. Of course not. And God is no different. We are God's children, and He promises to never leave us nor forsake us.[406] In fact,

Jesus tells us, *And behold, I am with you always, to the end of the age.*[407] As children of God, we are the most cared for, provided for, attended after, and watched over beings in the universe.

If you are trying to live an abundant life in your own strength, power, and might, good luck. You will eventually fail. God's power to live the life He intended for you doesn't come *from* you, it comes *through* you. It comes from Him. It comes based on your personal, saving relationship with the Lord Jesus Christ. And, sometimes, this power comes through us at our weakest moments—when we have no choice but to surrender to God.

TOOL #12
Hopelessness / Despair / Depression / Suicide

Bible Text

- "Come to me, all you who are **weary and burdened**, and I will give you rest. Take my yoke upon you and learn from me, for I am gentle and humble in heart, and you will find rest for your souls. For my yoke is easy and my burden is light." (Matthew 11:28–30 NIV, emphasis added)
- "For I know the plans I have for you," declares the Lord, "**plans to prosper you and not to harm you, plans to give you hope and a future**." (Jeremiah 29:11 NIV, emphasis added)
- "The Spirit of the Lord GOD is upon me, because the LORD has anointed me to bring good news to the poor; he has sent me to **bind up the broken-hearted, to proclaim liberty to the captives, and the opening of the prison to those who are bound;** to proclaim the year of the LORD's favor, and the day of the vengeance of our God; to **comfort all who mourn**; to grant to those who mourn in Zion—to give them a beautiful headdress instead of ashes, the oil of gladness instead of mourning, the **garment of praise instead of a faint spirit**; that they may be called oaks of righteousness, the

planting of the LORD, that he may be glorified." (Isaiah 61:1–3, emphasis added)

- "Therefore, since we have been justified through faith, we have peace with God through our Lord Jesus Christ, through whom we have gained access by faith into this grace in which we now stand. And *we boast in the hope of the glory of God*. Not only so, but we also glory in our sufferings, because we know that suffering produces perseverance; perseverance, character; and character, hope. And *hope does not put us to shame*, because God's love has been poured out into our hearts through the Holy Spirit, who has been given to us." (Romans 5:1–5 NIV, emphasis added)

Self-Test

Do you believe things have just gone too far, and there is no solution for the problems you face, the pain you feel, or the predicament you're in? Do you feel like there is "no going back" from where you currently are to receive forgiveness for your sins? Have you dwelt upon, or harbored in your mind, thoughts of self-harm or suicide as the only way out? If so, you are being duped!

Emotional Partners with . . .

Rejection, Depression, Despondency, Confusion, Unworthiness, Insecurity, Inferiority, Alienation, Abandonment, Loneliness, Isolation, Emotional Anguish, Anxiety, Torment, Internal Pain, Occult.

God's Opposite Emotion

Hope, Forgiveness, Love, Peace, Sound-mind

The Demonic Spirit of Hopelessness

The Enemy wants you to be hopeless. When you have arrived at this point, you can be sure that the Great Deceiver has been working on you for some time. You don't just wake up one morning feeling hopeless. It's a progressive state that is usually well-orchestrated against you.

Hope can be found in Jesus, but the devil doesn't want you to know that. He wants you to look at what you can see, not what you can't. The devil wants you to forget the fact that there is a loving and merciful God who is working out all things together for good for those who love Him and are called according to His purpose.[408]

We previously discussed an interesting story in 2 Kings 6:14–17 about the prophet Elisha as the King of Aram pursued him. The King of Aram was enraged at the prophet Elisha, to whom God disclosed the king's every plan. In his anger, the king sent multitudes of troops to capture Elisha. When Elisha's servant saw the king's army with horses and chariots surrounding their city, in great dispair, he stated, *'Alas, my master! What shall we do?' Elisha responded, 'Do not be afraid, **for those who are with us are more than those who are with them.'** Then Elisha prayed and said, 'O LORD, please open his eyes that he may see.' So the LORD opened the eyes of the young man, and he saw, **and behold, the mountain was full of horses and chariots of fire*** (God's angels) *all around Elisha* (parenthesis and emphasis added). Only then did his servant understand the real circumstances. When he saw beyond the physical realm, the situation completely reversed itself.

The devil wants you only to see the physical world. He wants you to experience hopelessness. But the spiritual world is infinitely more powerful than the world we can see. In fact, the physical world was created by the spiritual world—God. And God has dominion over both. So don't get stuck in the trap of feeling that there is no hope. Just like Elisha, God has His army of angels ready to respond to our earthly circumstances. So, have faith in the Lord, and refuse to believe Satan's lies. And remember, *And Jesus said to him, "'If you can'! All things are possible for one who believes.*

The Demonic Spirit of Despair / Depression

Interestingly, the late Derek Prince, world recognized counselor and teacher on spiritual warfare and deliverance, was himself delivered from a spirit of despair and depression—a spirit which tormented him for many years. The key to his deliverance was his coming to the understanding that the spirit of depression or heaviness he was trying to rid himself of, *was not of him, "but it was from another person, a* **demonic spirit**," he commented (emphasis added).[409] Mr. Prince stated, "I had struggled with this thing for years, until I recognized it was not myself, it was another person seeking to afflict me."

This understanding came to him as he read Isiah 61:3 (KJV): ". . . *the garment of praise for* **the spirit of heaviness**. . . "(emphasis added). Mr. Prince said the Holy Spirit revealed to him that this was his problem. He had "a **spirit** of heaviness, of depression."[410] For the first time he understood that the depression he had endured was a *demonic spirit*. For years Mr. Prince said he had been using the wrong remedy for his condition. He stated he had been crucifying the flesh, thinking that his flesh was the problem, when in fact, his problem was from another—the *demonic spirit of despair or heaviness*.

Mr. Prince stated, "One must understand, you're dealing with a person without a body."[411] A person with emotions, and a personality just like us, only in spirit form. Mr. Prince stated that once this was revealed to him, he was eighty percent of the way to victory. Mr. Prince said he only needed to come upon Joel 2:32 (KJV) that states: "*And it shall come to pass, that* **whosoever** *shall call on the name of the LORD shall be delivered...*" (emphasis added).

Mr. Prince shared that—with this understanding—once he called upon the name of Jesus for deliverance in his life, "it was like a heavenly vacuum cleaner came down over [his] shoulders and just sucked this thing out."[412] This immediate liberation is similar with the experience of many who have truly been delivered from a demonic spirit.

Mr. Prince stressed how extremely important it is to know whether one is dealing with a **spirit** or the **flesh** because the remedies for dealing with the flesh and dealing with a demonic spirit are completely different. He goes on to share, "I was dealing with the *spirit of heaviness* and I was trying to deal with it as if it were the *flesh*. But you can't crucify a demon, nor can you cast out the flesh."[413]

This is a common mistake that I believe many in the Christian community make, primarily because we are rarely educated on this spiritual battle and are even taught that we are immune from these demonic spirits. These are doctrinal mistakes that leave many desperate individuals attempting to crucify the flesh when the problem may be spiritual in nature.

The Demonic Spirit of Suicide

As we discussed earlier, demons often masquerade as emotions. They do this because it allows their presence to easily remain hidden, allowing them to cause extreme emotional torment for long periods of time. There are those in the deliverance ministry that believe the demonic spirit of suicide is one of these demons.[414] Feelings of despair, depression, hopelessness, and rejection can accompany this demonic spirit. In fact, according to Derek Prince, **the spirit of rejection** is one of the demonic spirits that often proceeds the spirit of suicide in one's life.[415] Once such spirits take up residence in one's mind, they can inflict such anguish and pain through their presence that their subtle push to suicide may seem to be an acceptable outcome. Remember, the devil and his hosts' objectives are outlined in Scripture: *kill, steal, and destroy.*[416] The spirit of suicide is the devil at his height. He creates within us a demonic problem and then provides us with his demonic solution—suicide.

Repeated Suicide Attempts

If you have opened the door to such demonic spirits, you *must* remove them from your life following the steps we have previously discussed. Have someone who is trained in this area deliver you from these demonic spirits, and then fill your heart and mind with the Word of God, so not to leave any room for the Enemy to return.[417] And finally, get in a congregation or group with other believers to help you maintain your freedom in Christ.

I once had a doctor friend comment about a mutual friend who had attempted suicide but survived. He stated that once a person unsuccessfully attempts suicide, oftentimes they will try again. I thought a repeated attempt was unlikely with our friend, because he was doing extremely well and had recently given his life to the Lord—which I have no doubt was sincere.

What I did not understand at the time was that although my friend appeared to be fine, I believe he had mentally and spiritually opened the door to a demonic spirit of suicide, and that the spirit remained within him. Because everything seemed normal, and he did not discuss any lingering compulsion for suicide, this topic remained hidden even to his Christian counselor. If someone is dealing with a demonic spirit of suicide, not getting rid of this internal demonic presence almost guarantees that these emotional feelings of pain, hopelessness, and despair will return, along with an overwhelming compulsion for self-destruction. Unfortunately, I believe it did, and my friend took his own life. Whether a demonic spirit was behind this suicide, I can't be sure, but I can't help thinking it was.

In addition to my doctor friend's insightful observation of the repetitive nature of suicide attempts, I read an interesting article that seems to reinforce this belief that suicide is a demonic spirit, and that such a spirit (if not expelled) may be generational in nature. This is often referred to by those in the deliverance ministry as a *familiar spirit.*

This insightful article discussed the story of a young girl who died from an apparent suicide. She had attempted to take her own life twice before and survived. What is very intriguing about this tragic story is that both this girl's mother and grandmother also committed suicide—but that was something this young girl was never told and was never made aware of. As discussed in Chapter Nine, a family member can open the door or give "legal access" to the Enemy in some area of their life through such conduct such as the occult, channeling, or invitation. This conduct can also give "legal access" to attack their children and grandchildren in the same area[418] with the same evil spirits, with the same torment, and in the same way as the parent or grandparent. Whether this was the case with this young girl, I have no idea, but is certainly makes one consider the reality of generational curses, or what is sometimes called "familiar spirits." (NEW footnote: Exodus 20:5, Exodus 34:7, Numbers 14:18, Deuteronomy 5:9).

Familiar Spirits

Some call these evil spirits that pass from generation to generation *familiar spirits*.[419] The Bible refers to demonic entities, as *familiar spirits* at least eight times.[420] The majority of these verses mention familiar spirits appearing when condemning the practices of the spiritual medium, fortune teller, wizard, and necromancer (those who pretend to talk to the dead but actually solicit familiar demonic spirits.) This specific type of demonic spirit is classified as a familiar spirit because it's acquainted with the person who has permitted or given a "legal right" for its spiritual presence in their life.

The word "familiar" is from the Latin word *familiaris*, meaning "household servant." So it's not hard to see how these spirits became known as familiar spirits—they are familiar with the person or family with whom they are associated. Some people believe these are the spiritual entities that are behind the addiction, poverty, depression, sexual bondage, and even suicide patterns that have persisted in many family lineages and bloodlines for generations. As we have previously stated in this book, such generational spirits need not remain in one's life. You can choose to resist these evil entities and break free from their hold over you and your family. Deliverance from such spirits through the Lord Jesus Christ is available to all who call upon His name.

This is something rarely discussed by those rendering professional mental help, in his area, probably because they are untrained and never received any instruction on dealing with these demonic entities. Prescription drugs and counseling are not a cure for demonic spirits, and therefore will have absolutely zero effect toward resolving one's mental torment, and one's compulsion to take their own life, if demonic in nature.

As previously stated in this book, spiritual deliverance through the power and authority of Jesus Christ, by someone who is trained in this area, and is working with a willing participant, is the only way to set one free from this (or any other) spiritual entity. Similar to an abscessed tooth that causes pain but never subsides until it is removed, so is the pain and torment of a demonic spirit that never leaves until it is completely delivered from one's life.

Without deliverance from these evil entities, the demonic presence can last for weeks, months, years, or a lifetime as previously discussed in Chapter Eighteen. And as discussed in Tool #8, this is one reason I believe some cases of PTSD may possibly be spiritually rooted. If the demonic spirits are the root cause, and they are never addressed or expelled, the condition will never go away.

Pigs Don't Get Delivered

An interesting story in the Bible can be found in the books of Matthew,[421] Mark,[422] and Luke[423] where Jesus confronts a maniac man that was full of demons who lived in the region of the Gadarenes. After crossing the Sea of Galilee with His apostles, the Bible tells us that a maniac man full of demons saw Jesus approaching on the shore, and immediately (the demons within the man) recognized Him as the Son of God, and cried out with a loud voice . . . *What have you to do with me, Jesus, Son of the Most High God? I beg you, do not torment me.*[424]

The demons begged Jesus not to command them into the abyss, but begged Him permission to enter into a herd of swine that was feeding on a nearby mountain.[425]

Interestingly, Jesus granted their request, and these demon spirits immediately left the man and entered into the bodies of the pigs (providing further evidence that demons want some type of physical body to work out their lust and torment). Instantly, this entire herd of pigs—which were quite normal and orderly only one minute before—after the demons entered them, stampeded directly over a cliff to their own demise.[426] One must ask, what in the world happened?

It appears obvious to me that the pigs, becoming indwelt by these evil spirits, went mad, and did what they had to do to rid themselves of these demons. It was an immediate and unanimous reaction by this entire herd of pigs (some believe two thousand in number) to run off the cliff and drown themselves to rid themselves of these demonic entities, rather than exist with these foul spirits inside of them. Remember, pigs don't get spiritually delivered.

But man is different. The Bible tells us that Jesus came to set the captives free.[427] Meaning, in part, that He came to set mankind free from these evil spirits and their influence. We do not have to die or take our own lives to rid ourselves of these demonic tormentors. But some do. They believe this is the only way to end the pain and torment they feel. But Jesus provided His church (through the sending of the Holy Spirit) power over these evil entities. We only need to surrender ourselves to the Lord and be delivered to be set free of these tormentors.

But Satan would rather you not know this. He would rather you believe that there is no way out of this condition other than suicide, or to have you live endlessly in this demonic state of pain and torment, constantly medicating oneself with alcohol, drugs, or some other substances to deaden this internal pain and anguish. Such a destruction of your life would, of course, rob you of all of the plans God intended for you and would be a win for the devil. *This is why it's critically important to know what you are dealing with* (a demonic spirit or the flesh) so that you may properly assert God's authority over your life, and become delivered from such bondage.

I believe that missing Jesus' message on deliverance is missing one of the great works the Lord came to make available to true believers in the body of Christ. That is, **our ability to take authority over and to cast out these evil entities and to set man free from their evil influences**.[428] Scripture plainly tells us that *these signs will accompany those who believe: in my name **they will cast out demons**; they will speak in new tongues . . .* [429] (emphasis added). Deliverance ministry was commonplace in the early church, a work of the Holy Spirit that is available for all who have confessed Jesus Christ as their personal Lord and Savior, and who walk with the Lord.

So pigs don't get delivered. People do. If you find yourself in such a condition as this, Jesus came to set you free. You can either find freedom from this torment with the promises of God or remain in your state of internal suffering and pain with the lies of Satan.

Suicide may be the method of deliverance for pigs, but Jesus is the method of deliverance for man.

If you are feeling hopeless, tell someone. Get help. Professional counseling may sometimes provide the needed relief. But if this condition persists over time with no relief, don't overlook the possibility of a spiritual component.

One final word on this topic—be sure to avoid isolation.

Avoiding Isolation

Have you ever watched a nature program and marveled at how effective and efficient predators are at killing their prey? They almost always use the same technique: They select their prey—usually one that has wandered from the herd—and separate their victim further from the pack before they go in for the kill.

Isolation has always been, and will always be, a technique of the devil. God made us social creatures. Being isolated from other people, allows the devil to attack and destroy us. God knows this and that is why we are told to be in *koinonia* (or community) with fellow believers. If you, or someone you know, is suffering from emotional issues—depression, PTSD, or loneliness— the last place you want them is alone or feeling isolated. Isolation magnifies the problem and lets the devil attack relentlessly and unabated. The simple act of connecting with others defeats this very effective and covert technique of the Enemy.

TOOL #13
Jealousy and Envy

Bible Text

- "Wrath is cruel, anger is overwhelming, but who can stand before *jealousy*?" (Proverbs 27:4, emphasis added)
- "But if you have ***bitter jealousy and selfish ambition*** in your hearts, do not boast and be false to the truth. This is not the wisdom that comes down from above, but is earthly, unspiritual, demonic. For where jealousy and selfish ambition exist, there will be disorder and every vile practice." (James 3:14–16, emphasis added)
- "Now the works of the flesh are evident: sexual immorality, impurity, sensuality, idolatry, sorcery, enmity, strife, *jealousy*, fits of anger, rivalries, dissensions, divisions, *envy*, drunkenness, orgies, and things like these. I warn you, as I warned you before, that those who do such things will not inherit the kingdom of God." (Galatians 5:19–21, emphasis added)
- "***You shall not covet*** your neighbor's house; you shall not covet your neighbor's wife, or his male servant, or his female servant, or his ox, or his donkey, or anything that is your neighbor's." (Exodus 20:17, emphasis added)

Self-Test

Are you negative toward someone because of what they have accomplished? Do you find yourself always comparing yourself against someone else, or picking apart and belittling someone else's accomplishments? Are you resentful of the advantage someone has over you due to their material goods or some other reason? If so, you are being duped!

Emotional Partners with . . .

Insecurity, Fear, Anger, Resentment, Anxiety, Covetousness, Lust

God's Opposite Emotion

Contentment, Peace

Jealousy, or envy, was the motive for Jesus' arrest by the chief priests of the day.[430] It was also the reason for the opposition to the gospel in Acts by the religious leaders of the day.[431] As Christians, we are called to avoid the emotions of jealousy and envy.[432] Jesus told us that what comes from within is what defiles us, listing envy among many fleshly attributes.[433]

So why do we have such a hard time with these emotions? Our flesh demands attention, and it is never satisfied. It wants more money, praise, power, and better relationships. But *why* does our flesh demand more? Because we falsely believe that more of these things—more of what others have—will make us happy, content, and fulfilled.

Even Jesus' disciples fell into this trap when they were arguing about where they would be seated in heaven: *And James and John, the sons of Zebedee, came up to him and said to him, 'Teacher, we want you to do for us whatever we ask of you.' And he said to them, 'What do you want me to do for you?' And they said to him,* **'Grant us to sit, one at your right hand and one at your left,** *in your glory.'* (emphasis added) *Jesus said to them, 'You do not know what you are asking.'*[434]

Another well-known Bible story that demonstrates jealousy and envy can be found in the Bible story of Joseph (Genesis, chapters 37–50). This story reveals how jealousy and envy can play out among siblings.

Joseph's father loved him more than he loved his other sons, so much so that Joseph's father made him a special coat, which infuriated his brothers. Their *jealousy* and *envy* of their brother Joseph was so great that they sold him as a slave. However, God was with him.[435] Joseph not only survived but was elevated to the second in command under Pharaoh as the governor of Egypt.[436] As only God could have planned it, this series of events ended up saving his family and much of the nation of Israel from a great famine.

If you have fallen into the trap of jealousy and envy, then listen to what Paul has to say: *Not that I am speaking of being in need, for I have learned in whatever situation I am to be content. I know how to be brought low, and I know how to abound. In any and every circumstance, I have learned the secret of facing plenty and hunger, abundance and need.*[437]

So be content with what you have. And if you start to become jealous or envious of someone, change your focus to the blessings that God has already given to you, and be satisfied.

TOOL #14
Unforgiveness / Resentment

Bible Text

- "Then Peter came up and said to him, 'Lord, how often will my brother sin against me, and I *forgive* him? As many as seven times?' Jesus said to him, 'I do not say to you seven times, **but seventy-seven times**.'" (Matthew 18:21–22, emphasis added)
- "And whenever you stand praying, *forgive*, if you have anything against anyone, so that your Father who is in heaven may *forgive* you your trespasses." (Mark 11:25, emphasis added)
- "So if you are offering your gift at the altar and there you remember that your brother has something against you, leave your gift there before the altar and go. First *be reconciled* to your brother, and then come and offer your gift." (Matthew 5:23–24, emphasis added)
- "For if you *forgive* others their trespasses, your heavenly Father will also *forgive* you." (Matthew 6:14, emphasis added)
- "Let all bitterness and wrath and anger and clamor and slander be put away from you, along with all malice. Be kind to one another, tenderhearted, *forgiving one another*, as God in Christ forgave you." (Ephesians 4:31–32, emphasis added)

Self-Test

Do you believe you have a legitimate right to be mad at someone? Have you held a grudge against someone for a month, a year, or a decade? Do you mentally run a highlight reel of someone's offenses against you, over and over again in your mind? Are you waiting for someone to approach you and *ask you* to forgive them for their actions before you offer them your forgiveness? If so, you are being duped!

Emotional Partners with . . .

Resentment, Anger, Malice, Hatred, Bitterness, Guilt, Wrath

God's Opposite Emotion

Forgiveness, Love

Forgiveness has nothing to do with being right. It has nothing to do with having a legitimate reason to be angry with someone, and it is not even based on a system of equality or merit. It is a voluntary act of the will. It is giving up your "legal right" to harbor anger, resentment, or hatred against someone. Again, fault has nothing to do with forgiveness.

Forgiveness is not based on emotion. In fact, it operates in opposition to your emotions. If you are feeling anger, malice, or hatred toward someone, then forgiveness is the last thing you feel like doing. But it is the weapon that extinguishes these destructive emotions and snuffs them out.

Truly forgiving another is, in essence, giving up your "legal right" to be angry at that person. Again, it makes little difference whether or not you have a legitimate reason to be angry. Let me give you an example.

A young man was selling his home. A nice couple came to look at his house and made an offer for purchase. The sale went through, and the young man signed over the deed. A week later, the young man drove home from work, pulled up in front of his old house, walked in the front door, and sat down on the couch. The startled couple asked the young man what he was doing in their home.

He replied, "I just wanted to come back inside and look around a bit at my old house."

"But sir, they said, you are no longer the legal owner of this house, you don't have the 'legal right' to be on this property." And they escorted him out the door.

Like this young man, once we truly forgive someone for their wrong against us, we forfeit the "legal right" to possess this ground called *resentment*.

Why go to such great lengths to forgive others? I can think of six reasons.

1. If we forgive others, then God will forgive us.[438]
2. So that we can freely experience the fruit of the Spirit.[439]
3. Because unforgiveness gives the devil a foothold into our lives.[440]
4. To eliminate a potential stumbling block in our prayer life.[441]
5. Because God forgives our great sins, we should forgive others' of their little sins.[442]
6. It *frees* us from the person that we choose to forgive.

There is a great parable that Jesus gives us in Matthew 18:24–35 about a man who owed the king a vast sum of money. The man was brought before the king to answer for an enormous debt he owed—a debt that he most likely could never pay. He pled for mercy at the king's feet, and the king showed mercy, ordering him to be set free. After his release, this young man came across someone who owed him a small amount of money. Ignoring the great compassion the king had just shown to him, he had the man jailed until he could repay the debt. When the king got wind of this man's unforgiveness for another's debt, he had this man brought back before him, and rightfully handed over to the jailors because of his refusal to forgive another's debt.

This example typifies the lesson, that if God in His mercy can forgive our enormous sins against Him, then we should also forgive another's sins against us.

> *A forgiveness ought to be like a canceled note, torn in two and*
> *burned up, so that it can never be shown against the man.*
> —Henry Ward Beecher

> *Forgiveness is an act of the will, and the will can function*
> *regardless of the temperature of the heart.*
> —Corrie ten Boom

TOOL #15
Rejection

Bible Text

- "For you did not receive the spirit of slavery to fall back into fear, but you have received the *Spirit of adoption* as sons, by whom we cry, 'Abba! Father!' The Spirit himself *bears witness* with our spirit that **we are children of God**." (Romans 8:15–16, emphasis added)
- "He predestined us for *adoption* to himself as sons through Jesus Christ, according to the purpose of his will." (Ephesians 1:5, emphasis added)
- "For my father and mother have forsaken me, but *the LORD will take me in*." *(Psalm 27:10*, emphasis added*)*
- *"I am fearfully and wonderfully made." (Psalm 139:14*, emphasis added*)*

Self-Test

Do you take suggestions as criticism? Does the least little comment made to you make you feel bad? Do you have a difficult time taking constructive criticism? Do you find it difficult to say, "I'm wrong?" Do you examine yourself continually, wondering if something is wrong with you or believing that you don't measure up? Do you constantly worry about what other people are thinking of you? Do you always feel like you're the outsider? If so, you are being duped!

Emotional Partners with . . .

Fear, Unworthiness, Insecurity, Inferiority, Alienation, Abandonment, Loneliness, Isolation, Suicide, Unforgiveness, Resentment, Guilt, Anger, Emotional Anguish, Anxiety.

God's Opposite Emotion

Adoption, Acceptance, Love, Joy, Peace

Author, writer, and president of Touched by Grace, Incorporated, Ron Wood, in his book *Deliverance—Our Legacy*,[443] captures the spirit of what I wanted to say for this particular tool better than I could have said it myself. With his permission, I'm reprinting this excerpt (on the spirit of rejection) in its entirety for you. Although this tool section is longer in length than my other tools, it clearly and beneficially describes the many aspects of the spirit of rejection—a weapon of the Enemy that affects many in our world, and keeps many from experiencing their fullness in Christ. Mr. Wood's reprint is as follows:

The Spirit of Rejection

Even if you can't explain it, you can describe it. It is a reality in our soul. What is rejection and what does it do to people?

Rejection affects adults as well. Many people have come to full age still carrying the scars of emotional, physical, or sexual abuse. These men and women look normal but inside they are filled with terrible insecurity, anger, or fear. Others are sitting on a ticking emotional time bomb of resentment and rebellion, just waiting to boil over into rage. These scars, if left unhealed, will render a person incapable of entering into committed, wholesome, long-term relationships.

One particular problem is very common. It undermines the confidence of many Christians and interferes with true fellowship between friends. It is a lying spirit from our Enemy called a spirit of rejection. Rejection is the worst pain the human spirit can suffer. Anyone who has been abandoned, suffered abuse, or endured discrimination can relate to this kind of anguish. Let's examine this assault from the devil so we can recognize this form of mental oppression.

The Mindset of Rejection

First, the spirit of rejection refers to the mindset ingrained into us which tells us that we are unloved, unwanted, or will never be good enough. This may start in childhood. This mindset makes us strive to earn our acceptance. It makes people feel driven to perform in order to be approved. This mindset makes people feel they are loved for what they do rather than for whom they are. It is demeaning. It robs people of peace. The sad thing is that no amount of achievement is ever enough to satisfy it.

In other people, the injustice of being treated unfairly or rejected or disrespected makes them boil over in anger. They quit trying to fit in, rebel against everyone, and try to break out of the box being forced on them. In refusing to be a victim, they may victimize others. Resentment covers their soul like a dark shroud. They wind up in an emotional prison of their own making.

The mindset of rejection is the result of having believed a lie. It is a syndrome of self-talk that comes from being programmed with falsehoods. Having been told a lie often enough, victims begin to say, "Yes, it's true." The lie becomes accepted when the victim agrees with the accusations. They become their own accuser. They have internalized the venom. The deceit becomes a self-fulfilling prophecy. The victim begins to accept being rejected and thus sabotages his/her own relationships.

This mental stronghold of rejection is powerful. It will be torn down only when we find God's Word about our case and choose to believe the truth instead of a lie. Only God's truth can set us free. The truth will connect us to God's love. God's love will cure our wounded soul.

The Wounds of Rejection

The spirit of rejection also refers to the residue within our personality of being deeply wounded. This mental or emotional scarring can occur due to being neglected, abandoned or abused. It can also come from being betrayed, being shamed, or being made to feel unloved. Racial discrimination often leaves scars of rejection. Children who were abused sexually suffer cruelly from this inner hurt. Divorce can also leave a lingering, festering wound. The fear of being rejected can make a person run from relationships. They reject others before they themselves are rejected. They spiritually "stiff-arm" those who try to get close.

Just like you can be injured in your flesh and form a bruise or a scar, so you can be injured in your inner man and develop a sensitive place or perhaps a hardened area like a scab on your feelings. When that irritated place gets touched, a reaction occurs. The Bible speaks of having a "wounded spirit." One symptom of having a wounded spirit is that you feel absolutely nothing, like you are dead inside. Another symptom is that you are hypersensitive in that area and can explode at the slightest provocation. God's unconditional love, realized and received, can cure this wound.

A Lying Spirit Called Rejection

The spirit of rejection is also a specific lying spirit, a demonic messenger from the devil. This spirit whispers to people that they are unloved, not wanted, or are being ridiculed. The devil inflames insecurities and fears. This demon seeks to undermine the Christian's true standing before God as a saved, cleansed, redeemed child of God. He does this by lying and attempting to deceive the believer regarding God's love, the atoning work of the cross, and our righteousness before God.

This lying spirit comes between family members and divides brothers and sisters and makes them feel isolated. The spirit of rejection pours gasoline on the fires of racial hatred. This demon is very successful in splitting up marriages, churches, and partnerships. These are vital relationships that the Holy Spirit wants to establish between friends. These relationships are necessary in the body of Christ in order for God's work to be done. Disunity, like divorce, often has this lying spirit as its agent provocateur.

The Spirit of Adoption

To understand the spirit of rejection, we need to understand its opposite, which is the spirit of adoption. Romans 8 speaks of God's antidote to the spirit of rejection. This cure comes from our heavenly Father, through the grace of our Lord Jesus, and is born witness to by the Holy Spirit. It is called the spirit of adoption. This is the Holy Spirit telling us that God the Father loves us and Jesus accepts us.

Sin and suffering cause people to be cut off from God and mistreat one another. Many unsaved adults are mad at God or are so deeply hurt that they blame God. This resentment keeps them from feeling God's love. Their image of God is wrong so they refuse to accept Him. God's grace offers us pardon even while we are angry and sinning. God knows we need to be healed of the consequences of our sins and the injuries of sins committed against us by others, even our parents. The spirit of adoption comes from heaven's throne. It can also be mediated by unconditional acceptance through other Christians. When we accept one another in Christ, relationships in Christ's body are formed. The Holy Spirit connects us together and affirms our self-worth. We are empowered to appreciate each other.

God's merciful provision for our healing comes by Christ's atonement on the cross. It is made real and effective in our lives when we confess our sins and receive His forgiveness. Then the Holy Spirit comes into our heart and testifies that we have become God's child. He does this by bearing witness in our spirit that we are adopted by God. This is the spirit of adoption.

The spirit of adoption goes beyond believing that God loves us; it is the actual felt love of God, so that we are enabled to know that God loves us. It ends loneliness, literally forever!

This marvelous work of affirming who we are in Christ is the work of the Holy Spirit, the Spirit of Truth. He only bears witness to what is true. He testifies in our spirit that we are truly loved by God. The Holy Spirit uses the Scriptures as well as the affirming voice of God to tell us the truth about ourselves. God's voice will cause us to know God's thoughts toward us. Those thoughts, always in agreement with the Scriptures, will reprove us of our sin and will affirm us as His children, but will never condemn us or drive us away. God will always tell us the truth in a merciful way. Our response is to believe what God says. Believing the truth about what Jesus did for us and believing the truth about who we are in Christ sets us free. We need to believe both aspects of the truth—about Jesus and about ourselves.

The truth is, God likes us! His love toward us is tremendous. He wants us to really know Him and He wants to dwell in our hearts. God wants us to have fellowship with Him without condemnation. He accepts us into His family by virtue of Christ's work on the cross. He gives us a new identity as His sons and daughters.

Unlike some earthly fathers who failed us, our heavenly Father will never abandon us. He will not cast away His children. God maintains a relationship with His offspring so that we need never fear being rejected by Him. His love is steadfast. It is covenant love.

Recovering from Rejection

God understands rejection and knows how to remedy its pain. Christ was rejected when He came to His own people and they would not receive Him. *He came to that which was his own, but his own did not receive him.* He endured rejection when He bore our sins. *He was despised and rejected by men, a man of sorrows, and familiar with suffering. Like one from whom men hide their faces he was despised, and we esteemed him not* (Isaiah 53:3, NIV).

In other words, He specifically included in His suffering the substitutionary pain that was required to relieve us of our rejection. He bore it so we don't have to. On the cross, He felt the pain of being cut off from His heavenly Father. *My God, my God, why hast thou forsaken me?* (Matthew 27:46, NIV).

God understands your feelings. Therefore, He can be touched with your pain and is ready to heal you. *For we do not have a high priest who is unable to sympathize with our weaknesses, but we have one who has been tempted in every way, just as we are—yet was without sin. Let us then approach the throne of grace with confidence, so that we may receive mercy and find grace to help us in our time of need* (Hebrews 4:15–16, NIV).

Diagnosing Rejection

Here's how to diagnose if you suffer from the spirit of rejection. Three areas to examine are circumstances, emotions, and thoughts.

Let's start with your circumstances. Did you have an alcoholic parent? Were your parents divorced? Were you abused? Have you been abandoned or betrayed in marriage? Have you suffered from discrimination? Have you had to break away from a controlling relationship? Have you been repeatedly de-valued as a person? If you fit any of these categories, then you could be a victim of the rejection syndrome.

Now let's consider your emotional hot buttons. Do you have great difficulty receiving correction? Do you take it personally and get offended? Do you resent all authority? Do you get angry for no apparent reason? Or, do you have an unnatural need for everyone to like you? Does the need for approval control your decisions? Does insecurity sweep over you? Are you plagued by chronic self-doubt? Do you wrestle with chronic bouts of loneliness? At times, do you despair of life, or are you tempted to take your own life? If so, then you probably battle rejection.

In addition to these diagnostic questions, ask yourself this about your thought life. What kind of thoughts run through your mind when you are with a group of people? Would you characterize these thoughts as mostly negative or positive? The spirit of rejection inserts these kinds of thoughts: "These people don't love me." "They won't talk to me." "I'm not worthy to be here." "I know they are judging me." "They don't really want me here." This is mental torment that typifies the spirit of rejection.

Inner Healing and Deliverance

If these questions point to your problem as the spirit of rejection, then you need to take it to God in prayer. If the problem persists, get someone to pray with you for deliverance. But first, realize this, rejection often carries with it unforgiveness toward those who have offended you. We might have been an innocent victim, but we have to take responsibility now for our reactions. We can't do away with our will and our choices or our reactions. We can be sinned against, begin to cherish a grudge, and as a result, begin to sin against our oppressors. Unforgiveness is itself a sin.

God's grace will enable you to make a choice, to give forgiveness to all those for whom you hold grudges. This is important! Freedom won't come without this vital step of forgiving others. In this case, your forgiveness must be explicit, by name, and it must be spoken aloud even if it is only to God, and even if it is for someone who is now dead. That does not matter. God is the judge of the living and the dead. Don't make any exceptions.

Don't allow any resentment to remain in your heart. Healing begins with a decision to repent and to give undeserved forgiveness. Give away grace and God will give grace to you. Repent of all bitterness and hatred.

When forgiveness is totally accomplished, it paves the way for successful inner healing. Inner healing is the actual curing of your soul of the wounds and traumas you have suffered and accumulated. The finger of God touches the sore spots and makes them well. This is the transformation of the inner man, the end to unrighteous reactions and automatic defenses. It is being at peace in Christ.

Inner healing must accompany deliverance. The place where damaged emotions have given way to this mindset of rejection must be torn down, or else deliverance will be merely temporary.

The house of your thought life must be swept and cleaned, then occupied with God's reassuring truth and love. Determine to think God's thoughts. This is a decision you must make in order to be free. Automatic judgments, racial prejudices, and defensive reactions need to be removed.

Take all negative thoughts captive. Don't let them rule over your mind. Replace them with words and images of faith that come from your heavenly Father. Take God's thoughts, God's attitude, God's will as your creed, not the words of this sinful world.

Repeat what the Scriptures say until they replace the lies you've heard. Soak in God's Word and let it renew your mind. Meditate on the Scriptures until faith, hope, and self-acceptance fills your personality. This takes time but it is something you can do for yourself.

Renounce the spirit of rejection and stand against it. To renounce means to take a stand against something that you had previously been identified with or had claim to. Like renouncing your citizenship, it is a legal action that has power to affect your status. Pray aloud and say with your own words that rejection will not rule over you.

Instead, ask God for His fatherly affirmation. Ask God to give you the spirit of adoption. Every child needs to hear the father's voice saying, "You're mine and I love you!"

After you've prayed against rejection, read the Scriptures, especially the epistles of the New Testament. They teach us our new identity in Christ, to *lay aside the old self* and *be renewed in the spirit of your mind* (Ephesians 4:22–23, NASB). Replace the devil's lies with God's Word. Soak your thoughts in the truth of who God is, what He has done for you, and who you are in Christ. Banish all self-doubts. Tell yourself the truth until you truly believe it. Find new friends in Christ who affirm you and love you with God's love. *See how great a love the Father has bestowed on us, that we would be called children of God* (1 John 3:1, NASB).

*The seventy-two returned with joy, saying, 'Lord, even the demons are subject to us in your name!' And he said to them, 'I saw Satan fall like lightning from heaven. Behold, I have given you authority to tread on serpents and scorpions, and over all the power of the enemy, and nothing shall hurt you. Nevertheless, do not rejoice in this, that the spirits are subject to you, **but rejoice that your names are written in heaven.**'*

—Luke 10:17–20 (ESV, emphasis added)

APPENDIX

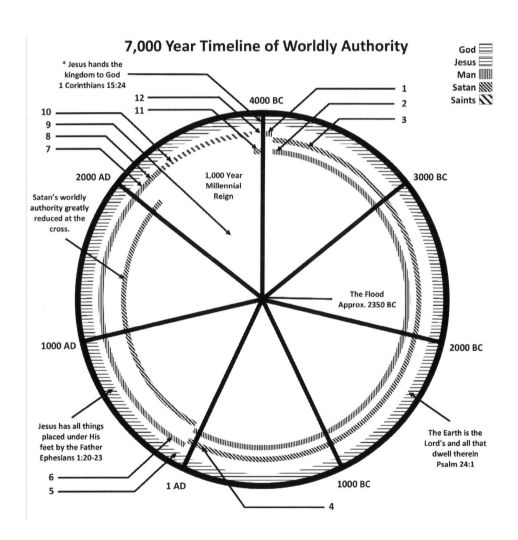

7,000 Year Timeline of Worldly Authority

God
Jesus
Man
Satan
Saints

* Jesus hands the
kingdom to God
1 Corinthians 15:24

12
11
10
9
8
7

2000 AD

Satan's worldly
authority greatly
reduced at the
cross.

1000 AD

Jesus has all things
placed under His
feet by the Father
Ephesians 1:20-23

6
5

1 AD

4000 BC

1,000 Year
Millennial
Reign

1
2
3

3000 BC

The Flood
Approx. 2350 BC

2000 BC

The Earth is the
Lord's and all that
dwell therein
Psalm 24:1

1000 BC

4

Chart Key

1. Adam and Eve: Given authority over the earth by God. (Genesis 1:28)

2. Fall of man: Adam and Eve sin and relinquish partial authority to the devil. (Genesis 3:6, 16–19)

3. The devil's earthly authority begins with the fall of man. (Genesis 3:15)

4. The devil tempts Jesus in the desert, stating to Jesus: "All authority has been given to me, and I can give it to whomever I choose." (Luke 4:5–6) (Approximately 30 A.D.)

5. Jesus on the Cross: Strips the devil, principalities, and powers of much of their worldly authority. (Colossians 2:15) Upon assentation to the Father, all power and authority in Heaven and Earth given to Jesus by the Father. (Matthew 28:18, 1 Peter 3:22) (Approximately 33 A.D.)

6. The Church: Regains its earthly authority through the coming of the Holy Spirit at Pentecost. (Luke 24:49, Acts 2:1–4, Matthew 16:18–19) (Approximately 33 A.D.)

7. Rapture of the Church: Church and Holy Spirit removed from the earth. (1 Thessalonians 4:16–17, 2 Thessalonians 2:7)

8. Tribulation Period: The devil is allowed to regain temporary authority over the earth. (Matt. 24:15, Revelation 13:12–16)

9. The devil is cast into the pit for 1,000 years. (Revelation 20:2)

10. Risen, saints return to rule with Christ for 1,000 years. (Revelation 20:4)

11. The devil is released to the earth for a short period. (Revelation 20:3)

12. The devil, fallen angels, and demons thrown in hell for all eternity. (Revelation 20:10, Matthew 25:41, Matthew 8:29)

*Jesus hands over the kingdom to God the Father. (1 Corinthians 15:24)

ABOUT THE AUTHOR

Richard (Dick) Oswalt has practiced law in the state of Kansas for over thirty years. In his early thirties, he had a bout with spiritual warfare that forever changed his life. "Growing up in the Presbyterian Church, I had never even heard the term 'spiritual warfare' let alone knew what it was," he remarked. Forced to confront an issue that he didn't understand or even knew existed, Dick spent the next twenty years developing his knowledge of the true nature of spiritual warfare, the spiritual laws that this war operates under, and why it destroys so many lives.

When Jesus said the Spirit of the Lord was upon Him to *proclaim deliverance to the captives* (Luke 4:18, BLB), one of the areas that He came to deliver us from was Satan's strongholds and bondages. The Bible tells us that Satan's objective is to kill, steal, and destroy mankind, and he uses his strongholds and bondages to do just that. This book is designed to teach the untaught on this important subject known as spiritual warfare—a subject every believer needs to understand—a subject greatly overlooked by the Church—and a subject the devil hopes you never learn. For those who refuse to believe such things exist, it matters not to the spiritual entities that roam the earth and inflict harm and torment on those who fall subject to their ways.

For more information on this and other titles by Richard E. Oswalt, J.D. please visit www.InTheDevilsToolbox.com.

NOTES

Introduction
1. Mark 16:17
2. Matthew 24:35, Luke 21:33
3. Mark 11:24–25, Mathew 21:22

Chapter Two
4. Revelation 12:7–9
5. Ephesians 2:1–2, emphasis added
6. 1 Peter 5:8
7. Revelation 12:3–4
8. With the exception of the angels who abandoned their original estate in the days of Noah, and that are bound in chains awaiting judgment. 2 Peter 2:4 and Jude 1:6.
9. Old Testament—Leviticus 17:7, Deuteronomy 32:16–17, Psalm 106:36–38; New Testament—1 Corinthians 10:20, Galatians 4:8
10. Mark 1:23–25, Mark 5:1–14
11. Matthew 10:1, 7–8, Mark 6:13, and Luke 10:17

Chapter Three
12. The Greek translation of the Old Testament known as the Septuagint used by the early Christian church likewise states: "In the beginning, God created the heavens and the earth."
13. Our prayers reach the throne room of God. See 1 John 5:14–15, 1 Peter 3:12, Revelation 8:4.
14. Ephesians 6:12
15. 2 Kings 19:35
16. 2 Kings 6:16–17
17. 2 Kings 6:15

18. 2 Kings 6:18
19. An excellent overview on the dangers of engaging in warfare against these entities in the second heaven (unless specifically instructed to by the Lord) can be found in the books: John Paul Jackson, *Needless Casualties of War* (CITY: PUBLISHER, YEAR). Additional resources on the requirement to be specifically called on by the Lord before engaging in such warfare: Rebecca Greenwood, *Authority to Tread* (CITY: PUBLISHER, YEAR); Don Dickerman, *Keep the Pigs Out* (CITY: PUBLISHER, YEAR); C. Peter Wagner, *Warfare Prayer* (CITY: PUBLISHER, YEAR); Michael Bradley, "Engaging with Demons in the 2nd Heaven" www.bible-knowledge.com/engaging-with-demons-in-the-2nd-heaven; John Paul Jackson, *Dreams & Mysteries – The Mystery of Spiritual Warfare*, https://www.youtube.com/watch?v=jG2rnSSC08M.

    "Engaging with Demons in the 2nd Heaven" by Michael Bradley, www.bible-knowledge.com/engaging-with-demons-in-the-2nd-heaven.

    John Paul Jackson, *Dreams & Mysteries – The Mystery of Spiritual Warfare*, https://www.youtube.com/watch?v=jG2rnSSC08M.
20. 1 Peter 5:8
21. Job 1:7 and Job 2:2
22. John 10:10, See also Enoch 15:11
23. Revelation 2:13

Chapter Four

24. "Gabriele Veneziano," Wikipedia, last modified February 29, 2020, https://en.wikipedia.org/wiki/Gabriele_Veneziano. Gabriele Veneziano, the Italian theoretical physicist, made his breakthrough discovery while working at the European Organization for Nuclear Research.
25. Holger Nielsen of the Niels Bohr Institute, Leonard Susskind of Stanford University, and Yoichiro Nambu of the University of Chicago.
26. "John Henry Schwarz," Wikipedia, last modified April 25, 2020, https://en.wikipedia.org/wiki/John_Henry_Schwarz. These three physicists who made the argument are John Schwarz of the Californian Institute of Technology, Joel Schrek of the Ecole Normale Superieure, and Tamiaki Yoneya of Hokkaido University.
27. The string theory was again modified in 1995 by Edward Witten, revealing an eleventh dimension known as the "M" theory. While not changing the above analysis, this finding certainly proves that we live in a multi-dimensional world.
28. Dr. Chuck Missler, "The Realm of Angels," Koinonia House. This article

was originally published in the March 2012 *Personal Update News Journal*. Dr. Chuck Missler also discusses the ten-dimensional universe in a video segment called "Angels: Volume One" recorded in 2011 published by Koinonia House.

29. The M-Theory, first introduced in 1995, suggests an 11-dimensional world (10 spatial dimensions and one time dimension)

30. Genesis 18:1–15

31. Genesis 19:1–5, 15–16

32. "Who's Who," Geneve internationale, accessed July 14, 2020, https://www.geneve-int.ch/european-organization-nuclear-research-cern-0

33. "The God Particle," Aspen Ideas Festival, accessed July 14, 2020, https://www.aspenideas.org/sessions/the-god-particle

34. Lewis Page, "'Something may come through' dimensional 'doors' at LHC," *The Register*, November 6, 2009, https://www.theregister.com/2009/11/06/lhc_dimensional_portals/. Additional resources on the Hadron Collider and particle accelerators: Lewis Page, "Dimensional portal incursion at the LHC!" *The Register*, April 1, 2010, https://www.theregister.com/2010/04/01/lhc_fifth_dimension_incursion/; Lewis Page, "Boffins hope for dimensional portal event at LHC by 2013!" *The Register*, February 1, 2011, https://www.theregister.com/2011/02/01/lhc_upgrade_shutdown_postponed/; "Extra dimensions, gravitons, and tiny black holes," CERN, https://home.cern/science/physics/extra-dimensions-gravitons-and-tiny-black-holes; Matt Ward, "Cern, the Large Hadron Collider and Bible Prophecy," Prophecy Update, https://www.prophecyupdate.com/cern-the-large-hadron-collider-and-bible-prophecy.html; Kristine Larsen, "ALICE and the Apocalypse: Particle Accelerators as Death Machines in Science Fiction," *MOSF Journal of Science Fiction*, vol. 2, no. 1, https://publish.lib.umd.edu/?journal=scifi&page=article&op=view&path%5B%5D=330. Additional information found at: Joseph Farrell, "Cern Admits It Seeks Contact with Parallel Universes," The Giza Death Star, October 16, 2020, https://gizadeathstar.com/2020/10/cern-admits-it-seeks-contact-with-parallel-universes/.

35. Ceri Parker, "7 things you didn't know about CERN and the strange world of particle physics," World Economic Forum, Global Agenda, September 7, 2016.

36. News and Information for End Times, Matt Ward, http://www.raptureready.com

37. God is the Creator of all things: Colossians 1:16–20, Psalms 115:15, 124:8, 134:3, 146:5–6. God (Jesus) has all things under His Authority and Control: Matthew 28:18

38. Psalm 91, Psalm 34:7
39. 1 John 4:4

Chapter Five
40. Luke 4:6–7 (NIV). See also Matthew 4:1–11, Mark 1:12–13
41. Genesis 1:26–28, Matthew 16:19
42. Colossians 2:15 (NIV) emphasis added
43. Matthew 28:18; see also Ephesians 1:20–23
44. Luke 4:18, Isaiah 61:1, John 8:36
45. 1 Peter 5:8–9

Chapter Six
46. Mark 1:32, 5:7, 7:25, 9:25, Luke 8:31
47. Matthew 10:1, 7–8, Mark 6:7, 13, Luke 10:17–20

Chapter Seven
48. Luke 8:4–8, also found in Matthew 13:3–9 and Mark 4:3–9
49. Luke 4:6–7, Matthew 13:18–23, Mark 4:13–20
50. 2 Corinthians 2:11
51. 2 Corinthians 11:3
52. Ephesians 6:16
53. Matthew 16:23
54. Matthew 16:18–19
55. Luke 22:31
56. Acts 13:22
57. I am aware that 2 Samuel 24:1 states, "Again the anger of the LORD was kindled against Israel, and he incited David against them, saying, 'Go, number Israel and Judah.'" This verse is an example of God's use of Satan, in His great wisdom, for His holy purposes.
58. Matthew 16:17, 2 Corinthians 11:3
59. Luke 4:6–7; see also Matthew 4:9
60. John 12:31, 14:30, 16:11, 2 Corinthians 4:4, 1 John 5:19
61. Galatians 5:22–23 (KJV)
62. Colossians 2:9–10 (NKJV)
63. John 3:16, Romans 6:1–12
64. Romans 7:19
65. Colossians 3:5–10
66. Ephesians 2:3
67. Galatians 5:19–21

68. Galatians 5:16–21
69. Colossians 3:2
70. Galatians 5:22–23a
71. 1 John 2:15–16
72. 2 Peter 2:19
73. Dr. Robert Lustig, Professor of Pediatric Endocrinology at the University of California, San Francisco. "Robert Lustig," Wikipedia, last modified July 3, 2020, https://en.wikipedia.org/wiki/Robert_Lustig. Dr. Lustig's specialty is in neuroendocrinology, which is the study of the interaction between the nervous system (brain, spinal cord, and nerves) and the endocrine system (the brain's regulation of the hormonal activity in the body.
74. In an interview with Ashley Mason discussing his new book *The Hacking of the American Mind* as presented on the University of California Television (UCTV—www.uctv.tv) http://robertlustig.com/hacking/.
75. Other sources citing the addictive nature: Butler Center for Research, "Drug Abuse, Dopamine, and the Brain's Reward System: Why Do People Use Alcohol & Drugs Even After Facing Consequences?" September 1, 2015, https://www.hazeldenbettyford.org/education/bcr/addiction-research/drug-abuse-brain-ru-915; William M. Struthers, Ph.D., *The Effect of Porn on the Male Brain*, Feb 1, 2013, https://www.equip.org/article/the-effects-of-porn-on-the-male-brain-3/; Carol Kopp, "Getting High On Shopping," December 7, 2005, https://www.cbsnews.com/newsgetting-high-on-shopping.
76. John 4:14, 6:35 (NIV)

Chapter Eight
77. Romans 7:4, Galatians 5:18, Romans 7:6, 2 Corinthians 3:11, 13, Colossians 2:14
78. Ephesians 2:8–9
79. John 13:34–35, Matthew 22:36–40, Mark 12:28–31, Matthew 5:17–30, Romans 7:6, John 15:12, 17,
80. Romans 8:3–4, Matthew 5:17
81. Romans 8:2
82. Matthew 22:36–40
83. John 13:34–35, John 15:12, John 15:17
84. 1 John 3:15, Matthew 5:22
85. Matthew 5:27–28
86. Romans 6:15
87. *Holman Bible Dictionary*, ed. Thomas Butler. (Nashville: Holman Bible Publishers, 1991), s.v. "Sin."

88. Romans 6:10, Hebrews 9:26
89. Colossians 2:14, Romans 10:9
90. Ephesians 4:26–27
91. Romans 3:10, Romans 3:23, 49, Psalms 14:2-3, Psalm 53:2–3
92. Acts 10:43, 1 John 1:7, 1 John 1:9, Act 13:38–39, Ephesians 1:7, Hebrews 9:15, Psalm 103:12, Romans 3:23-24, Act 2:38–39, Mark 2:10, Romans 6:23
93. Galatians 3:10, 13, Deuteronomy 27:26
94. Romans 7:6, Roman 6:14–15, Galatians 2:16, Romans 8:1–2
95. Matthew 5:21–22, Matthew 5:28, John 13:34-35, Mark 12:30–31
96. 2 Thessalonians 3:3, 1 John 5:18, Luke 10:19, Psalm 91:1-16, John 10:28–30
97. *Merriam-Webster*, s.v. "Trespass," accessed November 7, 2017, https://www.merriam-webster.com/dictionary/trespass.
98. Proverbs 15:26
99. Psalms 94:11
100. Matthew 5:28
101. Exodus 20:17 and Deuteronomy 5:21
102. Matthew 22:36–39
103. Hosea 4:6

Chapter Nine
104. Revelation 12:10
105. 1 Peter 5:8
106. Deuteronomy 18:10–13, Leviticus 9:31 and 20:6, 1 Chronicles 10:13, Proverbs 28:13
107. Leviticus 26:40–42
108. Deuteronomy 24:16
109. Ezekiel 18:20; see also Jeremiah 31:30
110. Proverbs 20:7, Psalm 103:17–18, 112:2
111. Mary L. Lake, *What Witches Don't Want Christians to Know [Expanded Edition]*, (CreateSpaceIndependent Publishing Platform, 2014).
112. Genesis 1:27, also, Transhumanism & the Human Enchancement Revolution, Tom Horn, ISN Mentoring Session aired on ISN Mentoring Network. Viewed on YouTube. March 7, 2020. https://www.youtube.com/watch?v=V-zKC00qvGE
113. The Evil Gene and the Lucifer Effect, Tom Horn, © 2020 Prophecy Watchers. Accessed December 23, 2020. https://podcasts.apple.com/us/podcast/tom-horn-the-evil-gene-and-lucifer-effect/id1162811009?i=1000495051338
114. Genesis 1:27, also, Horn, "Transhumanism & the Human Enchancement Revolution."

115. More on this topic can be found in Dr. Ed Murphy's book *The Handbook for Spiritual Warfare [Revised and Updated]*, (Nashville, Thomas Nelson Publishers, 1996).

116. Rod Dreher, "Exorcism and the Shaman's Apprentice," *The American Conservative*, November 26, 2018, https://www.theamericanconservative.com/dreher/exorcism-shaman-apprentice-demonic. Also discussed in Murphy, *Spiritual Warfare*, chapters 54–56.

117. Additional information on these topics and the topic of religious abuse can be found in Lake, *Witches*.

118. Isaiah 61:1, Luke 4:18

119. John 10:10

120. Mark 16:9, Luke 8:2. BIBLETOOLS.org notes that although Mark 16:9–10 appears in the King James and New King James versions, many other translations either label this section as an appendix or leave it in the footnotes, as does the Revised Standard Version of the Bible.

121. Job 1:12, Job 2:6

122. 1 Samuel 16:14, 1 Samuel 18:10

123. 1 Samuel 13:1–12

124. 1 Samuel 13:14

125. 1 Samuel 15:3

126. 1 Samuel 15:8–9

127. 1 Samuel 15:26

128. 1 Samuel 16:14

129. 1 John 5:18

Chapter Ten

130. Galatians 5:22–23

131. Matthew 21:12

132. John 11:35

133. *Webster's New World Dictionary*, fourth edition. (Boston: Houghton Mifflin Harcourt, 2010), s.v. "Emotion."

134. Randal L. Ross, *Tapping the Power of Your Emotions*, (Lake Mary, Fla.: Creation House Press, 1996).

135. 1 Peter 5:7 NIV

136. John 8:32

137. James 3:14–16, emphasis added

138. 2 Timothy 1:7

139. Jerry L. Tennant, *Healing is Voltage*. (Charleston, SC: Createspace, 2010).

140. Lorie Johnson, "The Deadly Consequences of Unforgiveness," *CBN News*,

June 22, 2015, https://www1.cbn.com/cbnnews/healthscience/2015/june/
the-deadly-consequences-of-unforgiveness.

141. Michael Barry, *The Forgiveness Project* (Grand Rapids, MI: Kregel
Publications, 2010).

142. Ibid

143. Philippians 4:8, Colossians 3:2

Chapter Eleven

144. 2 Corinthians 10:5

145. "80% Of Thoughts Are Negative…95% Are Repetitive," *The Miracle Zone*,
March 2, 2012, Date Accessed May 11, 2020, https://faithhopeand
psychology.wordpress.com/2012/03/02/80-of-thoughts-are-negative-95-
are-repetitive/.

146. 2 Corinthians 10:5

147. Ibid

148. Ibid

149. Ibid

150. Philippians 4:8

151. Galatians 5:16–26

152. 1 Corinthians 3:16

153. Proverbs 14:12, 16:25

Chapter Twelve

154. Jeremiah 17:9–10

155. Psalm 4:7, Isaiah 65:14

156. John 16:6, James 3:14, Leviticus 19:17

157. 1 John 3:20

158. Matthew 13:19, Luke 8:15

159. Romans 10:10

160. Mark 11:23

161. "80% Of Thoughts Are Negative…95% Are Repetitive," *The Miracle Zone*,
March 2, 2012. Accessed May 11, 2020, https://faithhopeandpsychology.
wordpress.com/2012/03/02/80-of-thoughts-are-negative-95-are-repetitive/.

Chapter Thirteen

162. 1 John 2:16

163. Genesis 3:6

164. Luke 4:3, 4

165. Genesis 3:6

166. Luke 4:5–8 (NIV)
167. Genesis 3:6
168. Luke 4:9–12
169. 1 John 2:16
170. Galatians 5:22–23
171. Colossians 2:10
172. Galatians 5:22–23
173. John 4:14, Ephesians 1:13–14
174. Amanda Prestigiacomo, "Transgenderism Not Supported by Science," *The Daily Wire*, August 23, https://www.dailywire.com/news/report-
175. Jeremiah 1:5, Psalms 139:13–14
176. Revelation 12:10
177. 1 Corinthians 15:55
178. John 14:6
179. 2 Thessalonians 2:11
180. Ephesians 1:13, Ephesians 4:30, 2 Corinthians 1:21, 2 Corinthians 5:5
181. Ephesians 1:13

Chapter Fourteen
182. 1 Peter 5:8
183. Ephesians 6:10–18
184. James 4:7
185. Ephesians 6:17
186. 1 Corinthians 3:16, 6:19–20
187. Frank and Ida Mae Hammond, *Pigs In The Parlor*, (Kirkwood, MO: Impact Christian Books, 2003). Murphy, *Spiritual Warfare*.
188. John 10:10

Chapter Fifteen
189. Matthew 28:18
190. Mark 16:17–18
191. Mark 4:39, Matthew 8:27
192. John 5:1–9
193. Luke 8:26–37
194. Mark 2:1–12
195. John 11:38–44
196. Luke 23:43
197. John 5:22–27
198. Matthew 28:18 (NKJV)

199. Luke 9:1, emphasis added
200. Luke 10:19
201. Acts 1:3, John 14:18, Acts 2:1–4
202. Acts 1:12–13
203. John 16:7
204. Acts 2:1–41
205. Acts 4:1–8
206. Psalm 51:10–12, 1 Samuel 10:6–10, Numbers 27:12–23, Judges 3:10, Micah 3:8, Isaiah 63:11, Nehemiah 9:20
207. Acts 2:1–4
208. John 3:1–16, Acts 2:38
209. Ephesians 1:13–14, Ephesians 4:30, 2 Corinthians 1:21–22
210. Galatians 5:22–23
211. John 16:8
212. Acts 9:31, Isiah 51:2
213. Galatians 5:18, Romans 8:14
214. Romans 8:26–27
215. John 14:26
216. 1 Corinthians 12:4–11. Spiritual gifts include, but are not limited to: 1. word of knowledge, 2. word of wisdom, 3. gift of healing, 4. gift of prophecy, 5. gift of faith, 6. the working of miracles, 7. the discerning of spirits, 8. different kinds of tongues, and 9. interpretation of tongues. I believe the gift of deliverance is not listed as one of the many spiritual gifts allocated to certain individuals in the body of Christ, because this is an ability that all believers possess, (when we are in a proper relationship with the Lord, and walking in His power and authority). I believe this ability to deliver ourselves from the grasp of the Enemy applies to not only us, but allows us to deliver others as well.
217. John 16:13
218. Acts 1:8
219. Colossians 2:10
220. Acts 3:2–10
221. Acts 9:33–34
222. Acts 9:36–41
223. Acts 14:8–10
224. Acts 20:9–12
225. Acts16:16–18
226. Acts 19:11–12
227. Mark 16:17–18 (NKJV), emphasis added

228. John 14:12–14 (NKJV), emphasis added
229. Bible Hub, https://biblehub.com/str/greek/1411.htm, s.v., "Dunamis." Word Hippo, https://www.wordhippo.com/what-is/the-meaning-of/greek-word-4aa80b3b9110a582b5f9eccb6e46fcfcce16e5eb.html, s.v., "Exousia."
230. Acts 1:8, 1 Corinthians 4:20
231. Matthew 16:25
232. John Paul Jackson, "Power and Authority," accessed June 24, 2020, https://streamsministries.com/shop/power-and-authority/.
233. John Paul Jackson, "The Difference Between Power and Authority," accessed June 24, 2020, https://streamsministries.com/shop/power-and-authority/.
234. Ephesians 6:18
235. Philippines 4:6
236. Acts 3:6–7, Luke 10:1–17, Acts 5:15–16, Acts16:16–18
237. Mark 16:15–18, emphasis added
238. Mark 16:17
239. Ephesians 6:12

Chapter Sixteen
240. John 16:23b, emphasis added
241. 1 John 5:14, emphasis added
242. James 4:6, 4:10
243. Romans 8:9
244. Jude 20
245. Deuteronomy 32:30, Joshua 23:10, Leviticus 26:8
246. Matthew 6:12, emphasis added
247. Matthew 6:14
248. *Merriam-Webster Dictionary*, (retrieved October 27, 2018)
249. Daniel 10:20

Chapter Seventeen
250. Matthew 24:35, emphasis added
251. "List of 3000 Promises in the Bible," *Believer's Portal*, https://believers portal.com/list-of-3000-promises-in-the-bible/. "How Many Bible Promises Are There?" Bible Info, https://www.bibleinfo.com/en/questions/how-many-bible-promises-are-there. According to one account, there are 3,573 promises in the Bible.
252. 2 Corinthians 10:4–5

Chapter Eighteen

253. *Webster's Dictionary*, http://webstersdictionary1828.com/Dictionary/deliverance, s.v. "Deliverance."

254. Luke 10:20

255. Mark 16:17

256. Graham, Billy. *Angels*, (Nashville, Tenn.: Thomas Nelson, 1995) pg 73.

257. Missler, *"Realm of Angels."*

258. Derek Prince, *They Shall Expel Demons*, (Grand Rapids: Chosen Books, 1998).

259. 1 Corinthians 3:16, 6:19–20

260. 1 Thessalonians 5:23

261. How do we know we have three distinct parts to our makeup? The Bible makes numerous references to the flesh or the body, and we are told that in Hebrews 4:12, "For the word of God is living and active, sharper than any two-edged sword, piercing to the division of soul and spirit, of joints and of marrow . . .

262. Nee, Watchman, *The Spiritual Man*, (Anaheim, Calif.: Christian Fellowship Publishers, 1968) chapter 15.

263. 1 Corinthans 3:16

264. Nee, *Spiritual Man.*

265. Galatians 5:17 (NIV)

266. Romans 7:18 (NASB)

267. Revelations 12:7–9

268. Jeremiah 17:9

269. Ephesians 4:26

270. Holy Bible Recovery Version, (Living Stream Ministry, 2002–2020) online. recoveryversion.bible.

271. Doris M. Wagner, ed. "Why a Christian Can Have a Demon," in *Ministering Freedom from Demonic Oppression: Proven Foundations for Deliverance* (Book 1), (Colorado Springs: Wagner Publications, 2002). Used by permission.

272. This story is found in all four of the gospels—Matthew 21:12–13, Mark 11:15–19, Luke 19:45–48, John 2:13–16

273. Luke 11:24–26. Eckhardt, "Demon."

274. Eckhardt, "Demon"

275. Prince, *Expel*

276. Ibid

277. Hammond, *Parlor*

278. Murphy, *Handbook*

279. Matthew 15:22–28, Mark 7:25–30, and Mark 10:51
280. Proverbs 28:13, 2 Corinthians 4:2 (NIV)
281. Matthew 12:29, Mark 3:27
282. Mark 16:17
283. Mark 9:29
284. Matthew 12:43–45, Luke 5:24–26, Luke 11:25
285. Matthew 16:18
286. Hebrews 13:8

Chapter Nineteen
287. Ephesians 6:10–18
288. John 14:6
289. John 8:31–32
290. John 8:34–44
291. John 17:17
292. Galatians 1:16, Acts 26:17
293. Exodus 2:11–12, Acts 8:1
294. Galatians 1:8
295. 1 John 4:1–6
296. Romans 6:23, John 1:29, 8:2–11, 1 John 1:29, Acts 20:28
297. Colossians 3:15–17
298. Hebrews 11:6
299. Ephesians 2:8–9
300. Romans 4:5, 5:1, Galatians 3:24
301. Acts 26:18
302. Hebrews 11:1
303. Romans 10:14–17
304. John 3:16
305. Hebrews 4:12

Chapter Twenty
306. Genesis 1:26
307. Revelation 4:11
308. Isaiah 43:21
309. Isaiah 43:7
310. Romans 6:23
311. Isaiah 59:1–2, 2 Thessalonians 1:8–9, Galatians 5:4–5, Genesis 3:23
312. John 19:30
313. Matthew 27:51

314. Psalm 51:10–12, 1 Samuel 10:6–10, Numbers 27:12–23, Judges 3:10, Micah 3:8, Isaiah 63:11, Nehemiah 9:20, Hebrews 11:5, 2 Kings 2:11, Genesis 5:24, Luke 1:41–44
315. 1 Thessalonians 5:19
316. Galatians 5:22–23
317. Ephesians 1:3
318. Colossians 2:10
319. John 4:14

The Devil's 15 Emotional Tools of Attack
320. John 10:10
321. 1 Peter 5:8
322. 1 Kings 22:22, 2 Chronicles 18:19–21
323. Matthew 13:19
324. John 10:10
325. Used by author's permission, Roy Sauzek, *The Death of a Pet—for Christians*, booklet, (Wellington, KS: Take His Heart to the World Ministries), http://www.takehisheart.com/pdf/deathpet.pdf.

Tool #1
326. Proverbs 1:7, Proverbs 8:13, Matthew 10:28, Ecclesiastes 12:13, Job 28:28, Psalms 33:8, Proverbs 14:26, Proverbs 14:27, Deuteronomy 10:12, Psalms 111:10, Psalms 25:14, Proverbs 3:7, Proverbs 86:11, Luke 1:50, Psalms 34:9, Proverbs 19:23, and Philippians 2:12–13
327. Philippians 4:19
328. 2 Corinthians 5:7
329. 1 Corinthians 2:16
330. https://www.dictionary.com/browse/legalism. Retrieved August 22, 2020.

Tool #2
331. Matthew 6:8

Tool #3
332. The account in Acts 1:16–19 says he fell headlong in a field; his body burst and his intestines spilled out.
333. Acts 1:13–15, 2:14–36, 3:1, 3:11–26, 4:8–26, 5:29–32, 10:34–43, 15:7–11
334. Acts 3:1–10, 5:1–15, 9:32–42
335. Acts 5:17–21, 12:6–11
336. Acts 10:1–49

337. David Reardon, "The Abortion/Suicide Connection," *The Post-Abortion Review*, 1993, https://www.afterabortion.org/PAR/V1/n2/SUICIDE.htm.

338. Reardon, "A Survey of Psychological Reactions," (Springfield, IL: Elliot Institute, 1987).

339. James 2:10

340. 1 John 1:9

Tool #4

341. Romans 8:14, Galatians 5:18

342. John 16:13

343. Hebrews 9:14, Romans 3:22–26, Acts 13:38–39

344. Mark 2:5–12, John 8:2–11

345. 1 John 5:19–20

346. Romans 10:9

Tool #5

347. Proverbs 22:24–25

348. Ephesians 4:26–27

349. Proverbs 25:28

350. Proverbs 14:29, 15:18, 16:32

351. Luke 11:4, Matthew 6:12

Tool #6

352. Josh McDowell, *More Than a Carpenter*, (Living Books, 1980)

353. Only the apostle John's life was spared. He was exiled to the island Patmos where he penned the book of Revelation.

354. 1 John 1:9

355. Luke 7:37–38

356. Luke 7:40–43

357. Luke 7:47

358. 1 Corinthians 15:55

359. Hebrews 2:15

360. Romans 10:9

Tool #8

361. Ephesians 1:13–14

362. Galatians 5:22–23

363. Colossians 2:9–10, Psalm 37:4

364. Daniel 10:13, Mark 5:10

365. Office of Public and Intergovernmental Affairs—"VA Releases National Suicide Data Report" June 18, 2018. https://www.va.gov/opa/pressrel/pressrelease.cfm?id=4074

366. "60 Minutes," season 51, episode 35, aired June 6, 2019, CBS.

Tool #9

367. Isaiah 14:12–15

368. Proverbs 16:18

369. Mark 7:21–22

370. Colossians 2, Galatians 1–3, 5:4

371. Luke 18:14

372. Philippians 4:6

373. Proverbs 16:18

Tool #10

374. John 15:13

375. *Merriam-Webster*, s.v. "Lust," https://www.merriam-webster.com/dictionary/lust.

376. Matthew 5:28, 1 John 2:16

377. Exodus 20:14, Hebrews 13:4, 1 Corinthians 6:9

378. 1 Corinthians 6:18, 1 Corinthians 6:9–10

379. Deuteronomy 27:20–23, Leviticus 18:6–18, 1 Corinthians 5:1–2

380. Leviticus 18:22–24, Romans 1:26–28, 1 Corinthians 6:9, 1 Timothy 1:8–11

381. Matthew 18:6, Mark 9:42, Luke 17:2

382. Leviticus 18:23, Exodus 22:19, Deuteronomy 27:21, Leviticus 20:15–16

383. 1 Corinthians 6:19

384. Prince, *Expel*, 188–191. Hammond, *Parlor*, 115. Murphy, *Handbook*, 136–143, 145, 147

385. Matthew 12:43–45

386. Luke 11:26, Matthew 12:45

387. Lawrence Mayer and Paul McHugh, "Sexuality and Gender," *The New Atlantis*, Fall 2016. https://www.thenewatlantis.com/publications/part-two-sexuality-mental-health-outcomes-and-social-stress-sexuality-and-gender.
    See also: Natasha Tracy, "Homosexuality and Suicide: LGBT Suicide – A Serious Issue." *Healthy Place*, April 12, 2013. https://www.healthyplace.com/gender/glbt-mental-health/homosexuality-and-suicide-lgbt-suicide-a-serious-issue. According to this study done on homosexual suicide rates, and suicide attempts, LGBT youth attempt suicide three times more frequently than their heterosexual counterparts. While a Canadian study

estimated that the risk of suicide among LGBT youth is fourteen times higher than for heterosexual youth. An additional report found that of transgender people, between 30–45% reports having attempted suicide.

388. Ibid

389. Ibid

390. Ibid

391. Prince, *Expel.*

392. Ibid

393. "Familiar Spirits," Spiritual Warfare Ministries, Accessed June 15, 2020 http://spiritualwarfare.cc/familiar_spirits

394. Three additional resources on this topic: Nick Redfern, "Incubus, Succubus & Nightmarish Encounters," March 9, 2019, https://mysteriousuniverse.org/2019/03/incubus-succubus-nightmarish-encounters/. Brent George, "A Brief History of the Incubi and the Succubi," March 4, 2017, https://sacspirit.com/2017/03/04/a-brief-history-of-the-incubi-and-the-succubi/. Alicia McDermott, "Incubi and Succubi: Crushing Nightmares and Sex-Craving Demons, Part 1," June 24, 2016, https://www.ancient-origins.net/myths-legends/incubi-and-succubi-crushing-nightmares-and-sex-craving-demons-part-i-006157.

395. Exodus 20:17 and Deuteronomy 5:21

396. *Merriam-Webster*, s.v. "Covet," https://www.merriam-webster.com/dictionary/covet.

397. Jeremy Wiles, Conquer Series, conquerseries.com, and Terry Cu-Unjieng, "A New Generation of Porn Addicts is About to Flood the Church—Are We Ready?" Conquer Series, https://conquerseries.com/why-68-percent-of-christian-men-watch-porn/.

Tool #11

398. Romans 10:17

399. Ephesians 2:8–9

400. Romans 4:5, Galatians 3:24

401. Acts 26:18

402. Galatians 3:26

403. Matthew 8:13, 9:18, Mark 11:23–25

404. Matthew 28:18

405. 2 Corinthians 12:10

406. Hebrews 13:5

407. Matthew 28:20

Tool #12

408. Romans 8:28
409. Derek Prince, "How Demons Can Cause Negative Thinking," PRMinistries, December 27, 2018, https://www.youtube.com/watch?v=UB2bHMYo2Gc
410. Ibid
411. Ibid
412. Ibid
413. Ibid
414. Derek Prince, *They Shall Expel Demons*, pg 106 (Chosen Books, a division of Baker Books, 1998), Frank and Ida Mae Hammond, *Pigs in the Parlor, a Practical Guide to Deliverance*, pg 113 (Impact Books, 1973/2003), and Derek Prince, *What You Need to Know About Demons—Your Invisible Enemies* (Chosen Books, a division of Baker Books, 1998)
415. Prince, *Expel*
416. John 10:10
417. Luke 11:25
418. Numbers 14:18
419. Prince, "Negative Thinking."
     Dr. Lance Wallnau, *Breaking Off Familiar Spirits, 3 Insights for Breaking the Cycle of Familiar Spirits in Your Family Line.* Lancewallnau.com/breaking-off-familiar-spirits/.
420. Leviticus 19:31, Leviticus 20:6, Deuteronomy 18:10–11, 1 Samuel 28:3, 9; 2 Kings 21:6, 2 Kings 23:24, 1 Chronicles 10:13, 2 Chronicles 33:6
421. Matthew 8:28–32
422. Mark 5:3–13
423. Luke 8:26–32
424. Luke 8:28
425. Luke 8:31–32
426. Matthew 8:32, Mark 5:13, Luke 8:33
427. Luke 4:18
428. Jesus and his disciples routinely cast demons out of people. Jesus tells us in Luke 4:17–19 that He came to proclaim liberty to the captives.
429. Mark 16:17

Tool #13

430. Matthew 27:18, Mark 15:10
431. Acts 5:17, 13:45, 17:5
432. Galatians 5:26, 1 Peter 2:1
433. Mark 7:22–23

434. Mark 10:35–38
435. Acts 7:9
436. Genesis 41:41–43
437. Philippians 4:11–12

Tool #14

438. Matthew 6:14–15, Matthew 18:21–35, Luke 6:37, Mark 11:25
439. Ephesians 4:30–32
440. Ephesians 4:26–27, 2 Corinthians 2:10–11
441. Mark 11:23–25
442. Colossians 3:13

Tool #15

443. Ron Wood, *Deliverance: Our Legacy*, (Touched by Grace, Inc., 2017).

Look for the second part of this series

In the Devil's Toolbox Part Two:
The Coming Deception—When the
2nd Heaven Invades Earth

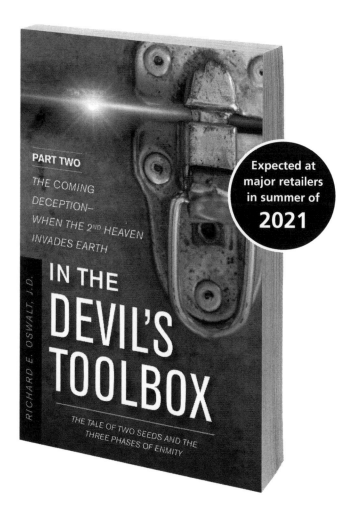

For more information on this and other titles
by Richard E. Oswalt, J.D. visit

www.InTheDevilsToolbox.com

Electric Moon Publishing, LLC is a custom, independent publisher who assists indie authors, ministries, businesses, and organizations with their book publishing needs. Services include writing, editing, design, layout, print, e-book, marketing, and distribution. For more information please use the contact form found on www.emoonpublishing.com.